THE SHADOWS OF EMPIRE

THE
SHADOWS
OF EMPIRE

HOW IMPERIAL HISTORY
SHAPES OUR WORLD

SAMIR PURI

PEGASUS BOOKS
NEW YORK LONDON

THE SHADOWS OF EMPIRE

Pegasus Books, Ltd.
148 West 37th Street, 13th Floor
New York, NY 10018

First Pegasus Books cloth edition February 2021

ISBN: 978-1-64313-668-4

10 9 8 7 6 5 4 3 2 1

Printed in the United States of America
Distributed by Simon & Schuster
www.pegasusbooks.com

For my grandfather
Kishori Lal Dhiri (1914–1990)
who spanned three continents and one empire

CONTENTS

INTRODUCTION

We are in the first empire-free millennium in world history since ancient times, but the world remains in the throes of a great imperial hangover. Empires are still shaping the twenty-first century in profound ways through their abiding influences on present generations. The purpose of this book is to identify these legacies and explain why understanding the world's history of empire can help to unlock many of the most troublesome conundrums in contemporary global affairs.

Even a cursory glance at the news suggests that the world appears to have gone mad or, at the very least, to have lost the semblance of regularity that makes us feel safe. Terrorism, Trump and Brexit have led many people to question the coherence of the Western world; Turkey and Russia slip deeper into authoritarian rule; war tears at the fabric of the Middle East and parts of Africa; a vast exodus of refugees flee for a better shot at life; and all the while China's economic tentacles spread further across the globe. Barely one-fifth of our way into the twenty-first century, it is not unreasonable to seek explanations as to what 'world order' means today, and how we can strive towards it.

Why turn to the apparently fusty legacy of empires to explain today's uncertainties? The end of the world's many empires is no longer at the forefront of our minds, overtaken by more pressing concerns about what lies round the next corner. And yet empires continue to haunt our minds in all manner of ways, stalking our subconscious understanding of who we are and of our place in the world. Empires have helped to construct national identities and carve out geopolitical realities and mentalities that prove hard to escape. This is as true for those whose great-grandparents were imperialists as it is for those whose countries have lived through subjugation and national liberation. Cities, institutions and infrastructure were built in the name of empires. Borders were hastily drawn and populations rearranged. Assets were stripped to enrich the colonizers at the expense of the colonized.

Merely to point out that the past has an influence on the present is too obvious. The real prize is in learning *how* this influence is being felt, and in working out what we can do to better fathom and manage the wars, terrorism, political shocks and global tensions that dominate our headlines. While this book is rooted in historical experiences, it is fundamentally forward-looking. It is not concerned with extensive retellings of imperial histories, although I will provide some summaries where necessary. Nor will I provide a running commentary on the minutiae of today's turbulent politics. Rather, this book straddles history and current affairs. It asks: how do the lingering half-lives of collapsed empires continue to shape such matters as security, foreign policy, international aid and global commerce today?

I will avoid picking any one national perspective, or picking sides in arguments that either categorically denounce or whitewash imperial legacies. Instead I will embark on a world tour, taking in the many varied post-imperial experiences of Europe, Asia, America, the Middle East and Africa. I will *not* argue that we are entering a new imperial age. Rather, my argument can be expressed concisely: twenty-first-century world order is a story of many intersecting post-imperial legacies. When these legacies collide, misunderstanding, friction, schism or even war can result.

This book is a plea to have greater awareness, as individuals and nations, of how our varied imperial pasts have contributed to why we see the world in such different ways. Our perceptions and beliefs concerning empires are coloured by our own inherited backgrounds, which is why there are rarely right or wrong answers to the questions that empires have thrown up.

Hence my own motivations for writing this book. My family roots are in Britain's former East African and Indian colonies, which means that my relatives were on the receiving end of British colonialism. Generations later, no matter how assimilated I might feel in contemporary Britain, I retain some identification with non-white regions of the world once subjugated by the British Empire. Innate, unspoken and familial, this is more an awareness of my roots than the stuff of rebellion. Indeed, I took a patriotic career path and signed up to serve the British Foreign Office in a role that would certainly have been closed to my ancestors.

The very fact that I could join the Foreign Office, and work on international security issues, shows that Britain has progressed substantially in the intervening decades since my family arrived after decolonization. Ethnic minorities in modern Britain can expect to receive far warmer welcomes than their parents did, which has meant that even though I was born in ethnically diverse and impoverished east London, I too could become an 'Englishman', just so long as I followed the cultural cues. Later, as a civil servant, I was proud to serve my country, but the experience left me with lingering questions around identity – both my own identity and Britain's national identity in a rapidly changing world, given what seem to me to be the lingering anachronisms in the mentalities of its elite institutions of state and academia.

And there my thoughts might have stopped, but for war erupting in Ukraine in 2014. I spent a year there, monitoring what was happening on the front line as part of an international diplomatic mission. We were not peacekeepers, so we had no means to stop the fighting, only to try and prevent things escalating further. Russia was clearly an aggressor, destabilizing a country that was part of its historical empire, with the goal of preventing Ukraine's government from drawing closer to the European Union – a club of democratic states that, despite lacking the motivations of the empires of old, had acquired its own empire-like traits, not least in its incessant expansion.

I was outraged that Russia would resort to war to stake its claims for influence in Ukraine. But the experience also convinced me how vital it is to tell different post-imperial stories, because they all matter in our diverse world – especially when they clash.

Returning from Ukraine, I became an academic, lecturing on the subject of wars past and present. Writing this book has afforded me insights into how people around the world interpret their inherited experiences of empire, and this forms the basis of what follows.

How did we get here?

It is a matter of great significance to live in a world without empires. By this, I mean the end of the *formal* empires of the past, where an outwardly expanding metropolitan core gobbled up territories via conquest. Nowadays, this kind of formal empire seems to be extinct. While certain countries will always be more powerful than others, the outright subjugation of one by another is now rare. Iraq annexed Kuwait in 1990, but was kicked out by a US-led military coalition a year later. Russia annexed Crimea from Ukraine in 2014, and while it was too strong to dislodge, this has not yet set a precedent for others. Rather, the ways in which powerful states dominate others have evolved to become more like *informal* empires of political and economic influence.

If empires had not existed, then it would have been necessary to invent something like them, to foster and upscale human progress. Empires have been vessels for order, modernity, culture and conquest since ancient times. Throughout history, civilizations have encountered one another at different stages of technological and political development. It is from here that the pattern of people imposing their will upon others arises. Some empires were notoriously more wicked than others, but the pattern itself holds true.

Understandings of empire changed, depending on who was doing the understanding, and when. The great English writer Samuel Johnson (1709–84) offered this definition in his *Dictionary of the English Language*:

> EMPIRE [*empire*, French; *imperium*, Latin]
> 1. Imperial power; supreme dominion; foreign command. Affect, ye fair ones, who in judgement fit, Your ancient *empire* over love and wit.
> 2. The region over which dominion is extended. A nation extended over vast tracts of land, and numbers of people, arrives in times at the ancient name of kingdom, or modern of *empire*.[1]

As Dr Johnson's definition suggests, the age-old notion of *kingdoms* building their realms by attaching adjacent territories to one another had evolved into ever more expansive empires.

Ancient empires, arising from early civilizations in Egypt, Mesopotamia, China and India, and from city-states like Athens and Rome, spread their visions of civilization and order by bringing nearby peoples into their orbit. These empires spread far and wide, across distances that seemed grandiose to their protagonists, BCE ('before the current era').

The monotheistic empires that developed alongside Christianity and Islam provided new impetus in the 'current era' (CE). Ancient polytheistic peoples had used empires to promote their own cultures. But the proselytizing of the Islamic conquests in the seventh century, and of the later Christian Crusades, channelled different energies. This spilled out into the wars between rival dynasties and denominations, which characterized Islam's split into its Sunni and Shia branches, as well as the schisms of the Christian Church.[2]

Nomadic empires, including those of successive generations of Mongols like Genghis Khan, Kublai Khan and Tamerlane, could cover enormous distances as they scythed through the locals, connecting different parts of the world as they went. Some nomadic warriors tried settling down in one place, but their empires ultimately lacked staying power.

Sprawling land-based empires, by comparison, were built around the core of an imperial centre and an established civilization. They became typical in the medieval and early modern eras, such as the Byzantine, Ottoman, Russian, Habsburg and Mughal empires. The most enduring of them lasted into the nineteenth and twentieth centuries, although by that point those that remained had reached their dotage. Creaky and old-fashioned, they had been overtaken by the latest imperial innovation.

Maritime colonial empires were, for a while, the way of the imperial future. From the late 1400s, European nations competed with each other to explore the full extent of the globe, in pursuit of knowledge and profit. Over time, these voyaging Europeans realized they could overwhelm local African, Asian and American kingdoms. Early on, Spanish conquistadors annihilated the Incas in South America and the Aztecs in Central America. The old inland empires in Asia and the Middle East could still hold their own against the Europeans. It was only in the 1700s and the 1800s, as the equilibrium between the world's empires began to tip decisively in the Europeans' favour, that they conquered much of the rest of the world.[3]

This shift was driven by advanced European nations experiencing industrial revolutions at home – bursts in productivity partly fuelled by resources extracted from the colonies. Colonialism, and in particular settler colonialism, is a specific form of imperialism. To reduce a territory to a colony was to claim exclusive rights over its sovereignty.[4] Settler colonies involved communities being dispatched from the imperial core to populate this land, in all likelihood to disempower or displace the previous inhabitants.

Occasionally those very settlers would fall out with their own imperial metropole (the parent state of the colony), usually because they wanted more lax independence.[5] This brings us to the birth of the USA, which ultimately proved to be a game-changer in the history of empires. Its Independence War was waged by settlers to kick out the British Empire, and the Declaration of Independence in 1776 became a rallying call to this end. Later US presidents took further steps to discredit the ability of Europeans to meddle in their affairs. After Britain fought America's fledging republic for a second time, its fifth president, James Monroe, issued a doctrine in 1823 that set out why the Old World should stay out of the New World. Nearly a century later President Woodrow Wilson used the tragedy of the Great War – which Europe's rival empires had brought upon themselves – to argue why colonies should be replaced by sovereign states.

The twentieth century turned into a story of collapsing empires. The First World War, or Great War (1914–18), claimed the Russian tsarist, Ottoman, Austro-Hungarian and the Kaiser's German empire – old dynastic empires of the mould that had predominated for centuries. The Second World War (1939–45) was waged to crush the nascent Third Reich, Japanese and Italian imperial projects. It also accelerated the decline of Europe's older overseas empires, and the British, French, Dutch, Belgian, Spanish and Portuguese lost their remaining overseas colonies after 1945.

Decolonization completely changed the world. Nationalism spread like wildfire, as those who had been subjugated by empires gained inspiration from each other's independence struggles. The torch-paper of anti-colonialism was lit by freedom fighters around the world, desperate to kick off the imperial yoke. Not all independence struggles were successful, but those that were birthed a host of new countries. The age of empires had inadvertently bequeathed nationalism to the world.[6]

The Cold War (1946–91) was the other defining event of this time. It was an ideological contest in which each superpower assembled global coalitions to support their causes. Whereas the USSR still held a land-based empire (which it had seized from the ashes of the old Russian Empire), the USA did not seek an equivalent. Instead, it engaged in a game that both superpowers were willing to play: seeking client states. No sooner had Asia, Africa, Latin America and the Middle East breathed in the free air of the post-colonial age than the superpowers came knocking with their own list of obligations: to support the communist or capitalist camps, and to receive money and arms in return.

The seemingly underhand ways in which power and influence were projected became an inflammatory topic. Kwame Nkrumah (1909–72) was a revolutionary who agitated against British rule in its Gold Coast colony. After independence, he named the new country Ghana, in homage to the pre-colonial name of a west African kingdom. He became Ghana's first president in 1960 and authored a tract against imperialism's newest mutation, writing:

> The essence of neocolonialism is that the State that is subject to it is, in theory, independent and has all the outward trappings of international sovereignty. In reality, its economic system and thus its political policy is directed from outside . . . Neocolonialism is also the worst form of imperialism. For those who practise it, it means power without responsibility and for those who suffer from it, it means exploitation without redress.[7]

Neo-imperialism and neo-colonialism are still bywords for explaining international bullying. As broad-brush terms, they can appeal to the instincts of fair-minded people the world over: that the 'big guys' shouldn't run rampant over the 'little guys' who want to choose their own path.

The extinction of formal empires came (for now) in 1991, with the fragmenting of the Soviet Union and the resultant creation of another brace of newly independent states in Eastern Europe and Central Asia. Today there are 193 fully recognized sovereign states,[8] effectively quadrupling the number in less than a century. A community of sovereign states seems to be a far nobler way of ordering the world, as opposed to carving it up for the un-ashamed benefit of the small handful of conquerors and colonizers. But while a world comprising sovereign states of apparent legal equivalence is all well and good in principle, in practice it cannot replace the hierarchical jockeying for influence that has always been the game of states.

Some states are so fragile or so small as to be effectively dominated by those that are more powerful. After the end of the Cold War, the USA became the undisputed heavyweight champion of the world. Today it is perhaps the world's *disputed* heavyweight champion. China's ascent to superpower status is now well recognized. A resurgent Russia is bent on resisting the serfdom of second-tier status, despite its relative economic weakness. Turkey, India and Iran are, in their own ways, carving out independent spheres of influence. The world of 2041 will look different from the world of 1991, when the US had greater latitude to act all over the world without facing challenge.

World affairs is not just a game of states, but of non-state actors too. Some of the knottiest problems in the world arise from nations that missed out on the great sovereign-state giveaway of decolonization. In less volatile parts of the world prospective separatists might opt for referendums, as the Scottish did in the UK in 2016 and the Catalans tried to do in Spain in 2018. There is even an alternative football World Cup for stateless people and nations that are not fully recognized, featuring the Turkish Republic of Northern Cyprus, Tibet, Abkhazia and Kurdistan.

In their frustration, some separatists resort to violence, as in Israel and the Palestinian Territories, for example. Civil war and terrorism can follow. Reflecting a newer international breed of terrorist, the jihadist movements of al-Qaeda and Islamic State have become today's barbarians at the gates. According to jihadist creed, they wage war against heretical Islamic sects and apostate post-colonial Muslim countries alike.

To bring order to the chaos, all manner of humanitarian non-governmental organizations (NGOs) and civil-society groups exist to fill the gaps that governments cannot. Sovereign states also sign up for membership in transnational clubs, which pool responsibilities and resources to tackle shared problems. The United Nations (UN), which looked positively sclerotic when its five-member Security Council became log-jammed over Syria's civil war that began in 2011, looks more dynamic if one focuses on the emergency responses of its Development Programme (UNDP), High Commissioner for Refugees (UNHCR) and other field bodies.

There is also an alphabet soup of regional organizations, such as the European Union (EU), the African Union (AU), the Shanghai Cooperation Organisation (SCO) and the Association of South-east Asian Nations (ASEAN). Ostensibly clubs for common economic interests, they also foster cooperation on other matters of common concern. In reality, however, the dominant voices in these clubs are those members who wrote the rules, paid in the most money and have been there the longest. The most powerful sovereign states still find ways to call the shots. A true regional government – let alone a world government – remains a pipe dream.

This brief canter past some of the pillars and problems of world order shows us what we have built, and what has arisen, in the absence of formal empires. For forward-thinking optimists, this is progress. For those with a historical eye, it is a mere rearranging of the same old problems that periodically beset humanity. We have to remember that, until relatively recently, the empires of the world had an instrumental role in the arrangement of international affairs; in assigning right and responsibility when it came to trade and governing; and in acting as vehicles for people to express allegiance, national pride and even religion. Empires – and reactions against empires – performed these roles for many centuries, and our empire-free world has barely begun.

Crediting or castigating imperial legacies

How the imperial past affects the present is a polarizing subject that provokes strong emotions, with some of us instinctively verging towards crediting empires and their legacies, whilst others castigate them. Are empires (and neo-empires) essentially responsible for the world's ills? Or, as regrettable as past inhumanities are, did the history of empires essentially create the modern world order?

It can be hard to strike a balance between these views. Empire is so out of fashion that it can be difficult to admit it ever had any positive legacies. Holding both thoughts in one's head – that yesterday's advancements also involved horrendous misdeeds – requires nothing less than an act of double-think. It is easier (and more emotionally comforting) to drift towards a polarized view.

It is now almost otherworldly to think that empire was for so long the default mode of political organization. Every empire was unique, but the notion of empire was ubiquitous and was largely taken for granted. Consequently for centuries empire was synonymous with world order. As the academic Dominic Lieven writes, 'in its time empire was often a force for peace, prosperity and the exchange of ideas across much of the globe'.[9] Empires governed disparate sets of peoples and often did so pragmatically rather than murderously, so long as these people proclaimed fealty to their overlords. Injustice was highly likely, but not inevitable in every part of every empire.

Empires propagated ideas, technologies, legal systems and forms of government, even if they were spread by empire-builders who remade other places in their own image as acts of grandiose vanity. In the end, the ultimate export was the sovereign state. Back in the day, there was greater diversity of political systems, from city-states to feudal monarchies and ungoverned frontier realms.[10] Now, just picture the rows of diplomats sitting at the UN, each with their country name on a board in front of them, and each representing a people encased within a set of borders.

To the extent that the state system is understood to represent progress, with decolonization came independence, and fuzzy frontiers were replaced by borders. Presidents, prime ministers and parliaments were set up. If these post-colonial states later fell into dictatorships and disorder, this was their waste of the gift of sovereignty: thus might the polarizing 'world order' argument go.

Globalization, and the interconnectedness that we take for granted today, was also pioneered by empires. The first Chinese Silk Road (BCE) connected Asia and Europe. Later empires, like those of the Mongols, Ottomans and Mughals, dominated trade across large areas. It was the seaborne expansion of European power that had a proximate impact on the present day (even if European explorers appropriated older trade routes used by Chinese, Indian, Arab or other merchants).[11] For a pro-market capitalist today, the debt to the imperial era is clear, from the trade in manufactured goods and raw materials, to the global monetary system.

In sum, even if old imperialisms look utterly distasteful to modern eyes, there is a far bigger picture of progress that links our imperial past to things that we take for granted in the present.

At the other end of the argument, while empires certainly influenced the way the world works, *this* is the problem. Empires are completely out of step with modern morality, and with the rights and freedoms that all people ought to enjoy. Therefore the beating heart of the modern world resides in the many struggles to overcome empires and oppression. The Davids of anti-imperial sentiment have ordered the modern world, not the Goliaths of empire.

Human progress has therefore involved sweeping away empires and colonies into the dustbin of history, but the struggle continues. Decolonization ought to have brought emancipation, but has in fact been further shackled by unequal power structures that hardened during the old imperial era. Rather than thanking the

West for transferring its ideas and technologies around the world, the spirit of protest *against* these standardizations motivates those who categorically castigate the legacies of the European empires, in particular, that persist today.

Hence 'empire', and its associated notions of 'imperialism' and 'colonialism', is for many people synonymous with inequity, racism, exploitation and the power politics of creating winners and losers. When judged against contemporary moral values, empires look inhumane and primitive. This is especially true if one considers their most terrible excesses, such as transatlantic slavery, as practised by Europe's colonial powers in Africa and the Americas; and the famines instigated by the British East India Company in Bengal, or by Russia's rulers against the Ukrainians, in which imperial elites looked on as their subjects wasted away before their eyes.

These legacies of exploitation and racism remain important today. Empires were built on hierarchies, so those in charge will have looked down their noses at those who were subservient. Racism could be used to justify slavery, torture and murder.

Protecting people around the world against prejudicial suffering has become a cornerstone of human-rights laws. The UN played midwife to the birth of new states during decolonization, and established a Decolonization Committee in 1961 for this reason. A year earlier, UN General Assembly resolution 1514 had declared that 'all peoples have the right to self-determination'. The UN played a crucial role at that moment of history, and during the transition to a post-imperial age.

But the nastier legacies of empires could not be banished through international declarations and free elections. Imperialism was as much an attitude as it was a tangible reality. A champion in post-imperial rehabilitation was Edward Said (1935–2003). The Jerusalem-born Arab Palestinian, who was later an academic in the US, delivered an insight into how empires had allowed Western superiority to be asserted materially, culturally and intellectually.

Worse, an imperial trick was to reprogramme those who had been colonized to believe that it was all in their interests, because 'Westernization' was being sold as the only route to modernity.[12]

Not every empire bothered Said equally: 'There are several empires that I do not discuss: the Austro-Hungarian, the Russian, the Ottoman, and the Spanish and Portuguese ... the British, French and American imperial experience has a unique coherence ... the idea of overseas rule – jumping beyond adjacent territories to very distinct lands – has a privileged status in these three cultures ... [Whereas] Russia acquired its imperial territories almost exclusively by adjacency.'[13]

This selectivity is inadequate for our age of greater competition between a rich variety of countries. Picking on Western European imperialism and American neo-imperialism with dedicated fury is not representative of the full range of imperial legacies that still matter.

Were Europe's colonial empires really in a different category of insidiousness from the Chinese, Russian, Ottoman and others? The histories of these inland empires have perhaps been seen more as part of these regions' organic heritage than as an alien invasion, although a Taiwanese writer might offer a stiff reaction to claims that the Chinese Empire has been integral to Taiwanese culture, just as a Ukrainian writer might well dispute the cultural heritage of the Russian Empire. If some empires are singled out for their inhumanities, then why not all of them? 'It seems strange to me to withhold this more balanced approach from the European empires as a matter of doctrine,' writes the academic John Darwin, who is concerned by the distorting impact of fixating on 'the moral and cultural aggression' of the Western world.[14] The West clearly did not have a monopoly over empire, since empires emerged on all continents for thousands of years.[15] Balanced narratives that take in the wider global view, and that avoid the emotionally comforting positions of polarized and selective stances, are important.

Rather than pick sides (which readers can do, if they so wish), the tone of accommodating diverse and contradictory perspectives is established here. How empires contributed to globalization *and* the traditions of protest this has provoked have together made today's world.

Old imperial habits die hard

The relationship between the USA and the Philippines offers an example of how legacies can long outlast the end of empires. For more than a century an empty bell tower had symbolized the unhealed wounds of conquest. Back in 1899, when the USA was an up-and-coming world power, American soldiers were commandeering the lands of yesteryear's superpower, the Spanish Empire. One such campaign was waged in the Philippines. Having seen off the Spaniards, Filipinos at first welcomed US rule, but later waged an insurgency in a bid for their freedom. A bitter war ensued. In 1901, in Balangiga village, Filipino rebels staged an ambush that inflicted dozens of US casualties. It was America's bloodiest military loss since Custer's last stand in 1876, during the Great Sioux War. The church bells of Balangiga rang out as the ambush unfolded. In retaliation, American soldiers later went on a rampage, killing numerous Filipinos and seizing the bells as a war trophy to take to the US.[16]

In 2018 the US government finally agreed to return the Balangiga bells to the Philippines. It was a proud moment for Philippines president Rodrigo Duterte. And it came not a moment too soon for the US, which Duterte had enjoyed criticizing, partly to show his public how tough he could be – but also because he was cultivating the Philippines' relations with the Pacific's new up-and-coming power, China. As the page was turned on one phase of history, another was beginning.

Obituaries of empires tend to follow a formula. The outlines of now-dead empires are traced in a succession of maps and their existence bracketed by a range of dates. The obituary is presented as that of a person: it lived from this-to-this year and, in the time afforded to it, is best remembered for the following list of triumphs, misdeeds and progenies ... All of which is essential historical data.

Empires, however, do not end overnight – they unravel gradually, fraying like a rope under stress, before the strands separate. Even then, threads of a bond with the past can remain in their physical and psychological legacies.

The unique imperial experiences of nations form part of their historical DNA. To carry on with the genetic analogy, just as we retain agency over our personal actions, because we are the products of both nature and nurture, so our inherited historical experiences work in a similar way, with our choices at times constrained by histories that we cannot change.[17]

It will become clear that an inheritance of past oppression leads to different perspectives than an inheritance of old imperial glory. All regions of the world experienced empires in some ways. In some nations, this experience still lies within living memory. In others, living linkages to old empires have only just slipped away. Regardless, there is no such thing as a singular inherited experience of empire – only a diversity of perspectives, both within and between nations: from a sense of debt, all the way to a sense of catastrophe; from denial, all the way to manifest destiny. The only possible conclusion is that of a plurality of experiences and interpretations of imperial legacies.

Some legacies are visible to the naked eye. Empires have contributed to the map lines of the world. As empires have risen and fallen, they leave in their wake certain distributions of power, demarcations of statehood, and lines in the sand that divide or unite people with each other, and with the natural endowments of the Earth. Movements of people. The drawing of borders. Trade flows for commodities and manufactured goods. Shared traditions. Common languages. Perhaps even traditional holiday destinations. All these things may have been shaped by imperial legacies.

Spotting the psychological legacies of empires requires a different kind of illumination. Unrequited pride, jealousy, enmity, blame and comradeship – these are the invisible forces that criss-cross the globe, linking so many of us in historical melodramas that continue to play out. The memories, experiences and scars of the past will have contributed to how people feel about themselves, where they locate their people in the wider world, and where such feelings as group pride and group blame are directed.[18]

Empires are only ever as durable as their governing philosophies. When the governing philosophy of an empire collapses, what is left behind: an empire that will collapse too? What remains of these philosophies after the end of empires contributes greatly to the texture of world affairs. Is there a governing class that seems unable to let go of the philosophy itself? How does this manifest itself – psychologically, religiously, politically?

In some cases, past brushes with empire may have been habit-forming for the elites of modern nations. These habits could relate to an expectation of superiority over others. Some former imperial centres, like London and Moscow, still try to project power with modernized versions of some of their old imperial tactics. Conversely, some post-colonial states owe the nature of their existence to being created in the wake of empire. From the Philippines to India and Kenya, anti-imperial rhetoric is still a powerful way for today's politicians to hold forth on all manner of themes. The same is true in Eastern European counties where memories of impoverishment under recent Russian domination still rankle. Striking one's own path, free from the vestiges of imperial dominion, remains a powerful political ploy in many parts of the world.

Old experiences may have contributed to path dependencies that persist in our post-imperial age. And we may not even

have noticed where these habits came from – only that the decisions of politicians and public today seem to be in tune with
the 'national character'. Imperial experiences are profoundly
character-forming. They have contributed to deeply buried and
unconsciously held attitudes. This, in turn, may give rise to
involuntary compulsions, and to itches that need periodically
to be scratched.

Finally there are the cultural legacies of empires. These can
be of profound importance, such as the endurance of the Islamic
faith in many parts of the world that were touched by past Muslim
conquests. Or of Britain's diffusion of culture across the Anglo-
sphere.

More trivially, nostalgia for an empire that once was can be
big business in the entertainment industry. Some viewers may
quite like to be reminded that their ancestors ruled vast realms.
The British are periodically fixated by dramas set in the Raj, the
former Indian colony, in series like *The Jewel in the Crown* (1984)
and films like *Viceroy's House* (2017). China's enormously popular
drama, *The Story of Yanxi Palace* (2018), fictionalizes the schemes
of the women of Emperor Qianlong's court as they compete for
his favour. urkish viewers were gripped by *The Magnificent Century* (2011–14), which depicted the court of the sixteenth century
Ottoman ruler Suleiman.

Period dramas set amidst empires can offer both cultural affir-
mation and an opportunity to refract modern concerns. This only
works because empire represents many people's heritage. Whether
we accept or reject it, or are simply unaware of this heritage, is
another matter.

We are not habitually raised with the stories of other people's
imperial heritages, which means it always takes real effort to see
the world through each other's eyes, and to notice the ways in
which the material and psychological legacies of empire influence
their circumstances and decisions.

The narrative of today

If our own century is to have a story, then it is curious to wonder what historians fifty years hence will opt for. Decolonization, the Cold War, the world wars, the age of empires, the industrial revolutions and the age of dynastic monarchies – each of these is a compelling story with which to encapsulate previous epochs. What description will future generations choose for today?

For those living in the present in any age, events are experienced in a disconnected and unforeseeable fashion. It is only in retrospect that historians can impose any sense of coherence on the past, teasing out the developments that provided crucial catalysts for change and choosing how best to characterize these dynamics. We would do well to bear in mind the words of J. R. Seeley, a writer on the British Empire: 'Great events are commonly judged by contemporaries quite wrongly. It is in fact one of the chief functions of the historian to correct the contemporary judgement. Instead of making us share the emotions of the passing time, it is his business to point out to us that this event, which absorbed the public attention when it happened, was really of no great importance, and that event, though it passed almost unnoticed, was of infinite consequence.'[19]

The obvious way to describe the present epoch is as the *information revolution age*. Widespread use of the Internet just so happened to coincide roughly with the year 2000 and the dawn of the current millennium, which adds to the sense of an opening of a new chapter for humanity. Certainly the ubiquity of the Internet has changed how many of the world's citizens experience politics, view world affairs, consume information, organize their social lives and locate their identities. This is game-changing stuff around the world. The information revolution and its influence will only spread, as data algorithms increasingly rule our lives and augment the human experience – at least, for those who can afford the latest technology products. Surely, then, this is how we should describe our age.

But it is already obvious that the Internet is not necessarily a tool for freedom, leading to globalized identities and connections that pay little heed to borders. Information always remains open to manipulation, no matter how liberating and novel the technical platform. Flooding people with information can be just as distorting as the censorship of old, even in democracies with a free media. Official narratives share bandwidth with citizen journalism (which can itself be punishable in places with controlling regimes, such as China and Turkey). Scandals besetting social-media giant Facebook over manipulation of its user data have shown that, if information is targeted at individuals to reinforce their biases over a number of political issues, the Internet is just a novel medium through which the age-old dark arts of propaganda are practised today. Nor is the Internet about to skip over national regulations. Try logging onto Facebook in China. Old-fashioned national protectionism has hardly drawn its last breath, and may well rear its head more prominently in the future.

So I am not convinced that information utterly defines our age. Those heralding the brave new world of connectivity would disagree with me. In *Sapiens: A Brief History of Humankind*, Yuval Noah Harari is even convinced that 'the global empire being forged before our eyes is not governed by any particular state or ethnic group'.[20] He argues that surely the more connected we are, the better placed we might be to employ our competitive impulses productively, seek the comparative advantages of production and perhaps even strive for the common good?

But no matter how rapid our technological advances might be, there are no full stops in history. One epoch does not stop before another starts – they blur messily into each other. All the trappings of modernity and its rapid techno-advances merely refract and refashion those elements of the human spirit that are unchanging. An obsession with what is novel can obscure a focus on what is being inherited from our immediate past. We should question whether the world has moved very far from George Orwell's sobering observation that 'The energy that actually shapes the world springs from emotions – racial pride, leader worship, religious belief, love of war – which liberal intellectuals mechanically write off as anachronisms.'[21] Whatever the criteria being used by people today to identify more of their own kindred spirits, it is hardly as if parochialism and discrimination have vanished from the world.

So while at first glance it seems utterly anachronistic to invoke empire as a lens through which to fathom our unfolding century, the empires of a bygone age cast a long shadow over how we think about ourselves and, as we look across the globe, how we think about and judge each other. Imperial legacies can be mundane, impacting on us in ways we might scarcely notice as we go about our daily lives. But they can also be of profound importance, helping to power the geopolitical tectonic plates upon which our fates depend.

The opening chapter explains how the USA refashioned the notion of empire in the latter part of the twentieth century into that of a largely unseen empire of influence. This is followed by chapters on the UK, the European continent as a whole and Russia, explaining the varying ways in which these places have adapted to the disappearance of formal empires. The next part of the book covers China, India, the Middle East and Africa, contrasting their experiences of adapting to the post-imperial world.

Throughout, it is the different experiences of dealing with imperial legacies that matter, not the similarities. Dealing with difference is essential to a relatively harmonious future for our world, and there are often no greater differences than our various imperial inheritances.

ONE

AMERICA'S IMPERIAL INHERITANCE

I never knew a man who had better motives for all the trouble he caused.

> Graham Greene (1904–91), *The Quiet American*[1]

There will be times when we must again play the role of the world's reluctant sheriff. This will not change – nor should it.

> Barack Obama, *Audacity of Hope* (2006)[2]

If we're going to continue to be the policeman of the world, we ought to be paid for it.

> Donald Trump, *Crippled America* (2015)[3]

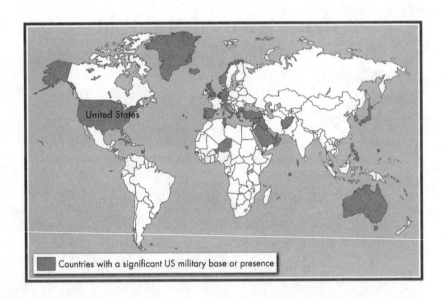

Map 1 The global military presence of the United States, 2019 (circles indicate countries or territories with a US base that would be too small to appear otherwise)

Opinions around the world differ sharply over whether the USA should conduct itself like a global empire, and whether doing so on balance helps to stabilize or destabilize the world. The virtues and vices of America's global role have been debated for the best part of a century. Fewer and fewer people alive today can recall a world in which the military, economic and cultural power of the USA has not been an overwhelming global reality.

America's imperial heritage is the historical key that explains why opinions are so strongly divided. Understanding how a nation that was born out of its anti-imperialist stance would end up adopting its very own imperial practices is a complex matter. By kicking out the British Empire, the fledgling American nation made the repudiation of its imperial inheritance a pillar of its self-identity. Notions of freedom became essential to America's national creed, whether this meant freedom of consumer choice, freedom from government oversight or freedom from tyranny.

At America's birth as a nation, the cause was unambiguous: freedom from the clutches of colonialism. However, traces of imperial DNA remained. Contradictory impulses, ignited in its past, still smoulder deep in America's heart, and they continue to shape its domestic character and its foreign-policy debates.[4]

This became clear as its power grew across North America and then around the world. In a burst of continental conquest, America captured lands between the Atlantic and the Pacific Oceans. Native Americans, Mexicans and European imperialists alike were kept out or swept aside. Liberty was denied to African slaves and their descendants. Starting in the nineteenth century, America's military began to wage a succession of wars of choice in far-flung lands. Its annexations and conquests stretched from Cuba to the Philippines. These American soldiers were unknowingly starting a military tradition of securing their country's interests by fighting in distant lands.

The tradition endures for America's 'imperial grunts', who now fight and die not for colonies, but for outposts from which the

USA can exert global influence.⁵ 'From the shores of Tripoli to the halls of Montezuma,' begins the US Marine Corps Hymn: Tripoli refers to the First Barbary War in 1805; Montezuma to the Mexican-American War in 1847. By remembering past wars, new US Marine recruits are reminded that they are expected to fight abroad today. Waging war abroad, for good or ill, has been essential to American military culture.

This has enabled America to stand tall at key moments in global history. During the Second World War, and again at the Cold War's finale, America appeared to be leading the world away from tyranny. Helping to reconstruct Western Europe and Japan after 1945, and presiding over the spread of democracy east of where the Berlin Wall had fallen in 1989, have been high points. These are the moments in history when America's heady mix of wealth, military clout and self-professed moral authority have positively altered the destinies of people far and wide.

These same compulsions have also led to disastrous interventions in Vietnam in the 1960s and 1970s, and Iraq in the 2000s. Two different generations have now witnessed America's military flounder in ill-begotten wars, each with the expressed intention of spreading democracy abroad.

Over a long span of time in world affairs, there can be no such thing as consistency of purpose or outcomes in the way America has defended its understanding of the free world. Inconsistency, however, seems endemic.

From invading Iraq, to its refusal to act decisively in Syria, America's global posture has lurched between dramatic over-engagement and equally dramatic under-engagement. After 2011, when the Syrian dictator Bashar al-Assad began to massacre his own people in that country's civil war, America remained on the sidelines, demanding that Assad step down, but not forcing him to do so. While the world was hardly clamouring for another American regime-changing invasion, the policy debates in Washington DC conveyed a sense of war-wariness and a hesitancy to intervene. Syria's war has raised an important question: if America cannot find effective ways to step in to punish those who are evidently unleashing evil, then who will? In the end, Russia's military stepped in to back Assad in September 2015, helping his army to win.

The US finds that it is damned if it does, and damned if it doesn't, get involved in the world's problems. Some Americans might be puzzled at how their country's expenditure in blood and treasure, with an annual defence budget approaching $700 billion, can be spent in maintaining world order when that very same world, in a pique of ingratitude, derides the USA as 'imperialist'.

While the USA does not self-identify as an empire, it has become the embodiment of an informal empire. Its global reach includes: military bases dotted around the world; fleets of globally deployable aircraft carriers; strategic alliances on every continent; orbital satellites that guide missiles; technology innovations with global consumer appeal; and economic power underpinned by the USA dollar as the world's reserve currency. The USA can dominate many parts of the world, or at least it can make its influence telling. For now it remains *the* country that can intervene militarily virtually anywhere to defend its vision of world order, and its notions of right and wrong.

Questions over *whether* America should be doing any of this have defined global politics for decades. They cannot be addressed without recourse to the origins of America's compulsions to be a superpower, which in turn reside in its imperial legacies.

Frontiersmen and colonizers: America's imperial experience

Relative to other places, the USA is a young country – although it has existed for nearly a quarter of a millennium, which is more than enough time for successive historical influences to have accumulated, each leaving its mark on the country's development.

With a little historical imagination, it is possible to picture the panorama of America's expansion. From English settlers establishing the Jamestown (Virginia) and Plymouth (Massachusetts) colonies along the east coast in the seventeenth century; to the Independence War that cast off the shackles of British rule in the eighteenth century; to the USA's expansion past the 'Wild West' and its incorporation of Texas, New Mexico, California and other states in the nineteenth century – a colonizing drive for continental control is the opening chapter in the American national story.

Empire is what the USA escaped from, and empire is what the USA later became. Not that you would know this from the way America has usually recited its own national story. As the Thirteen Colonies broke free from the British Empire, they birthed not only an independent country, but also a formidable founding myth.

The Boston Tea Party on 16 December 1773, when the Sons of Liberty revolted against British taxation, escalated into a full-blown insurgency. What followed is retold as the stuff of pure American patriotism. To invoke 'the spirit of 1776' is to summon an emotively powerful history that has passed into legend. Thomas Jefferson, the Founding Fathers and the Declaration of Independence intoning that 'all men are created equal' have provided the USA with its moral guiding light as an incubator of freedom. General George Washington's crossing of the Delaware River at the Battle of Trenton in 1776, immortalized in the iconic painting by Emanuel Leutze, is a potent visualization of plucky, freedom-seeking rebels striving against tyranny. British soldiers and their allies were sent packing, and in 1783 the USA was recognized by Britain as an independent country.

Americans have tended to interpret the founding myth in creationist terms – not religiously, but in the sense of their nation having arisen from sudden and seismic events, rather than having evolved with roots and antecedents that stretch back far further.[6] In this sense, America's institutions and ideals were painted onto a blank canvas. It was 'year-zero' in 1776, and questions of inheritance were less compelling than the idealism of a fresh start. As George Washington said in 1790: 'the establishment of our new Government seemed to be the last great experiment for promoting human happiness'.[7] The sentiment has stuck in terms of providing an undergirding for American patriotism.

Historians have pointed out that the events of the Independence War do not really offer a basis for extrapolating a lasting sense of national mission. Some historians are rather more blunt than others. Hugh Bicheno is unapologetic: 'Unfortunately it remains true that any criticism of the US is likely to be answered with a recitation about how much worse everywhere else is and always has been, a reflex drawing much of its vehemence from the Foundation Myth. One definition of immaturity is an inability to grasp that one's birth did not transform the world.'[8] Ouch! Is this at all fair?

The War of Independence was no straightforward fight between plucky rebels and a nasty colonial overlord. The USA was born from a competition between rival European imperial powers over North America, which was both a valuable prize in itself and a gateway to the Caribbean, to Central America and eventually to the Pacific Ocean.

When the Thirteen Colonies revolted against the British Empire's terms of trade, the French and Spanish empires were watching carefully. As George Washington's military campaign gathered momentum, France stuck in its oar, allying with Washington's rebels in 1778. Spain joined the fray the following year. Franco-Spanish naval actions challenged the Royal Navy, hindering its ability to blockade the rebels. On land, French forces played a role in wearing down the British. The British themselves were reliant on local allies and imported Hessian (German) troops. As befitted an imperial and not a national age, the fighting forces were a patchwork of professional soldiers, mercenaries and locals who happened to be caught up in the swirl of violence.

As well as an imperial war, it was also America's first civil war. A brutal schism tore American Patriots apart from the Loyalists to Britain's crown. Black soldiers and Native Americans were involved on both sides. The war was brutal, and whereas America's independence myth emphasizes the cruelty of British soldiers and the high-minded ideals of the Patriots, both sides fought bitterly. Violence, as well as Britain's imperial overreach, was central to America's birth.[9]

Paris, appropriately, was the location of peace negotiations that culminated in the November 1783 withdrawal of Britain's troops from New York. The USA was hewn from the rocks of imperial competition between Britain, France and Spain.[10]

The territory of the US recognized at the Treaty of Paris had boundaries from the Atlantic coast to the Mississippi River. Benjamin Franklin, negotiating for the US, wanted parts of Canada, which Britain refused to cede. The Spanish remained in Florida and the French in New Orleans. Mexico lay to the south-west, and Native Americans across the plains. Next to this, the Thirteen Colonies looked rather puny and vulnerable. The USA's success was far from a given at the outset.

This is where imperial legacies began to have a telling influence. The Patriots who waged the Independence War had rebelled against what they saw as the British Empire's malpractice, not against the principle of empire itself. This was still the imperial age, and the fledgling USA would need to find its feet in a world of empires. What transpired is striking: the basic imperial template, in which a metropolitan centre coordinated affairs between a collection of far-flung and autonomous outposts, became the template for America's westward expansion.[11]

Repudiating and then effectively replicating empire embedded a paradox deep into the American psyche. The implications of this became ever more telling as the USA found its feet.

Thomas Jefferson, then a delegate to the Continental Congress, had a guiding hand in the drafting of the Declaration of Independence and coined the phrase 'Empire of Liberty'. It was uttered in 1780, while the war against the British was still being waged. He characterized the Empire of Liberty as 'an extensive and fertile Country' that would busy itself with 'converting dangerous enemies into valuable friends'. Jefferson's motivations were to differentiate America's intentions from the European colonizers, and it was a neat phrase that remained in America's conscience. It would later be employed to suggest the USA's expansion was being pursued in the wider interests of humanity.

Jefferson later served as president (1801–9), presiding over a major act of expansion with the Louisiana Purchase of 1803. France, then embroiled in its own revolutionary war, and having purchased Louisiana from Spain only six years earlier, was persuaded to offload the territory to the USA for $15 million. The Louisiana Purchase doubled America's territory. It included lands that now form at least a part of fifteen states, all the way from Louisiana and Arkansas in the south, through the Midwest up to Montana, and even areas that are in present-day Canada.

President Jefferson also dispatched the Lewis and Clark expedition. The explorers Meriwether Lewis and William Clark set off from St Louis in 1804, making their way to the Pacific the following year, before returning to their starting point in 1806. The expedition produced the first detailed maps of the Missouri and Colombia river systems, providing cartographical knowledge that America found it useful to cite in lingering border disputes with Britain over Canada.

New Orleans still has some of its French-speaking Creole culture. At the time of Jefferson's purchase, the question of what to do with the locals had colonial connotations. 'Americans of 1803 were too close to 1776 to feel comfortable in imperialism,' observed the author Albert Weinberg. His seminal 1935 book highlighted 'the alchemy' that transformed 'a doctrine of democratic nationalism into a doctrine of imperialism', and eventually into the idea of manifest destiny.[12]

'Manifest destiny' was a phrase used to convey the USA's mission to cover its continent. It is credited to the journalist John O'Sullivan (1813–95), and gained traction in successive decades as a way for Americans to articulate the righteousness of their expansion. Manifest destiny owed a debt to Puritan conceptions of re-enacting the Exodus by settling in a new and promised land and, as such, contributed to America's evolving national identity.[13] The white settler population latched on to this sense of mission. It provided an ideology behind their keenness to expand in a manner reminiscent of European colonialism, now refashioned for the conquest of North America.[14]

At the start of the nineteenth century, however, the USA was still vulnerable to blockade by its ex-colonial master. The next war with the British Empire is remembered for the burning of the White House in 1814 by British soldiers. The US had declared war on 12 June 1812 in response to a partial blockade by the Royal Navy of US ports. James Madison (president 1809–17) employed a strategy in which American forces invaded Canadian towns and forts and attacked British merchant ships. The British fought with one eye firmly fixed on severing the trading link between the USA and Napoleonic France.

A notable legacy of this war are the lyrics of the 'Star-Spangled Banner', which was written as a poem by Francis Scott Key as he watched the Battle of Baltimore unfold in 1814. Fort McHenry was being bombarded by British ships as the lines came into his mind. Nestled in its lyrics are the following:

> O'er the ramparts we watched were so gallantly streaming.
> And the rocket's red glare, the bombs bursting in the air,
> Gave proof through the night that our flag was still there;
> O say does that star-spangled banner yet wave
> O'er the land of the free and the home of the brave?

Hostilities ended in 1815 with the US having held its own against Britain. The Republic's fifth president, James Monroe (1817–25), articulated just why the Old World and New World must remain apart. The Monroe Doctrine of 1823 implored Europeans not to interfere in America. As per its text: 'the American continents, by the free and independent condition which they have assumed and maintain, are henceforth not to be considered as subjects for future colonization by any European powers'. The historical context is important to bear in mind, since Spain's grasp over its empire was waning, precipitating independence for several Latin American countries. Monroe had real concerns of a free-for-all breaking out, if Spain's European rivals descended for the spoils.

The Monroe Doctrine was unequivocal on the following matter: 'With the existing colonies or dependencies of any European power we have not interfered and shall not interfere. But with the Governments who have declared their independence and maintain it, and whose independence we have, on great consideration and on just principles, acknowledged, we could not view any interposition for the purpose of oppressing them, or controlling in any other manner their destiny, by any European power ...' But Monroe did not preclude, and indeed encouraged, the expansion of America's population and the addition of new states. European imperialism was to be staved off, but American expansion was to persist.

The gleaming prize now captivating American settler imaginations was the Pacific coast.

No president better embodied this stage of expansion than the seventh, Andrew Jackson. During his time in office (1829–37) the seizure of Native American lands increased. Jackson signed the Indian Removal Bill in 1830, an act so draconian that it forced southern Native American tribes to accept resettlement to federal territory further west in exchange for their land. The Cherokee were marched off along the 'Trail of Tears', so-called because thousands perished in this forced removal. Gold had been discovered in lands they were forced to abandon, leading to a gold rush in Georgia, where white settlers prospered. The US Army pushed Native Americans into reservations (another name for concentration camps).[15] Iroquois, Shawnee, Mohawk, Apache and other tribes all suffered. Out on the plains some of the tribes fought the settlers hard and well, but they could not win.

The USA had concluded that liberty applied only to those capable of self-government, and deemed the Native Americans to have failed this test. Ethnic cleansing was accompanied by cultural appropriation. The bald-headed eagle, a symbol of spirituality to Native Americans, became a symbol adorning the coins and seals of the Federal Government.

The 'Wild West' and the gold rushes had an enduring influence on America's national culture long after the official closing of the frontier in 1890. Frederick Jackson Turner's *The Significance of the Frontier in American History* (1893) captured this: 'up to our own day American history has been in a large degree the history of the colonisation of the Great West'. Comparisons with European colonialism struck Turner as relevant. America was 'the pathfinder of civilisation', an agent fomenting the 'disintegration of savagery' in encountering 'the Indian and the hunter'.

Turner noticed a growing rift in ideology between the frontiersman and his European roots. 'At first the frontier was the Atlantic coast', but over time, 'The advance of the frontier has meant a steady movement away from the influence of Europe, a steady growth of indolence along American lines.' This impacted upon the character of the frontiersman: 'The separation of the Western man from the seaboard, and his environment, made him in a large degree free from European precedents [in] ideas, manners, customs.' This afforded such distinguishing traits as 'buoyant self-confidence and self-assertion'. Overall, the liberty inherent in a democracy was interpreted by the frontiersman as offering justification to be left alone by the Federal Government: 'The frontiersman was impatient of restraints. He knew how to preserve order, even in the absence of legal authority.'[16]

A pugnacious interpretation of liberty had been catalysed by America's frontier experience. Individualism, democracy and expansion were blending together into a potent mix of ideals, in which the ultimate purpose of democracy was the valuation of individualism, which could only be honoured by the government keeping its nose out of an individual's opportunities for self-betterment.[17] These ideals led to tensions between settler outposts, newly incorporated states and a Federal Government that was, at the time, relatively weak.

West of the Mississippi River, newly settled territories often had little traces of a functioning state, and this elevated the role of Protestant churches in staving off total isolation and barbarism amongst the settlers.[18] Settled territories needed to wait to be upgraded to states. Sometimes several decades would pass between their annexation and their formal inclusion in the USA.[19]

The story of Texas encapsulates these themes. It features the frontiersmen Davy Crockett from Tennessee and Jim Bowie from Louisiana. Both were to die at the Alamo in 1836, the legendary battle that still inspires Texan and American hearts as the archetypal tale of a desperate last stand, in which the Alamo's 185 defenders fought the Mexican army of General Santa Anna.

The battle for the Alamo came about as part of a rebellion of white settlers against Mexico's government. Texas was originally part of the USA's purchases from France, but it was traded away in 1819 to Spain in a treaty for the USA's acquisition of Florida. This left the Texans out on a limb and soon to be absorbed into Mexico (which was also a new country, gaining its independence in 1821 and later fighting off Spanish attempts to reconquer it). White settlers, some of whom had settled in southern Texas with their slaves, did not want to belong to Mexico, so they rebelled.[20]

Crockett and Bowie, neither of whom was a Texan, decided to fight and, ultimately, die with their white settler brethren.

Battles like the Alamo proved seminal to the USA, further stoking its martial spirit, creating a sense of 'us and them' in relation to Mexico, and providing a rationale for a full-scale war that resulted in further expansion.

Texas was annexed by the USA in 1845. A year later, President James Polk (1845–9) declared war on Mexico. The Mexican-American War (1846–8) was fought across the Rio Grande and involved major battles in Monterey and for control of Mexico City, which fell in September 1847 after Santa Anna's army withdrew. The border was duly changed, and California was formally annexed by the USA in the Treaty of Guadalupe Hidalgo in 1848. The sums paid by the US to Mexico as compensation for the annexation were soon recouped many times over, when gold was discovered in California, and as prospectors descended on the newly acquired territories.

Perhaps less well remembered is how America's victory against Mexico widened the eyes of slaveholders hoping to expand their own private business empires. The Mexican-American War was a watershed moment, displaying the ability of the US to deploy tens of thousands of its soldiers and capture huge tracts of territory a world away from Washington.[21] In its aftermath there could be little doubt of America's aptitude for conquest. Not all Americans held slaves, but those who did began to covet new slaveholding lands in Central America and the Caribbean. Slaveholders began to lobby for the USA to annex Cuba and other nearby islands.

Slavery and dreams of empire were inextricably bound together. Slavery was the ultimate manifestation of colonization, not of land but of people. The abolitionist Solomon Northup's personal odyssey of horror, documented in his book *Twelve Years a Slave*, closes with this observation: 'I doubt not hundreds have been as unfortunate as myself; that hundreds of free citizens have been kidnapped and sold into slavery, and are at this moment wearing out their lives in plantations in Texas and Louisiana.'[22] The terror of Northup's ordeal remains a heart-wrenching tale and a well-known example of one man's suffering amidst a system of slavery that had been an aspect of America's expansion.

Slavery was a clear example of an imperial inheritance: the transatlantic slave trade saw scores of Africans brought to the New World by European slavers. Slavery also provided the USA with its moment of reckoning in the Civil War.

President Abraham Lincoln's election in 1860 was bad news for US slaveholders. They felt he would be prejudicial to their interests, by quashing their dreams of America conquering new slaveholding colonies. In the election Lincoln had carried every state in which slavery was outlawed. California's admission to the Union also meant that free states now outnumbered slave states.[23]

As Lincoln explained in his Peoria speech of 1854, slavery was an imperial inheritance: 'Slavery already existed among the French at New Orleans; and to some extent, at St Louis. In 1812 Louisiana came into the Union as a slave state, without controversy. In 1818 or '19, Missouri showed signs of a wish to come in with slavery. This was resisted by northern members of Congress; and thus began the first great slavery agitation in the nation.'

To Lincoln's credit, he tried to be understanding of those who had inherited the practice of slavery: 'When Southern people tell us they are no more responsible for the origin of slavery, than we; I acknowledge the fact ... I have no prejudice against the Southern people. They are just what we would be in their situation. If slavery did not exist among them, they would not introduce it. If it did now exist amongst us, we should not instantly give it up.'[24]

The Union had to fight to make this point. It fought the Confederacy, which formed in 1861, composed of states from the deep south and upper south that wanted to secede from the Union. The matter of slavery was essential to the Confederacy, because the economies of the southern states relied on the cotton trade and its use of slaves.

The resulting Civil War lasted for four bitter years (1861–5). The decisive battle between the soldiers of the blue (Union) and the grey (Confederate) uniforms took place at Gettysburg in Pennsylvania. It was waged over three days (1–3 July) in 1863. Confederate general Robert E. Lee had invaded the north to try and threaten the Union's capital, Washington. His gambit failed, and the Confederacy never recovered its momentum afterwards. The two sides continued to slug it out until 1865, when Lee's army was finally defeated and forced to abandon the Confederate capital of Richmond, Virginia. Lee surrendered to Union general Ulysses S. Grant, bringing the Civil War to a close. It was a devastating conflict that killed an estimated 2 per cent of the total American population of the time, including at least 650,000 soldiers (and, in all likelihood, many more than that, given the imprecision of records).

Some of the scars of such a devastating war still haven't fully healed.

Gettysburg remains sacred ground. Visiting the huge site today requires a car to cover the area. Back on 19 November 1863, Lincoln effectively consecrated the battlefield: 'Four score and seven years ago our fathers brought forth on this continent a new nation, conceived in Liberty, and dedicated to the proposition that all men are created equal ... We have come to dedicate a portion of that field, as a final resting place for those who here gave their lives that that nation might live.'[25]

These fine words could not slam the door closed on a divided story. Quite the opposite – so much ill feeling had been unleashed. Lincoln himself was assassinated in April 1865, just days after Lee's surrender and the Civil War's end. This hardly spelled the end of black persecution, notably in parts of the south. As William Du Bois, one of black America's most vital intellectuals, ruefully observed: 'the granting of the ballot to the black man was a necessity, the very least a guilty nation could grant a wronged race, and the only method of compelling the South to accept the results of the war. Thus Negro suffrage ended a civil war by beginning a race feud."[26]

The legacy of slavery, this most pernicious of imperial imports, lingered painfully. Sparks still fly in modern America over the controversies around taking down Robert E. Lee statues and banning Confederacy flags. In recent years, as some of America's businesses and states have chosen to stop displaying the flag, seeing it as synonymous with slavery, some southerners have not taken this turn of events lightly, arguing that the Confederate flag (and the Lee statues) reflect their heritage. The politics of historical memory are still being fought over, a century and a half after the Civil War, even if the war's outcome had guaranteed the preservation of the Union.

America could not insulate itself from the practices of empire in its first hundred years: some of these practices came with the inheritance of its original settlers; other imperial practices remained prevalent in the world at large. They were interpreted and adapted by the USA in a novel way for its own conquest of North America and, during the next hundred years, in its global expansion.

Settling on the American way: from colonizer to influencer

After the Civil War, as the USA recovered its strength, it teetered on becoming a full-blown colonizing power. This false start deeply influenced how the USA saw its growing global stature.

In the latter part of the nineteenth century, with its population burgeoning, the USA began to experience an economic take-off, which was driven by reconstruction of the south, the winning of the west, railway construction and industrialization.[27] Territorial expansion continued with the 1867 purchase of Alaska from the Russian tsar for $7.2 million. There was only so much land that money could buy, and war would prove to be a greater catalyst for expansion.[28]

The Spanish-American War in 1898 would be the USA's coming-of-age moment as a Pacific power on the upswing. It was also the making of the multi-talented Theodore Roosevelt, who left his post as Assistant Secretary to the Navy in order to get stuck into the fighting. The US military had intervened to support a Cuban rebellion against Spanish colonial rule, and this was Roosevelt's opportunity for personal glory in the name of causes he advocated: freeing the Cubans from the Spanish, and proving to Europeans that the USA was no longer to be trifled with. Roosevelt formed the 'Rough Riders' cavalry detachment and gained personal fame in the battles that followed.

Around this time Roosevelt stirred his fellow Americans to action with the following speech: 'There comes a time in the life of a nation, as in the life of an individual, when it must face great responsibilities . . . We have now reached that time . . . The guns of our warships in the tropic seas of the West and the remote islands of the East have awakened us to the knowledge of new duties.'[29]

Another pro-war voice was the naval theorist Alfred T. Mahan, whose writings helped to persuade Americans that they needed to dominate the seas. He argued that the war was justified by 'the generally iniquitous character of Spanish rule in the colonies'. The USA would intervene on the basis of 'enlightened self-interest', refuting Spain's tyrannical rule while also inheriting the best of British imperial practices: 'Sea power, as a national interest, commercial and military, rests not upon fleets only, but also upon local territorial bases in distant commercial regions.'

To govern these foreign holdings, Mahan explained, 'territories beyond the sea can be securely held only when the advantage and interests of the inhabitants are the primary object of the administration. The inhabitants may not return love for their benefits – comprehension or gratitude may fail them.'[30] Such a condescending passage was unerringly similar to idealized European justifications for empire. Men like Mahan and Roosevelt were persuading Americans to step into the imperial breach.

America's military defeated Spain within a year of the outbreak of hostilities. As well as Cuba, the USA annexed other Spanish colonies, including the Philippines, Puerto Rico and Guam, seizing Hawaii for good measure too.

The US military initially arrived in the Philippines to ally with the locals against the Spanish, but American soldiers ended up fighting the Filipinos, who had no desire to exchange one set of occupiers for another. A bitter colonial war ensued there against local resistance: in this war, 4,234 Americans were killed (compared to just 379 in the war against Spain). In the way the US military conducted the Philippines war, the prejudices of racial superiority derived from its long experience of the 'Indian Wars' and of southern slavery were sometimes noticeable in US soldiers' perception of the locals as expendable. The US Army had prevailed in the Philippines war by 1902, and at least 250,000 Filipinos died along the way (a minority from fighting, many more from disease, with the total number of deceased likely to have been much higher).[31]

At the start of the twentieth century the USA seemed ready, capable and motivated to become an imperial power on a scale that could exceed its European forebears. The English writer Rudyard Kipling, thrilled at this prospect, penned the following lines in exhortation of the US war in the Philippines:

> Take up the White Man's Burden –
> The savage wars of peace –
> Fill full the mouth of famine
> And bid the sickness cease.

Kipling's words were only partially heeded. Not long after its coming of age as a colonizer, America decided to take up a different profession: as a global power that decisively influenced other places, rather than controlled them. A *Pax Americana* was established around Central America and in the Pacific, but it would end up looking quite different from the European seaborne empires.

No episode better exemplifies America's brazen assertion of its rite of passage than that over the Panama Canal, which the now President Theodore Roosevelt (1901–9) muscled in to create. In November 1903 the US recognized the Republic of Panama, with the quid pro quo that Panama's government signed a treaty that gave the US territorial rights over a twenty-mile-wide zone on either side of where the canal was later built. With the canal's completion in 1914, the US gained the ability to move its navy directly between the Pacific and Atlantic Oceans – an ability that proved telling during the world wars. Panama had been persuaded and strong-armed, not conquered.

The world wars were the platform onto which America stepped, reluctantly at first, in its transition to a global superpower. The Great War proved to be a false dawn. President Woodrow Wilson (1913–21) initially tried to keep America out of the war, but couldn't ignore international opinion turning against Germany in 1915, when a U-boat sank the passenger liner *Lusitania*, killing more than a thousand people (including scores of American civilians). Wilson eventually caved in to political and public pressure, and in 1917 American soldiers (known then as 'doughboys', due to their ration packs) deployed to Europe to help deliver the *coup de grâce* against the German Army.

What came next in fact reasserted America's anti-colonial credentials. Wilson wanted to be guarantor of a post-imperial peace without annexations. In his 'Fourteen Points for Peace' he announced a desire to dismantle the old colonial empires. Amongst his words was the line: 'we feel ourselves to be intimate partners of all the governments and peoples associated together against the imperialists'. At this moment in 1918, it looked as if the US might lead a post-imperial world order.

Congress, however, vetoed Wilson's ideas for a greater global role. America was not yet ready to preside over world affairs as moral guarantor and policeman. Wilson's efforts were not wasted, however. As the historian Susan Pedersen explains: 'that "Wilsonian moment"... mobilised publics from Poland to Samoa ... deciding the President's stirring words applied to them'.[32] The USA's anti-colonial founding myth had reverberated globally.

During the Second World War, America asserted itself on a global scale. Its drift into the war was gradual. The USA granted a 'lend-lease' deal to the UK, allowing it use of certain US military bases, which passed into law in March 1941. Churchill's pleas for wartime assistance from President Franklin D. Roosevelt (1933–45) previewed the changing of the guard that was set to occur between the one-time imperial master and its former colony. But it was the Japanese Empire's attack on the US fleet moored up in Pearl Harbor, Hawaii, on 7 December 1941, and its coordinated attacks across the Pacific, including on the Philippines, that provoked F. D. R. to bring America's military into the war. The eventual defeat of Germany and Japan, which the US military played a major role in achieving, was the springboard for the enduring US role in both Europe and Asia that persists today.

Post-1945 there was no return to isolationism; American 'empire by invitation' (a term used by historian Geir Lundestad) saw it establish a presence in West Germany and Japan. Democracy (under American tutelage) replaced empire as the foundation of order, bankrolled by US dollars spent in post-war reconstruction. In this regard, at least, the USA was following the well-trodden footsteps of past empires by guaranteeing the peace in order to justify its dominating influence.

By 1955 it was operating 450 military bases in thirty-six countries. A post-war global economic system was being refashioned from the old colonial one, this time with the USA at its hub.[33] America's material wealth, its sense of destiny and its notion of exceptionalism had impelled it to take on ever-greater global roles. The Cold War unfolded concurrently with decolonization, so American military and business interests filled the gaps created by the retreating European colonists. For example, the US inherited former British colonial military outposts, and eventually took the strain from France in its decolonization war in Indochina.

In the paddy fields of Vietnam the new-found imperial vigour of America's foreign policy met its match. The US military simply could not win, in no small part because America's ideologies had contributed to its misdiagnosis of the conflict. The American government had convinced itself of the need to embed democracy in South Vietnam, and to protect it from North Vietnam's communist regime. This logic was compelling for presidents John F. Kennedy (1961–3) and Lyndon B. Johnson (1963–9), under whose watches the US military became ever more involved. The problem was that Vietnam was experiencing its own civil war, after its nation had fractured under the intense pressures of its anti-colonial war against French rule. The US mistakenly imposed a binary logic of 'democracy versus communism' on a war that was too complex to allow for such reasoning. As many as two million Vietnamese, and more than 58,000 Americans, paid for these mistakes with their lives.

America's claim to be defending freedom abroad was further hobbled by discrimination at home. Young black American conscripts were fighting in Vietnam, but their communities still faced prejudicial treatment. The civil-rights movement would be catalysed by Martin Luther King, who was born in Atlanta, Georgia, in 1929 – a city that Du Bois had called 'the geographical focus of our Negro population'.[34] King's soaring rhetoric helped to deliver, for Americans at home, breakthroughs in their civil rights that mirrored the spirit of anti-colonial movements abroad. In doing so, it illustrated a persistently contentious matter, of some white Americans treating themselves as the 'core' of the nation and seeing the descendants of slaves as less than equal.

*

The Cold War was as much an ideological contest as it was a physical stand-off between the militaries of the superpowers. The Cold War Doctrine of President Harry Truman (1945–53) had set the tone by putting the US on a path to 'contain' Soviet global influence. 'Wherever the USSR placed an X the US placed an O,' reflected contemporary Senator Tim Kaine.[35] This led to decisions to intervene in the politics of countries like Guatemala, Congo, Cuba and Iran. The USA was convinced of its need to deny – to the freedom-denying communists – any opportunities for influence to shape political destinies around the world.

Moscow's old-fashioned territorial empire eventually struggled to compete with Washington's cutting-edge empire of influence. Buoyed by its research and development successes in the Second World War, which had already produced the atomic bomb, America continued to spearhead technological development in various areas. For example, there were advances in synthetic products (which, with the notable exception of oil, ended the need to seize other places for resources); transport (so that US influence and firepower could be projected from the skies); and communication (which enabled Hollywood movies and American radio to be broadcast globally). America increasingly projected its influence without the trappings of a formal empire, because technology allowed it to.[36]

Perhaps this is why President Ronald Reagan (1981–9) confidently denounced the USSR as 'the evil empire' – a wonderful rhetorical jab that pointed out Moscow's iron grip over Eastern Europe, while disavowing America from the slur of empire.

With the collapse of the USSR in 1991, Reagan and his successor, George H. W. Bush (1989–93), presided over the further expansion of America's global influence, its propagation of neo-liberal capitalist practices and the era of an undisputed US-led world order. Francis Fukuyama, the political scientist, captured the hubris of the time by writing that 'the end of history' had arrived, thanks to the collapse of the communist model and the triumph of American liberal capitalism.

It was not only hubris, but ingenuity, that had secured the USA such a dominant world role. Its military outposts, and its sponsorship of the NATO military alliance, provided the hard-power guarantee for exercising control over flows of trade, information and services.[37] Globalization, rather than colonization, had become the American way of ruling the post-imperial roost.

Refashioning the very notion of empire has helped the USA craft a world without formal empires. An American who looks at the world map and sees US military bases all over, sees US cultural and technology products with a global fan-base, and hears the English language spoken almost everywhere can easily reconcile all this with the USA's founding myths.

Freedom is not free, but it sure is ill-defined

When I lived in Washington DC in 2008, many young politicos would talk about America's global significance. One rather trivial conversation sticks with me. I was told with conviction over happy-hour drinks, by a very well-meaning man, that 'America was the world's first true democracy'. When I opined that perhaps Europe's political experiences might have planted essential roots, I was swiftly put in my place regarding the purity of the American model. Such self-assuredness was not in short supply in DC, the cockpit of America's informal world empire of commerce and influence.

I had moved to DC to work for the RAND Corporation, the US think tank that had been set up in 1948 to preserve academic input in US defence policy.[38] RAND's Europe office in Cambridge, UK, had given me my first job out of university and later sent me to their DC office, which inhabited an innocuous space atop a shopping mall near the Pentagon. I was there to help research and author a study into the US–Pakistan relationship, which, after 9/11, had become mission critical in the response against al-Qaeda. Contributing to this study with experienced US authors offered me great insights into how the US leveraged its global influence.[39]

In Washington I was struck by the contrast with London, which by comparison felt stooped in a faded glory. London's soot-stained statues were to its old imperial heroes. Washington's monuments were to its more recent global entanglements. The city somehow felt grander for it. I visited Arlington Cemetery to pay my respects to those killed in the Civil War, the world wars, Korea, Vietnam, Iraq and Afghanistan. The headstones, arrayed row by row and resplendent in an ethereal white, seemed in their totality to convey America's sincere belief that their service personnel have died through the ages in the defence of their freedom.

Patriotic nationalism, rather than imperialism, explains much of what makes America tick as a globally engaged superpower. Support for its troops, especially after 9/11, has become a unifying creed for many Americans, with the belief that their compatriots in uniform serving abroad – no matter the context – should be venerated for their service and sacrifice. This is a huge step up (and over-compensation, perhaps) from the Vietnam-era castigation of the unfortunate conscripts who had been forced to fight there, by Americans at home who wanted someone at whom to direct their anger and upset over the war. Part of the reason why there had been so much hurt and confusion in America about its role in Vietnam was that the war didn't seem to make any sense at all.

In the Second World War, when US military intervention tipped the scales against Germany and Japan, the cause of fighting for global freedoms was less ambiguous. The same was also true in the 1991 Gulf War, when the US military fought to liberate Kuwait. After 9/11 its many counter-terror and counter-insurgency-related deployments have unfolded across Asia, Africa and the Middle East, but they have less clearly been able to embody the 'freedom' rationale.

Self-defence and freedom have become conjoined rationales to sell the idea of these foreign commitments to domestic audiences. Some people accept this rationale. Others question why their military is so widely deployed around the world, and whether its global presence magnifies the terrorism threat to Americans.

As befits a nation with free speech, there is a thriving tradition of Americans who argue that their country's neo-imperialism lies at the root of many of the world's ills. Writer and political commentator Noam Chomsky has helped to shape the tradition. Chomsky was an MIT linguistics professor during campus protests against the Vietnam War in the 1960s. While he didn't join the protesters, the episode left its mark on his writing. In *Hegemony or Survival*, for example, he delivers a polemic against funding repressive regimes under the exigencies of the 'war on terror', and points to the continuities with US foreign policies during the Cold War of doing precisely the same in the name of blocking the global spread of communism, and as part of an 'imperial grand strategy'.[40]

Another critic astutely predicted the underlying motives behind the 9/11 attacks. Chalmers Johnson, a navy veteran turned professor, warned in 2000 that America risked suffering 'blowback' for its foreign and defence policies. 'Acts committed in service to an empire but never acknowledged as such have a tendency to haunt the future,' he warned, before complaining that 'we Americans deeply believe that our role in the world is virtuous – that our actions are almost invariably for the good of others as well as ourselves. Even when our country's actions have led to disaster, we assume that the motives behind them were honourable.'[41]

The charge of self-denial is important. It is an indication of its imperial inheritance that America shoehorns loose notions of freedom into its activities. A paradoxical blend of righteousness and self-assertion is conveyed by phrases like 'Empire of Liberty', 'Manifest Destiny' and 'The Indispensable Nation' (the latter coined by Madeleine Albright in 1998 when Secretary of State). This kind of language has deposited its influence in the American psyche over different generations. The enduring sentiment is that America has the right to its global influence because it is, ultimately, in the interests of the world for it to do so.

Free will, and assumptions around choice, are essential to this belief. America doesn't impose itself uninvited: from Germany to Japan in the 1940s, South Korea to South Vietnam in the Cold War, and Afghanistan to Iraq after 9/11, Americans have supported their sovereign partners. However, the logic of the late 1940s, in which American occupations came in the wake of total victory in the most devastating conflict the world has ever seen, applies itself awkwardly in other circumstances. America has become adept at engineering situations to prolong its involvement all over the world. Its base in Okinawa is a relic from the victory over Japan seventy-five years ago, but remains as a lynchpin in its coming Pacific stand-off with the Chinese Navy. It is all perfectly legal, since the US government negotiates a 'Status of Forces Agreement' with the sovereign governments that host its bases – although one wonders whether the SOFA proves too comfortable ever to leave.

America's democratic faith has indeed set limits over the extent to which it exerts direct rule over other people. Reconciling these lofty principles of democracy with the pragmatism needed in international affairs is essentially impossible. This is the tragedy of America's informal empire. It is why America becomes a target for global consternation and accusations of hypocrisy, and why such criticisms can leave Americans rather touchy. 'The belief in American innocence, of "original sinlessness", is both very old and very powerful,' academic Anatol Lieven has observed. 'This is in origin a New England puritan or "Yankee" myth stemming from the idea of the settlers as God's elect, born again in the New World and purged of the sins of England and Europe.'[42] Not all Americans bought into this myth, with white southerners historically suspicious of Yankee moralizing. Generalizations such as these can only ever be a guide, but they help to explain why

America's globally impactful decisions can be so unfathomable and unpopular to outsiders.

'Freedom' and 'liberty' are often invoked by Americans to make sense of their nation's birth, its political culture and its manifest destiny. But freedom and liberty are not abstract concepts that exist apart from history. Rather, they only ever make sense in the context of circumstance, geography and imperial inheritance. Wantonly transferring them from one context to another (for example, by democratizing defeated enemies in 1945, then trying to do the same in Iraq in 2003) precipitates disasters in which everyone suffers – both the Americans and those they are supposed to be helping.

Herein resides a blind spot in the American government's self-image: fixating on the good intent behind its actions rather than on their outcomes. So many American citizens can see this, but they cannot fundamentally alter the incentives and compulsions behind their country's globe-straddling presence.

Presidential roulette:
'America first' and insular imperialism

Every president brings his own proclivities to the job. But no matter what they personally believe before they start work in the White House's Oval Office, no president can retreat from the wider world. The psychological legacies of an imperial inheritance, and the physical responsibilities of managing an informal empire, do not discriminate between Republican and Democrat, hawk or dove. The imperial inheritance is open to different interpretations, and there is an endless supply of arguments to be forged from the ambiguities of America's global posture.

In the 1990s America was getting used to a world in which it had no challenger. Bill Clinton (1993–2001) was not a foreign-policy-oriented president, nor did he need to be. Early on in his presidency, Clinton was burned by America's failed intervention in Somalia's civil war and famine, immortalized on page and film as the *Black Hawk Down* incident. So Clinton's administration steered clear of the Rwandan genocide and was sclerotic in involving itself in Yugoslavia's disintegration. In the face of humanitarian catastrophes around the world, the moral righteousness to act crept into his presidency through figures like Madeleine Albright. Overall, however, America lacked a clear enemy against which to project its moralizing and military prowess.

While the broad optimism of Clinton's era as president extended into the new millennium, his successor was dealt the terrible fate of the 9/11 attacks. The wars of President George W. Bush (2001–9) have been perhaps the most divisive actions undertaken by modern America. His administration was full of ideologues who maintained both romantic notions concerning the exercise of American military power and a keen understanding of how doing so would perpetuate America's informal empire. Bush responded to 9/11 by listening to these ideological hawks and opting for a militarized response, and by identifying an 'Axis of Evil' of states that could threaten America (which seemed a different problem from the actual issue of al-Qaeda's network).

The cottage industry of Americans criticizing their own government burgeoned and gained a worldwide following, for example in the films of Michael Moore, and through the caustic comedy movie *Team America: World Police* (2004), which offered an interpretation of the absurdities of fighting terrorists across an informal empire. Bush seemed oblivious to the criticisms. A Texan, he embodied a maverick persona, mixed with earthy sensibilities, that made sense to a slice of the domestic electorate (he secured a second term in 2004), but left a large swathe of the rest of the world baffled as to why America would respond to the blowback against its global presence by extending it further.

Before taking office, Barack Obama (president 2009–17) astutely judged that in foreign policy 'our record is mixed', alternating between being 'farsighted' and 'misguided'. 'Such ambiguity shouldn't be surprising, for American foreign policy has always been a jumble of warring impulses.'[43] Obama toned down Bush's all-out approach and made a conscious effort to present to the world the softer side of America's values. He declared Iraq an unjust war and wound down US involvement there, but he did so to double down on the war effort in Afghanistan. By the second term of his presidency in 2012, the renewed war effort in Afghanistan had produced only negligible gains in stabilizing the country and defeating the Taliban. This perhaps explains Obama's reticence, bordering on inaction, when it came to the escalating civil war in Syria after 2011.

Each presidential administration reacts to the events of its time, but in doing so it offers its own interpretation of how America's global presence should be used. Which is why, even before he took presidential office, Donald Trump (2017–) was clear that he opposed America's endless foreign wars and burdensome international commitments. He would personify a sense of America shrugging its shoulders and not bothering itself so much with an ungrateful world.

Such is the game of presidential roulette – neither its own people nor the world at large can ever really guess what lies in store for them, and which imperial legacies matter the most. In Trump's case, it would revisit the legacies of the Mexican-American war.

Donald Trump's electoral victory in 2016 has been bitterly divisive for America. It has also coincided with a time in world history when America's global dominance, unquestioned for so long, has seemed less everlasting. The question for America's influence, and for its liberal world order, is what shape it will be in after Trump. When America awakens from the spell cast by Trump's temperamental presidency, will its moral authority around the world have been diminished beyond repair, with rivals like China and Russia stepping into the gaps it has left?

Before entering politics late in life as a maverick candidate,

Trump earned his wealth as a property baron and TV personality, displaying little worldliness or interest in much beyond America's shores. His empire had been a business one, which, ultimately, was perfectly in tune with how America has historically exercised its power via trade and finance. Trump was not greatly bothered by loftier ideals of democracy abroad or motivated by militarism.

While Trump's America did not suddenly retreat from all its global undertakings, the presidential enthusiasm for them was clearly lacking. Trump berated his NATO allies in Europe for not paying enough into their defence budgets, arguing that they had been free-riding since the Cold War on America's defence commitments to Europe. He cut off US military aid to Pakistan for being an inconsistent partner in the 'war on terror' (Osama bin Laden, after all, was shot dead by US special-forces soldiers back in 2011, after he was found squirrelled away in Pakistan). Trump ordered the scaling down of the US military presence in Afghanistan, where its troops were battling al-Qaeda and supporting the government it had installed after 9/11. And Trump withdrew US forces from Syria, where a relatively modest number of them had been battling ISIS. When forced to validate this decision, amidst concerns that ISIS was not yet totally beaten, Trump simply said that Syria offered to America nothing but 'sand and death'.

Much like gazing at the stock market, we can become fixated by short-term fluctuations in political events and by the impulsive decisions of a particular president. No matter how novel Trump might have appeared at the time, his proclivities reflected a particular interpretation of the instinct for America to step back from an ungrateful world, count its dollars and look after itself.

Just as the trajectories of old empires were dependent on the personalities and abilities of any given emperor or empress, so America's presidential system is somewhat beholden to the impulses of the person in charge. Even democratic checks and balances cannot overturn this basic fact of US political life. Back in an era of monarchies, it was commonly understood that one bad ruler in a pantheon of wise and worldly leaders could greatly endanger the empire's position and its standing amongst both friends and rivals.

The biggest post-imperial convulsions of the Trump era have been domestic. The varied facets of American imperial heritage include the role of white settlers in the early history of pan-continental expansion, and how the national character is shaped by these experiences.

For instance, it is impossible to grasp the defence of gun rights – and the argument that what is needed to stop a 'bad guy with a gun' is a 'good guy with a gun' – without recourse to historical myths of the gun-slinging frontiersman. The National Rifle Association (NRA) has five million members and, as well as being gun enthusiasts, they have earned a reputation for holding certain conservative political and cultural attitudes. National character has many facets, but at least one facet of America's identity, embodied by groups like the NRA, is that of the maverick who sees himself as a bold and plucky nonconformist. The Jacksonian tradition remains a symbol of a populist patriotism that reflects 'nativism, anti-elitism, anti-intellectualism, white identity, hostility to other races' – in other words, 'rugged frontier individualism'.[44]

This is perhaps why the Trump administration made sure to kick back to 2028 a proposed change to the $20 bill, in which Andrew Jackson's image was supposed to be replaced by the slave-turned-activist Harriet Tubman.

A key Trump campaign pledge was to build a wall along the US–Mexico border to keep out alleged illegal entrants to the US, while at the same time ejecting those migrants who had already illegally settled in America. Their country's imperial foundations have clearly influenced how some US citizens perceive the changing demographics of their country. Policies like building a wall with Mexico only have resonance in the context of a long history of tension between the two countries, which was once settled by war, but has since been expressed through mutual stereotyping and blame for common, shared cross-border problems.

Changing demographics explain why these issues concern some parts of white America. According to the US Census Bureau, in data released in 2018, 'the non-Hispanic White-alone population is projected to shrink over the coming decades, from 199 million in 2020 to 179 million in 2060 – even as the US population continues to grow. Their decline is driven by falling birth rates and a rising number of deaths over time among non-Hispanic Whites as that population ages.'[45] Polling from the Public Religion Research Institute, also from 2018, examined attitudes concerning the US becoming a majority non-white nation by 2045. It found that 64 per cent of Americans polled thought it would be a mostly positive change, and 33 per cent thought it would be mainly negative. When these responses were broken down according to political affiliation, far more Republican-supporting respondents (64 per cent) thought this change would be mostly negative.[46]

The leader who comes next in the presidential roulette that is American politics must find imaginative and responsible ways of handling this diversity of opinion. The defensive reactions that some Americans held to the country's changing demographics, and around conceptions of 'whiteness', gave Trump a basis to employ xenophobic language and, in the 2016 election campaign, to assert (against all the evidence) that Obama was not American, but a Kenyan Muslim. The divisiveness of this language has contributed to a polarization in politics and social discourse.

More broadly, it is likely that the imperial backstory to America's formation as a state will play a big role in influencing its future domestic character, as its changing demographics rebalance the outcomes of white settler conquest, two centuries after the fact.

America relearns to share the world stage

The 'American experiment' had its own strong admirers back in the day, including many foreigners who admired its libertarian political systems. America's enthusiasm, energy and vitality have meant that it was able to view the wider world without the baggage of older civilizations. The Europeans who crossed the Atlantic Ocean had to start afresh, and to become the world's primary superpower a mere two centuries later has been a stratospheric ascent. Nevertheless, that ascent was heavily influenced by an imperial inheritance that had accompanied them across the Atlantic, and that will remain a part of America's national character as the world enters a new cycle of great power competition.

The size of China's economy is projected to substantially overtake America's between the 2030s and the 2060s.[47] During this period its imperial inheritance will influence how America perceives and manages greater competition from China. The early signs are that the habits of informal empire have not at all prepared America for a world in which it may no longer be top of the global pecking order as the sole and undisputed superpower.

Trump has provided one indication of what this might look like, by escalating a trade war in 2019 over what he has alleged are China's unfair trade practices (such as undervaluing the renminbi currency to outcompete US firms). As the balance of world order shifts, how ill-tempered America might become will also be reflected in newer arenas of contestation.

Silicon Valley has been the latest engine-room of America's global influence. The cultural and economic reach that America's tech giants offer has opened a new phase in the USA's global influence and interests. It is just over a decade since Facebook, Amazon, Google and others began to dominate a large share of commerce and socializing around much of the world, offering a twenty-first-century manifestation of the projection of influence, ideas and control. This is not 'empire-building', unless one uses the term analogically, but it is an arena of global influence that reflects some of America's neo-imperial impulses in a new form. America has enjoyed a dominant technological and cultural role in the waves of globalization of the 1990s and early 2000s, but it will play a less dominating role in future waves, as the diversity of global influences multiplies far beyond the Western world.

To retain a leading world position, America cannot take for granted its global appeal, and may have to work doubly hard to remind others why it earnestly believes itself to be unlike the great imperial powers of the past. Doing so without retreating into isolationism requires skilled leadership, something that the USA urgently needs as the post-imperial world matures.

TWO

BRITAIN'S GRANDEUR AND GUILT OF EMPIRE

One must never forget that one is a Sahib, and that some day, when examinations are passed, one will command natives.

Rudyard Kipling (1865–1936), *Kim*[1]

... he had grasped the truth about the English and their Empire. The Indian Empire is a despotism – benevolent, no doubt, but still a despotism with theft its final object.

George Orwell (1903–50), *Burmese Days*[2]

Some said it was a snub to Britain. Some said it was a symbol of the part-Kenyan President [Obama's] ancestral dislike of the British Empire.

Boris Johnson, 2016, in response to Barack Obama's removal of a bust of Winston Churchill from the Oval Office[3]

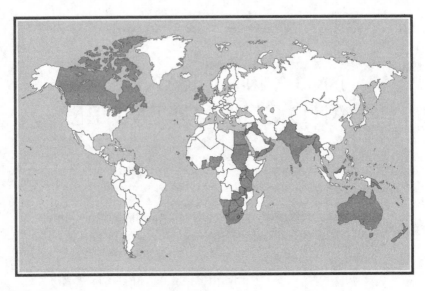

Map 2 The British Empire at its peak, *c.* 1925

Table 1 Remaining British Overseas Territories, 2019

Territory	Location
Anguilla	Caribbean
Bermuda	Caribbean
British Antarctic Territory	Antarctic
British Indian Ocean Territory	Indian Ocean
British Virgin Islands	Caribbean
Cayman Islands	Caribbean
Falkland Islands	South Atlantic Ocean
Gibraltar	South of Spain
Montserrat	Caribbean
Pitcairn Islands	South Pacific Ocean
South Georgia and the South Sandwich islands	South Atlantic Ocean
Sovereign Base Areas of Akrotiri and Dhekelia	Cyprus
St. Helena, Ascension and Tristan da Cunha.	South Atlantic Ocean
Turks and Caicos Islands	Caribbean

The problem with having ruled the largest empire the world has ever seen, upon which the sun never set, is that any achievements afterwards tend to pale in comparison. Britain, a relatively small and isolated island, has played an outsized role in how the modern world developed. It spread the English language, which now has the greatest number of non-native speakers in the world. It planted seeds that later germinated into the thriving modern countries of Australia, Canada, New Zealand and the USA. It has diffused its parliamentary political system to Asia, Africa and beyond. And its financial system, which connected London to these places, still reaps riches for the UK. After an imperial experience that lasted five centuries, Britain settled into post-imperial retirement a few decades ago. As its last imperial generation put their feet up, what legacies can we say the Empire has bequeathed to future Britons?

The half-life of an empire leaves residues of its existence long after its demise. In the post-imperial age this doesn't necessarily lead to straightforward attempts at resurrecting that empire, but to enduring habits and post-imperial behavioural tics in later generations. Put simply, these are the values and lessons from imperial history – both good and bad – that still compel our publics and our politicians. Put uncharitably, this is the historical baggage that stops us thinking with clarity at crucial moments of decision as the world changes.[4]

For Britain, its post-imperial hangover is still being experienced for better and for worse. Britain still benefits from its imperial legacies, ranging from its global economic power with London at the hub of financial industry, to the appeal of its universities and the diversity of its populace. These outcomes partly flow from the physical legacies of the Empire, including the influential connections that Britain developed around the world, and how these continue to renew its global networks of commerce and consumption. People from across the world love to come to Britain (and especially London) to spend their money, whether as tourists, students, workers or investors, precisely because they feel they are visiting one of the enduring centres of global life. Modern Britain has successfully harnessed many positives from its imperial past.

However, the Empire has also deposited lingering mentalities that periodically hinder Britain's progress – notably two of its most consequential foreign-policy decisions of the millennium thus far: the invasion of Iraq in 2003 and the Brexit vote in 2016. A different kind of post-imperial malaise loomed behind each decision. In the case of Iraq, the government of the day believed that British military power could contribute to remaking the Middle East in a Western image, despite Iraq being the source of one of the world's oldest empires. In the case of Brexit, a slim majority of the voting populace chose to leave the EU, partly from a desire to restate Britain's pride in its sovereign autonomy, and to prevent Britain becoming an appendage of Brussels.

Neither decision has anything *directly* to do with imperial legacies – too much time has elapsed between the problems generated by the end of empire and the present day. Nevertheless, the more subtle ways in which the Empire has deposited its influence *are* discernible in both of these decisions, as they also are in a host of other burning issues facing Britain. Abroad, Britain's imperial history textures the way it engages with the economically ascendant India and China. At home, when it comes to Britain's strategies against thwarting home-grown jihadists inspired by al-Qaeda and the Islamic State, some of the trickiest questions relate to how post-imperial experiences have affected immigration patterns and community integration at home.

The question is not so much *if* five centuries of being an imperial power have influenced the character of modern Britain and its ways of thinking and doing things – the answer is surely a resounding 'yes'. The pertinent questions are *how* this influence manifests itself across a host of different issues, and whether a greater consciousness of imperial legacies can positively contribute to Britain's development.

What matters are the unspoken assumptions and expectations generated by a history of successful imperialism, and how these mental legacies of empire became closely entwined with the physical legacies that manifest in Britain's domestic make-up and in its global connections.

The first step in unravelling these conundrums is understanding what the British Empire was. The British historian Arnold Toynbee once quipped that history is 'just one damn thing after another', and a potted history of the Empire must explain how its territorial reach and its governing philosophies changed over time.

'Our Island Story': Britain's experience of empire

Until relatively recently it was normal for energetic, industrious and militaristic nations to expand outwards, seizing the riches that awaited, and spreading their own vision of civilization far and wide. The British Empire developed in an unplanned manner by cobbling together scattered territories. Contemporaries thought its gradual acquisition eventually helped its longevity: 'The British Empire is the outcome of a slow and organic growth,' wrote J. Saxon Mills in 1918. He saw a contrast: 'most empires that have been the result of conscious and ambitious design – whether the designer was an Alexander, or a Napoleon or a Kaiser Wilhelm – have been short-lived'.[5] What were the other secrets to Britain's imperial success?

Much is rightly made of Britain's island geography, which has physically and psychologically demarcated its inhabitants from conquerors and continental trends alike. While the British Isles after the Roman invasion was completely reshaped by successive waves of invaders, from the Vikings to the Normans, for around the last thousand years Britain has forged its destiny free from foreign occupation, which afforded it the opportunity to direct its energies towards its own expansion.

For medieval English kings, nearby France offered the most

inviting territories. Vanity and kingly desires for the prestige of an ever-larger realm were driving impulses. There was a defensive logic too, which was to prevent the French linking up with the Irish, Scots and Welsh and encircling England. France served as England's forward line of defence, right until the ups and downs of the Hundred Years War (1337–1453), during which the English triumphed at the Battle of Agincourt in 1415, but by the war's end had lost its French territories.[6]

Opportunities for expansion further afield arose in the fifteenth and sixteenth centuries, when seafaring English explorers established overseas colonies and trading posts. This was not undertaken through a coherent goal of empire-building or of government policy, but by individuals seeking adventure and profit. Walter Raleigh and Francis Drake, freebooting conquerors during Elizabeth I's reign, gained fame for their daring voyages. Men like these sought official charters and licences from the Crown to stamp English authority on their acquisitions and to fend off their rivals.

By now the Spanish Empire's dramatic expansion posed the biggest threat to England's own ambitions to expand. But the Spanish Armada's failure in 1588 to land on English shores showed just how tough seaborne invasion was, in the face of the determined Royal Navy (which had been formally established four decades previously). War with the Spanish did much to catalyse the English national spirit and spur further conquest.

The scope of English ambition was embodied by Richard Hakluyt, who lobbied for the English colony that was established in 1606 in Jamestown, Virginia. It was the New World's first permanent English settlement and it extended the Protestant Anglo-sphere.

Commerce was the fuel of empire-building, but war was the engine that drove the process. Protestant England's competition with Catholic France and Spain became defining features of wars to come, and furthered England's transformation into Britain.

The Act of Union (1707) bound Scotland to England and Wales in political union (supplanting a dynastic union, which England feared would be abandoned by the Scots in favour of a Catholic claimant to the throne). England was ruled from 1714 until 1837 by an imported German Hanoverian Protestant dynasty, after the childless reign of Queen Anne. France and Spain meanwhile supported Jacobite uprisings in Scotland and Ireland, seeking to restore a Catholic monarch to the English throne. Culminating in the 1746 Battle of Culloden, fought near Inverness, the Jacobite claim was vanquished. As for Ireland, the French invaded in 1796, catalysing a rebellion that was brutally crushed by Britain, and paving the way for the 1801 Act of Union with Ireland.

The distinction between kingdoms and empires is not absolute. For example, the kingdom of England had brought Scotland, Wales and (for a time) Ireland into Britain. And then, by conquering places far away as well, the whole entity eventually renamed itself 'Great Britain'. Why was it later convincing to call India a British colony, but over time less convincing to describe Scotland as an English colony? Some Scots may well disagree with this qualification, but would perhaps agree that many modern countries are former empires now in disguise.

British national identity was thus forged from a patchwork of separate national identities. The expansion of the British Empire offered a profitable rationale for the Union. As the historian Linda Colley notes, a mixture of 'circumstances impressed [Britons] with the belief that they were different from those beyond their shores'.[7] Protestantism, monarchy, war and imperialism imparted upon Britons a worldview in which they saw themselves as distinct from those in continental Europe, against whom their triumphs were mounting.

The Seven Years War of 1756–63 was a triumphant turning point for the Empire. The war with the French and Spanish had gone global and was now unfolding across North America, the Caribbean and India. Britain emerged from the Seven Years War having beaten the French in Canada, India, West Africa and the West Indies, and the Spanish in Havana and Manila.

Robert Clive's victory, on behalf of Britain's East India Company, in the Battle of Plassey in 1757 against the Nawab of Bengal (and his French allies) opened India's riches to British conquest. All told, the scale of these victories changed the Empire's character. Until then it had operated as a maritime commercial network, and as a vehicle to expand the Protestant Anglo-sphere; now the British ruled Catholics in Quebec and a myriad of other races and religions in India and elsewhere.[8]

The Empire's destiny was further altered by the loss of the Thirteen Colonies in America's War of Independence. America's rebels were helped by the French and Spanish to bloody the noses of the British. The eventual loss of the American colonies delivered a seismic shock to British imperialists, who interpreted this as a catastrophic schism between the two main branches of the Anglo-Saxon world, something that added a bittersweet taste to subsequent Anglo-American relations.[9] Canada remained British. Australia came under Britain's influence in 1788, and New Zealand in 1840. But the Empire's overall focus had shifted from colonies of émigrés, to ruling over people who were culturally, ethnically and religiously distinct.

Industrial revolution helped to power the Empire after the loss of the American colonies. Britain harnessed its economic potential – and resources taken from its colonies – like no other economy of the age could manage. Abundant reserves of coal, for example, proved a huge advantage in modernizing Britain's naval power, by making its warships faster. This was vital in such a sprawling Empire, which again needed to be defended when the situation on the European continent turned against Britain, with the rise of Napoleon after the French Revolution. Britain played a leading role in negating the French threat, culminating in the Battle of Waterloo in 1815 that ended the Napoleonic Wars. At the subsequent peace conference, the Congress of Vienna, the British walked off with the lion's share of the spoils. Not only was Britain on the winning side, but an era of shrunken French power beckoned. This reaped for Britain a geopolitical dividend. Unlike Napoleon, Britain did not covet dominion of the European continent, parts of which remained under Austro-Hungarian, Russian and Ottoman rule at this time. Instead, Britain used the opportunity to further expand its far-flung Empire.

Queen Victoria's long reign (1837–1901) saw the Empire approach its apex. Russia became Britain's major rival during this era. British and Russian empires fenced for influence in South and Central Asia, in what became known as the 'Great Game'. During Prime Minister Palmerston's tenure, the Crimean War (1853–6) saw Russian expansion checked by British alliance with the French and the Ottomans. As the century came to an end there was an absence of war among the great powers of Europe. Europe's rivalries were held in balance by the delicate diplomacy of the Concert of Europe, a loose conglomeration of powers that agreed to use diplomacy as a first resort in sorting out any rivalries and complaints against other nations.

Peace in Europe meant that Britain could further focus on its colonial consolidation abroad. *Small Wars: Their Principles and Practice* (1896), written by Colonel Charles Callwell, provides a useful summation of the military arts as seen through British gunsights at the time. He writes of 'expeditions against savages and semi-civilised races by disciplined soldiers, campaigns undertaken to suppress rebellious and guerrilla warfare in all parts of the world'.[10] As ghastly as this language is, this was also the era when Britain abolished slavery. Having for so long been involved in the gruesome transportation of African people to America's colonies, Britain's about-turn came in 1834. It took years for abolition to come into real effect, just as it had taken years of prior campaigning by William Wilberforce, a parliamentarian and evangelical, to argue against slavery. In yet another contradiction, as slavery was ending, Britain began to formally annex parts of Africa.

Such were the contradictory impulses behind British imperialism. It was fuelled by various drives: the civilizing ambition of spreading modernity; Christian missionary zeal; the military logic of pitting British mettle against weaker natives; and the naked profiteering of being at the centre of a web of trade. All these impulses were at play and it was not always easy to align them. Britain was now a global superpower, but these deep contradictions bedevilled the entire enterprise. As Charles Napier (who consolidated British rule in India) intoned: 'It is true we have won the Empire most unjustly, but it is now impossible to abandon our position. We may not retreat, and can only hold our ground by skill and courage.'[11]

Repression was part of the toolkit, as British soldiers periodically suppressed rebellions across the Empire. In 1857 the Indian mutiny against British rule erupted, and was only suppressed because enough sepoys (Indian soldiers) stayed loyal to their British masters. In Africa, the British also found their control could be bitterly contested, for example when suffering a military defeat in 1879 at Isandlwana in South Africa by a Zulu army, which had none of the technological advantages of the British soldiers they overwhelmed. When General Gordon was killed by locals in Khartoum in 1885, the episode shocked the public when the news reached home.

The British public preferred to lap up stories of valour, ingenuity and success across the Empire. Even those members of the public who were largely apathetic to imperial affairs could not ignore the fact that their country was a superpower. Enthusiasm at home for the Empire was deeply entwined with patriotic pride for the monarchy, and reached fever pitch as Victoria was proclaimed 'Empress of India' in 1876, and at her Diamond Jubilee celebrations in 1897.

Yet the turn of the century saw the Boer War tarnish Britain's lustre, as its army took several years to subdue a rebellion of

Dutch-origin farmers in the Transvaal. Different methods were being used to govern and hold on to each part of the Empire. Some territories were annexed outright. Others were ruled as 'dominions' (Canada, Australia, New Zealand and South Africa) and were granted some measure of self-rule, whereas the 'dependencies' or 'protectorates' were not. Overall, by 1914 the British Crown's sovereignty extended across eighty territories, covering eleven million square miles and including more than 400 million people, which, in a world population of an estimated 1.7 billion at this time, was a significant percentage of humanity.[12]

The ties holding together all of these distant lands and peoples began to fray and snap under the pressure of the world wars. The Great War stoked the fires of national awakening and challenges to British rule. The failed 1915 Gallipoli campaign, where Australian and New Zealand (Anzac) soldiers played a major role in Britain's war against the Ottomans, led some Anzacs to question British rule. The Fenians' 1916 Easter Rising was aggravated by Irish soldiers' experiences on the Western Front. Indian soldiers who fought in the trenches, suffering more than 74,000 deaths among their comrades, were horrified by news of the 1919 Amritsar Massacre, when scores of Indian civilians were killed by General Dyer's troops, laying bare the essential hypocrisy of British rule in India.

Paradoxically, after the Great War, the Treaty of Versailles granted Britain (and France) even more colonies. The Germans lost theirs, and the Ottoman and Russian Empires had collapsed entirely.[13] In the inter-war years the Empire seemed to grow larger than Britain's ability to defend it. Britain started to rely on the Royal Air Force, which was formed in 1916, to suppress uprisings in places like Iraq. The prototype R-101 airship, *Empire of the Clouds*, symbolized British optimism and hubris. This giant blimp was a marvel of aeronautical engineering for its time. It was supposed to connect the various British overseas territories, but it crashed on its maiden voyage in 1930, killing all the assembled dignitaries, in a tragic metaphor for the badly over-stretched Empire.

A decade later the Second World War precipitated the Empire's final downward descent. In 1939 Britain again went to war to defend its empire against new rivals and upstarts. The British public sometimes exhibits a patchy knowledge of its imperial history, perhaps because most prefer to reflect on their country's contribution in the Second World War. It is a story that still holds a part of the national psyche in rapture, and Brexit-era Britain has entertained itself with films like the Churchill biopic *Darkest Hour*, and with *Dunkirk*, the story of the British Expeditionary Force's retreat from Europe in 1940. Britain's 'finest hour' in resisting the Nazi German war machine rightfully remains an inspiring story, although the myth of 'standing alone' underplays how soldiers, sailors and sustenance from the colonies bolstered Britain's war effort.

The British Empire's actions in the Second World War may well be its biggest gift to the modern world, because it played a vital role in fighting imperial Japan in Asia and the Nazi German Empire in Europe, which Hitler was building on a basis of genocidal racial hierarchy. Perhaps this is another reason why the Second World War matters so much to British historical memory: it showed its own empire in action against unquestionably more aggressive and inhumane rivals.

It is also far easier to comprehend the six-year event of the war, with its clear beginning and end, than it is to take in the Empire, which was a five-centuries-long state of being and of mind. Moreover, Britain's post-war fall from imperial grace happened just as an English-speaking former colony rose to superpower status. The transatlantic 'special relationship' with the US has hardly been plain sailing but, overall, the rise of the US has magnified Britain's importance in a way afforded to no other European ex-empire. All this has lastingly influenced Britain's self-identity and sense of global purpose. France, by contrast, was occupied by Germany during the war and, once liberated, did not follow on the coat tails of a new Francophone superpower. None existed. Instead, France faced painful decolonization wars in Algeria and Indochina at precisely the same time it was investing more of its hopes for the future in the European Economic Community (EEC).

In the 1950s Britain still had grand ambitions to remain a powerful and independent world player, able to operate independently of America. Despite the country's wartime exertions, the war's outcome had not undermined, but had in fact vindicated, British confidence.[14] This flimsy façade was exposed by the Suez War debacle in 1956. It was the moment that Britain's status as a global superpower was revealed as fiction. Prime Minister Eden's government conspired with Israel and France to end Egyptian General Nasser's seizure of the Suez Canal from the company that ran it. Eden was blindsided by America's angry response: President Eisenhower sought consensus with the USSR at the UN, to order an end to the attack on Egypt. Britain was rebuked, its troops withdrawn in ignominy. A new world order, in which the superpowers held most of the cards, had dawned. Britain was left on the sidelines, eventually settling into a subordinate role to the US during the Cold War, and later grudgingly joining the EEC. Meanwhile its colonies were being dismantled.

After Suez, the Empire's fragmentation gathered pace. For a while it looked as if Britain might anchor its empire in Africa. Since the nineteenth-century 'scramble for Africa', the continent had condescendingly been considered by some colonists so backward as to be incapable of self-rule. The reality was that African independence movements were gaining momentum, inspired by other anti-colonial struggles. Britain's African holdings one by one came free: Ghana (1957), Nigeria (1960), Sierra Leone (1961), Tanzania (1961), Kenya (1963), Gambia (1965) and – after the bitter Rhodesian War – Zimbabwe under Robert Mugabe (1980). The British were out of Africa.

Decolonization gathered pace not only due to Britain's declining material capacity to grip the colonies, but also because its ideals were bankrupt. The Empire was built on a belief of superiority of a certain strata of Britons to rule others, with attendant theories to explain the economic dynamism and creativity of the colonizers. British colonists thought that in the future non-Europeans could emulate these accomplishments, with the appropriate tutelage. An analogy was used, of colonies as 'children' that were tutored by and then grew independent from their 'parents'. This was prevalent in Britain (especially after its American settler colony had decided it was grown-up enough in 1776 and left home).[15] For example, *The Economist* magazine wrote in 1862 that colonies 'would be just as valuable to us . . . if they were independent', adding that 'uncivilised races' still needed 'guidance, guardianship and teaching'.[16] By this logic, non-Europeans needed to follow the instruction sheet of modernity and emulate its accomplishments.

Thus, if interpreted from a stubborn and prideful British perspective, the independent states hewn from the colonies had come from a wellspring of British effort – a view soon eclipsed by the drive and desire of newly independent peoples to walk their own path.

Some former colonies managed this with aplomb; others suffered kleptocratic rulers who mismanaged the opportunities of independence; or they suffered persistent violence. Where Britain's retreat was hasty and led to violence, the wounds of colonial rule continued to bleed for generations, as India and Pakistan's awful schism had shown since 1947, and as Israel and the Palestinians also experienced. Some former colonies gained independence through hard bargaining with the departing British. There were some orderly transitions of power and other blood-drenched catastrophes, such as in Kenya during the Mau Mau uprising in the 1950s.[17] Violence also surged in Cyprus around independence, over whether the island would unite with Greece. But by the handover of Hong Kong to China in 1997, the British Empire was over.

Between pride and embarrassment

As Britain entered the new millennium there was anything but consensus as to what it meant to have once been an imperial superpower. Chris Patten, Hong Kong's last British governor, offered a blandishment for 'the most humane and well intentioned of the colonial powers', and for an empire that ended with 'the usually peaceful and successful preparations for independence of scores of new countries as free and plural societies'.[18] Other Britons poked fun at the absurdity of it all. As the comedian Eddie Izzard joked: 'We stole countries; that's how you build an Empire. We stole countries with the cunning use of flags! Just sail round the world and stick a flag in [because] "no flag no country!"...' Satire may well be a good recipe for later generations of Britons to digest their imperial history, because opinions around its legacies seem so polarizing.

The seesaw of Britain's view of itself can tip between pride at its accomplishments as an empire, and apologetic embarrassment at the Empire's blatant inequities. Both views have their sympathizers. The British Empire undoubtedly diffused institutions and ideas that remain with us, wiring together distant parts of the globe in a preview of modern globalization. Of this matter there is little doubt, say those who derive lingering pride from the scale and sweep of Britain's past global influence. But the terms of trade were exploitative and accompanied by repression and snobbish racism, say those who carry a lingering imperial guilt for the Empire's abhorrent evils.

This debate around the British Empire's legacy leads to a circle that cannot be squared, even if provocateurs periodically attempt to do so. To take two best-selling books as examples. Niall Ferguson's *Empire* portrayed the diffusion of modernity as a theme of overriding importance. Liberal capitalism was spread globally by Britain, and even if nasty things happened along the way, 'the question is whether there could have been a less bloody path to modernity'.[19] In contrast, devising his critique from the vantage point of modern India, Shashi Tharoor has argued precisely the opposite: that the damage wrought by the Raj was too great for it to merit any redeeming features. He warned that 'the need to temper British imperial nostalgia with post-colonial responsibility has never been greater'.[20] And the title of his book? Fittingly, *Inglorious Empire*.   .

When the live wires of this debate cross, sparks fly. In 2015 Cecil Rhodes' statue at Oxford University's Oriel College became the focal point of activists who wanted to exorcise the vestiges of Empire from stone and spirit. They were inspired by South African students who sought to scrub Rhodes' name from their campuses too. Rhodes had been the quintessential imperialist. He was the namesake behind the Rhodesian colony (which later became Zimbabwe) and contributed to the Boer War's outbreak. The statue was left *in situ*, however, due to Oxford University's intransigence. Fearing its own backlash, Cambridge University announced in 2019 that it was commissioning its historians to investigate whether the university had previously profited from the slave trade, and would consider making appropriate reparations if this was found to be the case.

The pages of newspapers and academia alike remain susceptible to firestorms of anger if anyone attempts to rehabilitate colonialism. In 2017 US academic Bruce Gilley published a modern 'Case for Colonialism' in *Third World Quarterly*, arguing that self-rule had in fact led to misrule in parts of Asia and Africa. Subsequent British debate on this matter was divisive. 'Don't feel guilty about our colonial history,' argued Professor Nigel Biggar in *The Times*.[21] This in turn led to torrents of anger and criticism that he could even entertain such a notion.

Tussling over the politics of historical memory is par for the course in a country that fosters free speech. Some bemoan the straitjacket of political correctness that prevents the British from deriving any residual pride from having maintained the Empire.

Others are disgusted at Britain's global exercise of hard power. It is easy to become snagged by one case or the other. While 'unremitting guilt' and 'unwilling pride' each make for compelling polemical positions, neither gets us very far in identifying the lingering after-effects of Empire and their repercussions on Britain's role in the world today.

The Empire defies straightforward characterization, and lasted for too long, spread over too large an expanse, for it to be easily encapsulated in a simple formula. It cannot be categorized as either a solely murderous and exploitative entity or a benevolent enterprise that diffused institutions and modernity. It was all these things at different times and in different places, and its historical record cannot be simplified to suit a political agenda.

Nor did the Empire reach an abrupt end in a single catastrophic instant; instead, it unravelled over several distinct episodes, gradually depositing its various legacies into the British psyche. So there was no single moment of public reckoning when the Empire collapsed. The historian Andrew Thompson writes that the period from the 1950s to the 1970s 'saw the concept of empire increasingly shorn of many of its more positive meanings' for the British, but there was no 'flipping point' when this happened.[22] Each milestone event in the decline, such as the Suez debacle, influenced the public mood rather than providing a grand sense of finale.

Today the impact on the national psyche of having ruled so much of the world has neither faded nor has it been faced. British schools tend not to teach imperial history, with the exception of a part of the geography syllabus for fifteen- and sixteen-year-olds, thus leaving British children shorn of detailed historical knowledge of their country's imperial past.[23] Schools largely steer clear of the knotty subject of the Empire, perhaps because there is no consensus as to whether to present the facts in a positive or negative light, and because neutrality is a difficult stance to adopt, given the intense passions the subject evokes. In multicultural Britain, many people have direct family experiences of being at the

receiving end of colonialism, making the matter even more sensitive. Conversely, when Britons were polled by YouGov in 2014
about whether they think of the British Empire as something to
be proud of, 59 per cent agreed that it was.[24] There can simply be
no national consensus over what the Empire still means for Britain and how to remember it.

Consider the totemic figure of Winston Churchill: was he the
saviour of his country or a colonial villain? A left-wing writer can
declare that 'Churchill was no hero – he was a vile racist fanatical
about violence and fiercely supportive of imperialism'.[25] Defenders
of Churchill explain how his character was formed by his boyhood
imperial endeavours, and that his views on race and attendant hierarchies mainly reflected his environment. Lawrence James writes
that 'imperial geopolitical considerations were always uppermost
in Churchill's mind'.[26] In Richard Toye's estimation, Churchill
'married the belief that non-white races were currently inferior
with the conviction they had potential to advance'.[27] Churchill was
a product of his time, as was the Empire, which is why they appear
in such a poor light, if judged according to present-day moralities.

From Ireland to Iraq:
war, terrorism and imperial legacy

To say that Tony Blair is a divisive figure would stretch even the
habit of British understatement. His decision for the UK to join
the USA in the Iraq invasion has sullied his reputation beyond
repair for a swathe of Britain's populace. That decision, and how it
came to relate to the problem of jihadist terrorism, can only truly
be understood when one factors in the impact of imperial legacies.
The connection here is indirect, but it forms an essential facet of
what went so wrong in Blair's calculus on Iraq, and in the abiding
battles against jihadist terrorism taken on by the British state.

A balanced examination of the Blair era must also account for
what he got right in managing other, more direct imperial leg-

acies. A month after Blair came to office he attended the handover of Hong Kong to China on 30 June 1997, which closed a chapter on Britain's post-imperial obligations to the Chinese government. The following year he presided over the peace treaty to end the conflict in Northern Ireland, which was signed on Good Friday, helping to bring to an end a long era of violence and a prolonged British Army presence in Northern Ireland, which had long been a post-imperial scar on modern Britain.

Conflicts that are rooted in the bloody politics of imperial history are perilously difficult to resolve; such is the accumulated weight of past embitterments bearing down on later generations. Untangling this mess had bedevilled Blair's predecessors and, while they had made progress in modernizing London's relationship with Dublin, getting the various communities in Belfast to agree to peace was tricky. Blair understood the roots of the conflict, given that his mother was a Protestant from Ireland's County Donegal. Perhaps this gave him an edge in negotiations with the Democratic Unionist Party (DUP) and Sinn Fein, who ultimately agreed to put the violence behind them and to share power in a devolved authority that was created in 1998.

Twelve years later, my first Civil Service responsibility involved supporting British negotiators during the devolution of policing and justice powers from London to Belfast, which was announced on 10 February 2010. By this time Northern Ireland enjoyed an open border with the Republic of Ireland, and the end of violence had seen military checkposts dismantled. It seemed as if Britain was making progress in updating its relationships with both Ireland and Northern Ireland for the post-imperial age.

After the horrific 9/11 terrorist attacks, Britain stepped in to assist its wounded US ally, not least because among those who lost their lives were sixty-seven British victims. America's government, reeling from the failure of its understanding of al-Qaeda, the perpetrators of 9/11, began flailing for an adequate response to the attacks. For its part, Britain's government response would be influenced by imperial legacies, not least its perception of its historical relationship with the USA. This was rooted in belonging to the Anglo-sphere, and in Britain's tendency to cast itself as Greece to America's Rome – a reflection of the torch passing from *Pax Britannica* to *Pax Americana* in the twentieth century. This legacy entrapped Blair's government into thinking it was Britain's business to involve itself fully in America's poorly planned invasions.

Another legacy was evident in the British state thinking it was even feasible to project military power far away, with the aim of fostering Western values. Before long, Britain's military was campaigning in its old imperial stomping grounds of Afghanistan and Iraq, where the British Empire's soldiers had once fought. These were the places that America had chosen to invade in its response to 9/11. These invasions were instigated to defeat al-Qaeda in Afghanistan, and to target Iraq's apocryphal weapons of mass destruction – but, in the end, the outcome of each occupation was determined by training local armies, building new governments, toggling down Western flags and leaving. For America, it felt like Vietnam redux. For Britain, it was eerily resonant of an imperial past, of its nineteenth-century defeats in Afghanistan, and the colonial wars that had culminated in handovers of power to newly independent states like Iraq in the twentieth century.

'History doesn't repeat itself but it often rhymes' – so goes the line that is attributed to the American author Mark Twain. It is not that the British state purposefully dusted off its old imperial handbooks after 9/11; it is more about the absent-minded reappearance of assumptions about the wider world held by its political elites, who defaulted to certain courses of action that had past precedence.

From Britain's perspective, at least the Afghanistan war had the clear rationale of targeting al-Qaeda's training facilities. So, could Britain have committed UK forces to the operation in Afghanistan only, and sat out the Iraq War? Instead Blair employed his rhetorical skills to make the case for the Iraq War on behalf of the USA, despite an estimated million members of the British public flooding into central London in 2003 to protest against the war. History has largely vindicated their emotive response to the weak case for invasion. Even within the British establishment, regrets cloud its reflections on the Iraq War. The Chilcot Report, the government's official inquiry into Britain's commitment to and execution of the Iraq War, and the Butler Report into British intelligence's failings over Iraq, have documented how the war was mismanaged by the government, the bureaucracy and the military.

Blair spoke in public after the Chilcot Report was published in June 2016. His once-youthful face, as it had appeared when he became prime minister in 1997, had aged considerably. Anguish seemed etched into his expression. Again he dissected the sequence of events leading to his decision to take Britain to war in Iraq, his legally-trained mind in full flow. For Blair, the relevant backstory was Saddam Hussein's flouting of UN resolutions, and the tradition of humanitarian interventions established by the US and UK in the 1990s.[28] Blair accepted that circumstances in Iraq had proved very different and that things had gone wrong. 'There will not be a day of my life where I do not relive and re-think what happened.' But he also appeared to advocate perpetual interventions: 'The West has a big decision to take: does it believe it has a strategic interest in the outcome of the struggle in the Middle East and elsewhere around the issues of Islamist extremism? My view obviously is that it does.'[29]

Blair's tragedy was his unwitting inheritance of old imperial compulsions. He and his national-security officials had not acted out of malice – they had acted in a way that was consistent with their country's imperial pedigree. Blair wanted to place Britain at the centre of events of global consequence – a pose habitually adopted by his forebears. The curious brew of altruism and brazen self-interest that accompanied the Iraq War was an updated version of motives that had once animated imperial-era statesmen:

Britain would punish an errant local leader, use its military to civilize and spread modernity, and solidify Western influence. Even if the idea was hatched in Washington DC, Blair had accepted and encouraged the core assumption that it was the West's job to democratize the Middle East.

British forces were deployed as if being sent to a colonial outpost that they had only recently vacated, and in a way this was true. In 1920, after the collapse of the Ottoman Empire, the League of Nations had authorized Britain's mandate over Iraq. Keen for access to Iraq's oilfields, Britain acted as kingmaker in establishing Iraq's monarchy. Nominal independence came in 1932, but Britain retained bases, influence and a stake in Iraq's progress. In 1958 the monarchy was overthrown by the Ba'ath Party, a nationalist political movement that was later led by Saddam.[30]

After he was overthrown in 2003, Iraq was run by the Coalition Provisional Authority, a body staffed by US and UK officials. At this point Iraq collapsed into civil war along ethnic fault lines that dated back to the British-mandate era. Back then, Iraq was cobbled together from a Shia south, a Sunni middle and a Kurdish north. Saddam's murderous rule had since made things a lot worse, by his favouring of Sunnis over the other groups. After he was deposed, armed groups from the Sunni and Shia communities mobilized to secure their stake in the new Iraq. Britain's military tried to secure Basra, the southern Iraqi city, but was too poorly resourced, and too ignorant of its surroundings, to have a real chance of success.[31] Whereas Blair and the British state could at least grasp the dynamics of Northern Ireland's sectarian violence, in Iraq they didn't have a clue.

Britain appears to have retained only a sketchy and selective understanding of the modern implications of its old imperial roles, and little sense of their resulting legacies. Military occupations miles from home, in which Western troops subdued the locals, who were then to be civilized by an influx of Western expertise, reeked of an unwelcome repetition of empire.

However, a different set of imperial legacies has borne down on Britain's domestic security. The day of reckoning with this awful reality came on 7 July 2005 when a home-grown terrorist cell of four British citizens (three of Pakistani heritage, the fourth a Muslim convert of Caribbean heritage) detonated suicide bombs that killed fifty-three people on London's transport network. Mohammad Sidique Khan, the cell's ringleader, detailed his motives for the bombings in a video – 'We are at war and I am a soldier. Now you too will taste the reality of this situation' – before praising Abu Musab al-Zarqawi (al-Qaeda's leader in Iraq), Osama bin Laden and al-Qaeda figurehead Ayman al-Zawahiri. The last-named issued his own edict after the attack: 'I talk to you today about the blessed London battle, which came as a slap to the face of the tyrannical, Crusader British arrogance.'

Through the hard-won efforts of Britain's security agencies, the threat of further al-Qaeda attacks was contained. But terrorism returned with a vengeance under the black flag of the Islamic State (IS). In 2017 the UK suffered a series of attacks by British citizens who claimed an affiliation to IS. This included an indiscriminate stabbing spree along London Bridge, and a suicide bombing in Manchester that killed and maimed people at a pop concert.

Britain's imperial past did not cause its involvement in the Iraq War in 2003, and this in turn did not cause the jihadist threat to the UK. Historical acts from different eras do not connect to each other with such straight lines, but the past bears down on the present by imbuing it with certain meanings rather than others. Imperial history is especially divisive: it imparts one set of meanings to those who, like the British, were recently successful empire-builders, but holds different implications for those who were colonized or subjugated, such as those in Iraq or Ireland. Britain's failure to grasp this after 9/11 contributed to terrible failures in the way it involved itself in the so-called 'war on terror'.

Brexit and immigration in a post-imperial light

Prime Minister David Cameron had already placed one bet on the UK's post-imperial fate: with the Scottish independence referendum. On 18 September 2014 more than two million Scots voted *against* the motion for Scotland to become an independent country, with 1.6 million voting to leave the UK. The outcome was relatively close and, rather than learn a lesson in the precariousness of referendums for settling such profoundly important issues, two years later Cameron placed another bet, this time on the UK's membership of the EU. He had hoped the outcome would favour remaining in the EU, therefore silencing his populist right-wing critics who wanted to assert Britain's sovereignty by leaving. This time the numbers came up short for Cameron. Those voting to leave the EU (17.4 million) had beaten those voting to remain (16.1 million). From this point on, Brexit would be Britain's future.

The origins of this instinct to leave the EU, however, resided squarely in the past, and in the uncertainties around Britain's post-imperial role. There were proximate reasons why so many people voted to leave the EU, such as the relative deprivation of Britain's post-industrial working class, the uneven yields of globalization and (in the minds of some who voted for Brexit) a desire to reduce immigration from Eastern Europe's EU member states. But perhaps over and above any single reason, Brexit was a defensive reaction to Britain's changing character. The historian Linda Colley's observation still holds: 'Whereas the Germans and French ... see a Europe without frontiers as an opportunity, the British are far more inclined to see it as a threat.' History reminds the British that 'they have fought against Continental European states in the past; but their apparent insularity is to be explained also by their growing doubt over who they are in the present. Consciously or unconsciously, they fear assuming a new identity in case it obliterates entirely the already insecure identity they currently possess.'[32]

This insecurity had been compounded by Western Europe cohering into a trading bloc. This unfolding process had bedevilled British politics by forcing the following questions: Should Britain participate? And did this mean its political, economic and cultural future now resided in continental Europe? Imperial pride directly hindered Britain's involvement in the 1950s, when it took a snobbish attitude to European integration, partly because it was still investing hopes in its remaining imperial bonds. Britain did not participate in talks over the formation of the EEC in 1958 because of a reluctance to pool its sovereignty, and because it thought the EEC might stumble. By the 1960s it had become clear that the economic costs of staying out of the EEC were too great, and the tension between economic necessity and political resistance intensified.[33] Britain tried to join, but Charles de Gaulle said 'non' in 1967. It was not until his resignation two years later that Britain got another opportunity, and the UK eventually joined the EEC in 1973.[34]

The Maastricht Treaty of 1992 opened a welter of new uncertainties in Britain. The euro currency was launched, but even though the UK opted out of this, the right wing of the Conservative Party was becoming irate at the prospect of the EU having a decisive influence on Britain's future. A splinter group of Conservatives formed the UK Independence Party (UKIP) in the 1990s, on a platform of getting the UK out of the EU. These Eurosceptics always argued that the majority of British people silently harboured similar desires, but for a long time this seemed like a fringe argument.

In June 2016, with Cameron's referendum, the Eurosceptic fantasy became the country's reality. Having been at the centre of the world for so long, it seemed that becoming just an appendage of the EU was not befitting a proud and sovereign nation – or so Brexit's intellectual architects felt, with many of their more specific arguments being linked by this theme. Some of Brexit's backers drew on old notions of Britain's natural allies being its former settler colonies, with their shared cultural and historical roots. The idea of 'CANZUK' – the closer association between Canada, Australia, New Zealand and the UK – unofficially resurfaced as something for post-Brexit Britain to pursue.[35]

Inherent in these arguments was a harking-back to a greater British past. Supporters of Brexit argued that it had been wrong for Britain in the 1970s to have prioritized the EEC over its historical and cultural ties to the far-flung Anglo-sphere and the wider Commonwealth.[36]

Perhaps the most impactful of imperial legacies on Britain's domestic development has been immigration. For decades it has been a motivator of British parochialism, and it remains the issue that has stoked the anxieties of some to safeguard Britain against change. When the Empire was thriving, British émigrés spread all over the world, especially into its settler colonies – but the tables were turned during the Empire's unravelling, as waves of immigration from the Commonwealth eventually changed the ethnic composition of the British populace itself.

As one gazes at modern Britain, it is like a mosaic of the former Empire, especially in major cities like London, Birmingham and Manchester. Some of Britain's migrant communities arrived due to decolonization, including Indians, Bangladeshis, Pakistanis and other South Asians; Somalis, Kenyans, Tanzanians, Ugandans, Nigerians and other Africans; with Palestinians, Iraqis, Kurds and others from the Middle East also coming. And so on. Communities from the former empire arrived in Britain at different times and in differing circumstances. Some fled instability at home, like the East African Asians who arrived after the Ugandan dictator Idi Amin evicted them in the 1970s. Somalis who fled after their country's collapse in the 1990s also chose the former imperial metropolis. Overall, Britain gained a myriad of immigrant communities.

For the white British majority populace, the pace of change

would have looked rapid. In 1990 the populace had some three million non-whites (including 840,000 Indians, 500,000 Caribbeans and 476,000 Pakistanis) and few Eastern European.[37] As the Census noted, whereas in 1991 the white populace of England and Wales was 94.1 per cent, twenty years later it had dropped to 86 per cent.[38] Not an overwhelming change, but more noticeable depending on where in the country one lived. There had been earlier waves of Irish and Jewish immigration, but Commonwealth immigration involved a reversal of the colonial encounter in a way that seemed to unsettle some Britons.[39]

The pangs of discomfort that Britain has experienced while adjusting to these changes would test the country's liberal character. In 1968 the politician Enoch Powell decreed that he saw the 'River Tiber foaming with much blood' due to immigration. These words reflected a line of thinking that he had held ever since he opposed the 1948 British Nationality Bill, which had facilitated large-scale non-white immigration by allowing Commonwealth subjects to be treated as British citizens. 'The UK and the Commonwealth do not constitute one country,' he said, believing that different races could not live in harmony and might end up in ghettos, adding that 'not merely years but generations will pass before this sudden and large influx has been fully assimilated into society'.[40]

Ultimately, Britain's liberal character prevailed over Powell's scaremongering. But another of his tics has continued to force spasms in British political life, outlasting his death in 1998. Powell was an ardent anti-European, arguing that 'I do not believe that the British people should consent to be a minority in a European electorate.' At the time he thought the UK's entry into the EEC was a fatal betrayal of British pride and sovereignty. As his biographer notes of Powell: 'Having entered politics as one of the last ardent imperialists, he soon sloughed off the skin of Empire and spent the rest of his career berating his fellow countrymen for their failure to completely renounce the myth of Europe.'[41] Enoch

Powell was a one-man exemplar of how the retirement from empire could find new outlets in targeting Europe, and how this blended with unease around immigration.

The themes of immigration and Europe came together in a witches' brew during Brexit. The EU's rules on the free movement of people meant that Poles, Romanians and others could work and live in the UK if they chose, which many did. Often energetic and enterprising young people, they seized the new opportunities open to them for travel and work. Who, after all, would not want a better life for themselves than their parents had? For Britain's anti-EU membership lobby, watching all this unfold, the game was now afoot. Their winning argument around Brexit was simple: Britain must leave the EU to take control of immigration, and to honour its own national identity.

Brexit has shown how a modern political campaign can resonate with under-acknowledged and untamed post-imperial feelings that have mutated throughout a populace. Many people voting for Brexit did so in an earnest reflection of their emotions, not by re-reading history, or from a balance sheet accounting how much trade Britain does with the EU, but because the Brexit campaign's emotional simplicity resonated with them. The immediate outcome of the referendum is that Brexit has left Britain in a sticky situation of uncertainty over its future global position.

Britain's post-imperial place in the world

Back in 1948, Churchill, on a speaking tour after losing the office of prime minister, offered a striking vision of Britain's influence in the world. 'As I look out upon the future of our country in the changing scene of human destiny, I feel the existence of three great circles among the free nations and democracies. The first circle for us is naturally the British Commonwealth and Empire ... Then there is also the United States ... And finally, there is United Europe.'[42]

Taking stock today of Britain's global position, with the Empire dismantled and replaced by the symbolic bonds of the Commonwealth; with the US 'special relationship' having to bear the strain of globally unpopular presidents, such as George W. Bush and Donald Trump; and with Brexit leaving Britain out of the EU – post-imperial Britain may well begin to feel rather isolated in a world that is increasingly dwarfed by Asia's rising powers, not least after the financial crisis that began in 2008 sealed European economic fates as to where to look for money.

Here, once again, another set of imperial legacies will be felt. Rising powers in Asia present the irony of another colonial table being turned, since Britain will have to face the inconvenience of its past imperial conduct in India and China. Imperial ties cut both ways, and some in India may well see Britain through the jaundiced eyes of a former colony. China, the world's richest rising power, presents an altogether tougher challenge – not sharing a common language with Britain, and with its authoritarian government. While China was never colonized, British gunboat diplomacy destabilized it in the nineteenth century. At this time the British were engaged in the opium trade, and were willing to inflict violence on China to protect the profits to be gained from selling opium to the Chinese people – which is far from an auspicious backstory to future trading relations, unless everybody concerned agrees to let bygones be bygones.

Britain faces dilemmas over how to position itself to reap the rewards of modern Asia's wealth, but at least the British economy can fall back on another of its imperial legacies: that it sits at the centre of a web of global commerce. At the twilight of Empire, Britain's continent-spanning influence was transformed into a network of financial centres spanning Hong Kong, Dubai, the Caribbean islands and other former colonies or Overseas Territories. An astonishing 45 per cent of global financial movements still pass through this network, in which the City of London uses offshore banking in a manner akin to the anonymity prided by Swiss bankers.[43] The City's 'square mile' of banks and insurance companies rose in tandem with the Empire, based on the networks between various colonial outposts. Its success was the financial secret behind Britain's accelerating global dominance in the eighteenth and nineteenth centuries.[44] Today, London remains Britain's shop window to the world and a major global financial hub. And while Brexit will not bring this to an end, it will accelerate questions around how Britain adapts its global role in the future.

The end of the Empire did not force Britain into global obscurity, and nor will Brexit. Britain's economy was the fifth-biggest in the 2017 world rankings, and its influence in global commerce, culture, higher education and other sectors remains considerable. Imperial legacies have contributed in some way to many facets of modern Britain, from the confidence that borders on arrogance of some of its contemporary elites, all the way to the pleasant, outward-looking Britain that has reaped for itself many of the rewards of globalization. Today Britain is 'internationalist' rather than 'imperialist', but what it means to be internationalist will itself continue to be a subject of debate.

In order to help the country stake out its future geopolitical ambitions, and to understand the evolution of its own society, Britain needs to ask tough questions of itself, to enquire further into the parts of its history it has preferred to neglect, and to re-examine some of its venerable institutions in a different light (including its military and national-security establishment, its oldest universities, its financial system, the honours system, and so on). Such conversations are best conducted in a temperate tone, succumbing neither to triumphalism nor to self-flagellation over what the Empire once was.

One place to start is by considering the extent to which Britain's confidence – evident when presenting itself around the world in matters of global security, development aid, business and suchlike –

still subconsciously draws from an imperial wellspring. Armies, businesses and even charities market a British brand of expertise, values and self-assuredness that did not pop into existence from a void of history. Britain has long been a country 'measured by the overseas actions of her statesmen and businessmen', as the writer Bernard Porter notes.[45] This is why Britain retains a preternatural instinct to project its influence globally, while at the same time suffering from an inability to articulate persuasively why any of this is in the national interest.

Each year the Queen's Christmas speech to the nation thanks those Britons working in international development, and in response to emergencies and conflicts around the world. One might reflect on the irony of Britons working in zones of instability when some of the roots of this instability exist in the lingering mess created by the British Empire. Or on the cynicism of British business interests that often accompany these more benevolent arms of global outreach. But Britain is hardly a country that sits on its hands, when there is profit to be made and problems to be solved around the world – and this industriousness is one of its great imperial legacies.

Generational change in Britain means that its population will, later in this century, lose its direct memory of the Empire. Whereas Queen Victoria reigned over the Empire's peak, Queen Elizabeth II's long reign, which began in 1952, has spanned Britain's transformation away from being an imperial power. The twilight of her reign offers another moment of reflection with regard to the physical and mental legacies of empire, and to the relationship between monarchy and empire. Whereas once the monarch had an empire to rule, the post-imperial age has further rendered the monarchy into a symbolic institution, and one that will need continual reinvention in order to have any relevance at all to modern Britain, beyond being a historical curiosity.

A Britain with an imperial past needs some sort of global mission, or else some of its deepest held and most defining instincts will be unrequited. A Britain that becomes much more inward-looking and projects its influence only through multilateral institutions is hard to envisage. While Brexit forces a rearrangement of this influence, most obviously in relation to Europe, in its private and public international engagements Britain will continue to position itself influentially in a range of networks of ideas and commerce. At the same time the ethnic diversity of modern Britain, and the ascent of ethnic-minority Britons to positions of influence in society, will renew the manner in which Britain can naturally present itself to the wider world. Some of the clues to its post-imperial place in the world reside amongst the positive legacies of empire.

THREE

THE EUROPEAN UNION'S POST-IMPERIAL PROJECT

Day after day I could see the cohesive effect of the Community idea . . . Although all the delegates retained their well-marked national characteristics, they were now working together on the same quest.

> Jean Monnet (1888–1979), reflecting on the
> Coal and Steel Community, created in 1950[1]

Today in Brussels they are again playing imperial marches . . . Now they do not invade with weapons. We know full well that Brussels is not Constantinople, nor Moscow, nor Imperial Berlin, nor even Vienna. From Brussels there is never conquest; it only ever administers colonies.

> Viktor Orbán, Prime Minister
> of Hungary, October 2018[2]

The EU itself is first and foremost a peace project . . . By the way, I've been wondering what that special place in hell looks like, for those who promoted Brexit, without even a sketch of a plan how to carry it out safely.

> Donald Tusk, President of the
> European Council, February 2019[3]

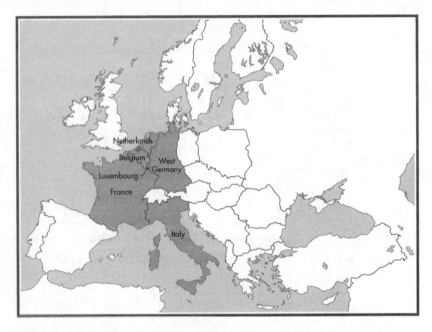

Map 3 The EEC at its foundation, 1957

Map 4 The countries of the EU, 2019

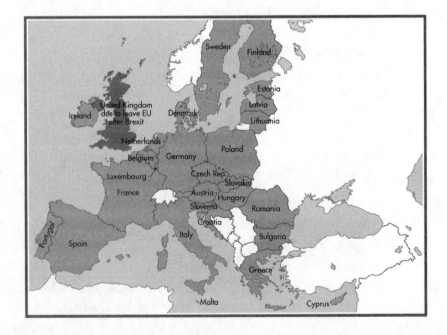

For many young EU citizens with no memory of war, peace in Europe means not presenting your passport when travelling from one member state to another; driving past empty border posts, for instance, where scrutiny and suspicion once ruled the day. Or peering out of a train as it rolls on between countries, to see relaxed policemen on the platform outside. Airport immigration officials who glance only briefly at a fellow EU citizen's passport. And so on. Mundane luxuries for an EU citizen travelling for work or fun. For businesses in Europe, such openness might have become integral to profit, but for the history of the continent as a whole, it is nothing short of profound.

From the wreckage of the collapse of the Roman Empire, Europe's history is war-ravaged, scarred by centuries of debilitating rivalries between the kings and queens of old, across battle lines that were compounded by different Christian denominations. As this era ended, Europe's nation-states took on the baton of war, with the revolutionary megalomania of conquerors like Napoleon and Hitler magnifying the bloodshed. For Europe to suffer such wars now is unthinkable. Peace, relative prosperity and cross-pollinating populaces are the new norm across much of the continent and, when placed against the long arc of history, this is a significant turnaround.

Clearly the EU did not bring this about, but it has catalysed and institutionalized Europe's peace. Credit should go where it is due: since the 1950s, the 'European project' has grown from humble beginnings as a *community* of common interest around coal and steel production between six Western European countries, to a *union* of nearly thirty member states. The 2012 Nobel Peace Prize was awarded to the EU. As the citation read, the EU had reconciled 'former archenemies Germany and France'; it had 'strengthened democracy in Greece, Spain and Portugal'; and it had done great work 'after the end of the Cold War, when a number of Central and Eastern European countries joined the EU'.[4] All good fodder for high-minded speeches by EU officials. 'The EU's secret weapon,' said then-European Council President Herman Van Rompuy, was 'an unrivalled way of binding our interests so tightly that war becomes materially impossible, through constant negotiations on ever more topics between ever more countries.' In sum, the EU has become a 'perpetual peace conference'.[5]

Upon scrutiny, some of this rationale resembles Swiss cheese. The vital EU contribution – enshrining peace via economic inter-dependence and negotiations – has failed to stir European hearts to the same extent as the story of the military defeat of Nazi Germany in 1945. America's contribution to the war effort, and the tax dollars it spent to rebuild Europe, were also part of the story, as were the US and European soldiers who faced off the Russians during the Cold War. Since the end of the Cold War, the jury is still out as to whether the EU's eastwards expansion has helped or aggravated East–West relations. Russia has even started wars over the EU's inclusion of so many former Soviet states, as detailed in Chapter 4.

In another hole of the Swiss cheese is Greece. In the mid-1970s its transition to democracy was boosted by the process of joining the EU. Brussels set up all sorts of hoops for the return of Athenian democracy, after a spell of military rule. Three decades later, after the 2008 financial crisis, Greece fell foul of the EU's insistence that it must impose austerity in order to balance its books. Germany, the EU's biggest economic power, was most insistent – after all, the German and Greek economies were now tethered to one another, after both countries adopted the euro currency. Greece's leftist populists, horrified at the imposition of austerity, argued that Europe's prosperity was decidedly discriminatory.[6] Anti-austerity riots gripped Greece in 2011, a reaction by people frustrated at rising unemployment, laws limiting cash withdrawals from banks to prevent capital flight, and so on.

Populist politicians in other parts of Europe watched the chaos in Greece and decided it was open season on Brussels. Immigration was the *casus belli* for right-wing populists, who have

habitually heaped blame on their own apparently feckless politicians, and on the EU's open borders, for allowing in refugees
and economic migrants. Italy's 'Five Star Movement' became the
country's largest political party in 2018. The 'Alternative for Germany' did not poll quite so well in 2017 – but that it polled at all,
in a country with a fascist past, was astonishing. France's 'National
Rally' party, led by Marine Le Pen, did not win either, but she
still got one-third of the votes. In Hungary, the nationalist Viktor
Orbán won power in 2010, six years after Hungary joined the EU;
scapegoating Brussels for an assortment of problems was part of
his vote-winning strategy.

To the plethora of Europe's populists, who argue for guarding
their particular vision of national culture against different kinds of
alleged 'dilutions', proving their arguments has mattered less than
making them *feel* real enough to provoke fear. Their insularity usually runs contrary to the EU's openness, and their often-traditional
worldviews contrast with the EU's push to the future.

How did it come to this? How did the 'European project', with
its noble intentions, create a backlash? Hubris in Brussels, and
the EU's overstretched ambitions, offer some answers. Helping
France and Germany to bury the hatchet from the 1950s onwards
is a world away from an economic and political union between
so many unique states in this millennium. Introducing the euro,
and granting free movement of people between places with starkly
differing incomes and levels of wealth, has shifted the European
project into different territory from its origins. Whilst the EU's
more optimistic supporters paint this as a Darwinian evolution
towards a 'United States of Europe', to those people it has alien-
ated it can feel more akin to a Kafka-esque metamorphosis.

Europe's populists have zeroed in on this. For all their appall-
ingly small-minded xenophobia, some of them do have a point:
the European project may have overstepped the markers of what
is feasible, in terms of unification and enlargement. And it is not
only virulent xenophobes who harbour such suspicions. When

52 per cent of Britain's voters opted to leave the EU in 2016, Brexit served as a warning of how un-compelling the EU's trajectory has become for a lot of ordinary people.

Consequently, if one was to gaze into the crystal ball of the EU's future, only a thick cloud of uncertainty would be visible. It is becoming trickier to predict what European unity will look like for future generations, who will have no memory at all of war-ravaged Europe. Even if the EU's complete collapse is unlikely, it may lose further member states, or be forced to curtail some of its uniting and enlarging ambitions. Is there any way to shed light on this future?

The EU:
post-war and post-imperial

The EU is clearly more idealistic than it is imperial. Herein is a lesson from history – and it is not the history lesson preferred by hubristic EU officials. Whilst the EU sees itself as a *post-war* unity project, it is also a decidedly *post-imperial* project. Imperial legacies offer a missing piece to the puzzle of explaining why it has always been tricky to unify Europe, why attempts to do so have made some nations feel unduly subjugated, and why Europe always used to have frontiers rather than fixed borders.

To be clear, this is not the same thing as accusing the EU of being an empire, as is the wont of populists like Orbán, who want to score cheap political points. Instead it highlights how Europe's long-established imperial instincts are deeply embedded in the continent's DNA. Imperial legacies have tended to be ignored, rather than properly interrogated, by the EU's advocates.

José Manuel Barroso, President of the European Commission (2004–14), did take a stab at addressing this issue: 'Empires were usually made through force with a centre that was imposing a *diktat* on the others. Now, we have what some authors call

the first *non-imperial empire* . . . 27 countries that *freely* decided
to work together, to pool their sovereignties.'[7] Putting aside its
oxymoronic wording, 'non-imperial empire' is a step closer to
acknowledging the EU's empire-like characteristics. The term
never caught on, unsurprisingly; Donald Tusk instead opted for
a more anodyne term, 'peace project', to sum up what the EU is
all about.

Whether the EU does or does not resemble an empire is dis-
putable. What is indisputable is that it follows a lineage of past
attempts at imposing European unity. This was given an implicit
nod by French president Emmanuel Macron and German chancellor Angela Merkel when, on 22 January 2019, they delivered a
joint statement of faith in the EU, and in Franco-German relations – they did so in Aachen, where the medieval Frankish King
Charlemagne set out to build an empire. Merkel and Macron's
event also coincided with the fifty-sixth anniversary of the Élysée
Treaty, a milestone in Franco-German reconciliation signed by
Charles de Gaulle and Konrad Adenauer.

Memories of the 1950s and 1960s will not resonate for ever.
In the long run, the recent symbolism of such anniversaries
may matter less than the distant connotation of imperial legacy.
While Europe has laudably moved away from the worst of its
immediate past, Europeans cannot cherry-pick from their historical experiences when seeing how the past leads to the present.
Europe is both post-war and post-imperial – by extension, so is
the EU.

There are two imperial traditions lying deep in the cellar of
Europe's past. Each has its own vintage, and each has diffused
particular legacies and, between them, they have shaped Europe
into what we recognize today. There is both the tradition of trying
to build empires *within* Europe; and the tradition of Europeans
conquering colonies *outside* Europe. These imperial pursuits eventually overlapped, as rivalries between European powers spilled
into colonial competition.

Europe: between empire and enlightenment

Empire-building in Europe is as old as antiquity, when Greek and Roman history involved expansions of power, order and influence from city-states over surrounding territories. Ancient Greece was as much defined by war as by its philosophers, odysseys and tragedians.[8] The Romans were defined to a greater extent by their martial and empire-building traditions. The word 'empire' comes from the Latin *imperium*, which meant 'sovereignty' or 'rule', the methods of which evolved greatly during the Roman Empire's long existence. By the end of the first century BCE, *imperium* may have referred to areas under direct Roman rule. As the classics scholar Mary Beard explains, it also meant 'something closer to "the power to issue orders that are obeyed"', and hence to the Romans claiming right of way in the *imperium*.[9]

At its geographic peak, around 120 CE, the *imperium* spanned Europe, North Africa and the Levant, providing an early reference point for conquest across the Mediterranean. Future empire-builders who looked back to Rome for inspiration would have noted its modernizing and civilizing missions. The *Pax Romana* involved extending peace and stability. As new lands became Roman provinces, their peoples became Roman citizens, and some were recruited as legionnaires. Some senators and emperors also had non-Roman origins (Hadrian, for example, came from the Roman province in Spain). There was a lot of diversity across the empire with, for example, the eastern part remaining culturally and linguistically Greek rather than Latin.[10]

The Roman Empire experienced a great schism when its western and eastern wings split. Barbarian hordes chipped away at, and then brought about, the outright collapse of the western empire. The eastern empire lived on – 'Byzantium', as it was known – to convey its Greco-Roman influences, and in 330 CE Emperor Constantine proclaimed his capital in Constantinople (now Istanbul). He had also legalized Christianity. Previously the Romans had treated Christianity as a heretical sect, throwing its adherents to the lions in front of the cheering crowds in coliseums. Three centuries after Jesus Christ, Christianity was being openly practised in Byzantium.

Empire and Christianity became fused in Europe's cultural and political history hereafter. Constantine's conversion was a huge shift and, for a while during his reign, it looked possible that he might conquer lands further east, which could have entrenched Christianity in the Middle East. But he died of illness in 337 CE; Byzantium's great imperial rival, the Persian Empire, duly cracked down on Christians in its midst. Constantine had hitched Christianity to the powerful vehicle of Byzantium, but in doing so he may have precluded the religion's spread further east.[11] In this way the boundaries of what has historically been understood as Christendom were set.

Religion, and its role in the formation of European identity, can be a sore topic for modern generations who place their faith in secularism and science. Depending on where in modern Europe you look, Christianity holds varying levels of appeal. Donald Tusk's quote at the start of this chapter – in which he wondered if there was 'a special place in hell' for those in the UK who had sold Brexit without planning it – is also interesting for its invocation of *Hades*. Many Brits were outraged at Tusk's gall; but why should they have been, if heaven and hell have lost their theological conviction? In Tusk's native Poland, Catholicism is widely practised, but the UK is an increasingly secular country.[12] Even then, Christianity's vocabulary and iconography offer a common cultural reference point, and being condemned to the fiery pits of hell is evidently still a worthy insult.

Unifying Christendom became a dream for conquerors long after Rome's fall. Charlemagne, whose kingly realm encompassed the Franks (who were the French and Germans, before such national identities existed), is one example. In 800 CE Charlemagne was crowned 'Holy Roman Emperor' by the Pope. This title invoked an aspiration to carry forth the torch of ancient Rome in Christendom's name. Byzantium still lived on in the east and continued to influence the Vatican in the 700s, when popes might be Greek or Syrian. This changed with Charlemagne's crowning, which involved a bargain between the Frankish kings and the Pope, and heralded the Westernization of the papacy.[13] Charlemagne's Carolingian Empire only proved to be short-lived, but it refreshed the dream of re-uniting Europe.

Unifying Europe would, however, elude all who tried. Common causes did exist, notably the Crusades, which prompted medieval Europe's kings to heed papal calls for common action against the expanding Muslim empire. Recovering the Holy Land was a cause that animated generations of Europeans, for instance around the time of Saladin, the Seljuk Turk, who led the capture of Jerusalem in 1187. The periodic wars between Europeans and Muslims would culminate in a seismic event: the fall of Constantinople to conquest by the Ottoman Empire in 1453. This spelled the destruction of the Byzantine Empire after ten centuries of existence, which had the additional effect of leaving its Greco-Roman imperial legacy up for grabs by new heirs.

The title of Holy Roman Emperor remained a focal point for European unity. This crown remained hotly contended by Europe's monarchs, keen to assert their moral authority over Christendom and plot a path to continental dominion. Its wearer inherited neither a territorial empire, nor gained the authority to control Europe's other monarchs, aside from being the 'first amongst equals'. To be the Holy Roman Emperor was a symbolic entitlement to authority, and it lasted from its medieval origins in Charlemagne's coronation in 800 CE until the title was abolished by Napoleon 1,006 years later.

The Holy Roman Empire was 'a model for the federation of European peoples ... an umbrella organisation; it united in the loosest possible form ethnic groups of greatly varying size and held them together by the most diverse of ties', according to the historian Friedrich Heer.[14] How about this for a 'rotating presidency' – Europeans of various nationalities wore the Holy Roman crown as it passed between different dynasties. It was often worn by Habsburg royals whose line connected different dynasties across Europe, making them the unelected pan-European elite of their day.[15]

Spanish King Charles V managed to unify a sizeable part of Europe under his rule through a mixture of inherited titles, dynastic unions and conquest. This was in the mid-sixteenth century, when European leadership also demanded a robust defence against the Ottoman Empire. Charles V belonged to the Habsburg dynasty and was also Holy Roman Emperor. For a while the Habsburg line connected Spain and Austria. In later centuries the Habsburg line and the Holy Roman crown passed to the Austro-Hungarian Empire, making Vienna an imperial powerhouse.

By now Europe was an 'enlightened' continent. The Enlightenment involved the opening of European minds to scientific knowledge and technological advancements, closing the door to the superstition and spirituality of the medieval era. A facet of Europe's 'Age of Reason' was its reconnection with the heritages of ancient Greek and Roman accomplishment. Italy, at this time comprising many city-states, became a focal point for Europe's advancement, and from cities like Florence the 'Renaissance Men' of science and literature looked to the ancients for stimuli, inspiration and cultural ballast.

Until a few decades ago it was *en vogue* for Europeans to learn about the so-called 'grand narrative', which traced a line between ancient Greece and Rome to Europe's Renaissance, thus overcoming the medieval era of European backwardness.[16] It was certainly a good story to puff up European confidence, and to explain Europe's later domination of the world. Historians like Hugh Trevor-Roper connected ancient Hellenistic and Roman civilizations to the rediscovery of antiquity in Renaissance-era Europe.[17]

Peter Frankopan, a modern historian, is sceptical of this lineage: 'In truth, France and Germany, Austria, Spain, Portugal and England had nothing to do with Athens and the world of ancient Greeks, and were largely peripheral in the history of Rome from its earliest days to its demise.' He explains, 'the Renaissance was not rebirth. Rather, it was a naissance – a birth ... For the first time in history, Europe lay at the heart of the world.'[18]

Nevertheless, ancient Rome's legacy influenced Europe's colonialists because it associated empire-building with spreading order and civilization through conquest. The principles of the *Pax Romana* were picked up by early-modern Europeans, some of whom were also imbued with the moralizing impulse of spreading Christianity through their colonial exploits.[19] There was an evident idealism behind spreading European civilization globally, mixed with the more proximate influences behind colonialism, which were profit and pride.

Competition between Europe's monarchs for resources and influence abroad grew intense. There was a promise of great reward: colonialism played a role in spurring the development of early-modern European states, offering outlets for Europeans to use their prowess in naval technology, to indulge their curiosities through exploration, to profiteer and eventually to occupy foreign lands outright, after trouncing the natives with Europe's modern armies. The competition between Europeans took on new dimensions after the Church split. The Reformation of Christianity began in Germany in the early 1500s, with Martin Luther's challenge to the papacy; as it spread, it led to a serious challenge to Catholicism by the new-found Protestant Church. Battle lines were drawn between Catholic and Protestant monarchs in Europe and around the world.

The formation of European states (in forms that are more recognizable today) occurred at the same time as Europe's overseas empires were built. Seizing empires outside Europe became synonymous, from around the sixteenth century, with building powerful kingdoms and nations at home. Profits from these colonies made these European nations richer, which helped to consolidate domestic power. The habit of building Europe's wealth by venturing far outside its own continent was being established. Moreover, Europeans from many different nations were facing the broadly comparable challenges of securing a foothold in new environments, which forced them to define themselves culturally and racially in their encounters with non-Europeans.[20] Indeed, despite the fact that European colonialists competed bitterly with each other for America's, Asia's and Africa's spoils, it was not unforeseen for them to cooperate militarily on some occasions against the natives.[21] Over time, much of the world was divided into rival European spheres of influence.

The legacies of European colonialism are vast and enduring. The exportation of European languages, ideals and culture has decisively shaped the rest of the world, while the importation of foreign profits and peoples has decisively shaped Europe. The transmission of influences from the colonial era has been a two-way exchange. Those historians who argue the opposite – that Europe's destiny was primarily forged by Europe-centred events, with colonies as a sideshow – have remained influenced by outdated notions of Europe as the centre of the world.[22]

Capturing the big imperial legacies that have accrued over the last 500 or so years of European history requires a case-by-case consideration of different European nations' experiences. Because Europe never unified during this time (and, if anything, became more competitive, due to rival bids for colonies), there are limits to which the continent has collectively been impacted by imperial legacies. Instead, each European nation that made a bid for continental mastery, or set out to seize colonies, had its own imperial experiences, resulting in unique legacies.

How modern Europe was shaped
by its imperial exploits

Portugal was at the vanguard of maritime exploration. From the edge of Europe, with fewer than one million people, and somewhat cut off from Mediterranean commerce, the Portuguese nobility took matters into their own hands to make their nation more significant. The ruling monarchs saw their naval explorers as warriors of Christ, blessing their voyages with both royal and religious sanctification. In the early 1400s Henrique the Navigator sailed to the Azores, Cape Verde and kicked off West Africa's exploration. As Portuguese horizons expanded, so did the possibilities for seeking glory at the expense of the locals. In 1415 a Portuguese fleet sailed through the Straits of Gibraltar and seized Ceuta, a Moroccan port, a feat that astonished other Europeans. Vasco da Gama's explorations later helped to expand Europe's horizons further, when his ships reached India in 1498. The following year da Gama sailed back to a glorious reception in Lisbon.

In 1510 Goa was seized by Portuguese conquistador Afonso de Albuquerque. He encouraged creating a Goan Christian populace through intermarriage with the locals, and Goa remained a Portuguese colony for more than 400 years. Portuguese voyages also reached Brazil in 1500, China in 1514 and Japan in 1543.[23]

Spain, though, would outdo the accomplishments of its Portuguese neighbour. The monarchs of Castile funded the voyages of Christopher Columbus. In 1492 he was convinced he had sailed to the Indies and was unaware that he had reached the New World. Thereafter, rivalry between Spain and Portugal grew over the Americas. The papacy had to step in and mediate, blessing these Iberian voyagers and helping to broker their spheres of influence, because colonization was 'very largely a Church–State venture', as the historian Anthony Pagden writes.[24] The Treaty of Tordesillas (1494) kicked off repeated negotiations about drawing a horizontal line through the Atlantic Ocean. Brazil was in Portugal's sphere; hence Portuguese became Brazil's official language. Elsewhere the Spaniards were supreme: conquistador Hernán Cortés invaded Mexico in 1521 and Peru in 1533. The gold and precious metals found there offered a large incentive. And the religious rationale had strengthened because Iberian monarchs were also involved in a war effort to evict the Muslim Moors from Europe. In 1492, as Columbus discovered the Americas, the Moors were forced out of Grenada in Spain, ending their al-Andalus caliphate.

The Spanish Empire reached great size and strength under King Charles V. Earlier, the Castilian monarchs Ferdinand and Isabella had linked the Spanish crown to the Habsburg line, and so Charles V became Holy Roman Emperor and gained control over parts of Austria, Germany, Italy, Belgium, Holland and rulership over the Czechs. He also led Catholic Europe's defence against the Ottomans. His successor, Philip II, seized the Portuguese crown in 1581, thus combining its overseas empire with the Castilian (an arrangement that lasted until 1640).[25]

Charles V, Philip II and their heirs saw Lutheran Protestantism as a threat not only to Catholicism, but also to their empire. Over time the Spanish Empire was drained by fighting Protestant Europeans in the Thirty Years War (1618–48). Eventually Spanish influence in Germanic lands slipped away. In 1700 the last Spanish Habsburg king died heirless. The Spanish Empire persisted in weakened form, but started to lose its colonies to upcoming rivals like the British and, much later, to the USA. Today the prevalence of the Spanish language, deposited by colonialism across so much of the Americas, and increasingly spoken in the USA, is amongst its greatest imperial legacies.

Austria, and Vienna in particular, became the centre of Habsburg rule after Spanish control waned. The Habsburg line had rather innocuous origins in a Swiss canton, before acquisitions through marriage and war won the Habsburgs several thrones, and eventually the Holy Roman crown, with Austria stamping its presence over Central Europe.[26] Vienna became the quintessential imperial capital of the day, with Catholicism and dynastic tradition binding the empire together, and Empress Maria Theresa (ruled 1740–80) being the embodiment of this order. Her daughter, Marie Antoinette, later became Queen of France after marrying Louis XVI, reminding us that modern notions of 'nations' were still a work in progress and were subordinate to sweeping dynastic unions.

Over time, more lands were glued together to create the Austro-Hungarian Empire, notably after Hungary's dynastic union with Austria, which began in 1867. At this time Hungary covered a much larger territory than its present-day incarnation, and that included Romania, Croatia and Slovakia. It had also been a battleground against the Ottoman Empire's attempts to expand into Christian Europe. Emperor Franz Joseph ruled for almost seventy years over a patchwork of lands, and his empire trundled on until the Great War. It was the assassination of another Franz (Ferdinand) that triggered war in 1914. He was its first casualty – and the Austro-Hungarian Empire itself expired in 1918 as the war tore it apart.

Austria today is a minnow; even more starkly so when one considers the grandeur of its imperial past. True, the empire was never 'Austrian' – it was multi-ethnic and diverse and was ruled by dynastic entitlement, not common identity. Baroque architecture across Central Europe reminds us of the old imperial era, and cities like Prague and Lvov retain an Austro-Hungarian feel. Vienna still has an air of cosmopolitanism and consequence for world affairs, hosting international bodies like the IAEA (the world atomic energy body) and another global multi-state club, the OSCE (Organization for Security and Co-operation in Europe), but despite this, sometimes trying to unearth the impact of its relatively recent former imperial power is difficult.

*

France, by comparison, is still heavily and obviously influenced by its imperial past. The ups and downs of its imperialism mirror the vicissitudes of French history. The Bourbon dynasty's rule had its golden age under the 'Sun King', Louis XIV. In the 1600s France conquered its first overseas empire in India, North America and the Caribbean, only to lose a lot of it in the Seven Years War (1756–63) to the British. So great a blow this was to its prestige that France's monarch started a new war in 1778 to reverse the outcome of 1763, but France was bankrupted by the costs of doing so.[27] The resulting privations on the French were a reason why the monarchy fell out of favour: anger was building, ultimately leading to the French Revolution of 1789 and the executions of Louis XVI and Marie Antoinette in the Bastille in 1793. France, for so long a pillar of Catholic dynastic rule, had become a revolutionary state.

This was a key moment in European history, in no small part because of the way it fused ideas of enlightenment and a renewed drive for empire. France's revolution was the platform for the rising military and political star Napoleon Bonaparte. Earlier in his military career the young Napoleon had led an army that occupied Egypt, enhancing his personal reputation (even if French rule there lasted just a few years). His real glory came later, in a revolutionary rampage across Europe, as his *levée en masse* armies exported the French Revolution across Europe. Napoleon proclaimed himself Emperor of France in 1804, and two years later abolished the Holy Roman Empire (although he made sure to marry the daughter of the Habsburg king, for good measure). It was all part of his doomed bid for hegemony over Europe.

Facing a British naval blockade, Napoleon introduced a 'Continental System' of standardization across his European empire to help pay for his war effort. All this ended with France's defeat in the Battle of Waterloo in 1815. Napoleon later died in exile, and France lost its colonies. But the legacy of French empire-building, and its fusion with modern ideals, endured. Republicanism and secularism could be as powerful a basis for empire-building as Catholicism and monarchy had been.[28]

Later French colonialism, in the nineteenth century, would shape the world in ways that are still recognizable today. The French rapidly rebuilt an overseas empire: Saigon was occupied in 1859, leading to the creation of French Indochina. Back in Europe, the French Army was trounced by the newly unified Germany in 1871. So to restore some Gallic pride, France's military turned to colonial campaigns in North and West Africa in the 1880s. The prevalence of its language in these regions is testimony to the enduring impact of France's assimilationist idea of including its colonies in a 'Greater France'. Algeria became the focal point of French settler colonization. In the 1950s, France was still so loath to give up Algeria, despite a growing independence movement, that it fought a bitter war there. Its imperial past remains a controversial topic, and when President Macron (too young to recall colonialism at first hand) announced in 2018 that France should return looted items from its former colonies, he was met with a mixed response amongst the French.

Controversies around colonial legacy remain in Belgium. A newer nation, it unified in 1830 and, keen to join the European club, set out to acquire colonies. King Leopold II notoriously ran the 'Congo Free State' as a private venture, creating a vicious regime that used soldiers to punish and kill countless Congolese for failing to work themselves to the bone on rubber plantations. In Belgium itself, statues of Leopold II still stand tall, despite the awful colonial record. Perhaps this is because the colonial legacy was quickly overtaken by bad events at home. Just five years after Leopold II's death in 1909, Belgium was the victim of German aggression in 1914, and again in 1939, in the world wars. Anglo-American wartime narratives duly recast the plucky Belgians as victims, inadvertently scrubbing colonial memories from prominence.[29] Today Belgium hosts major international institutions like NATO and the EU – no doubt a nod to the country's wartime suffering. For Europeans, Belgium is a small and unthreatening country. Congolese history remembers differently.

Germany, by contrast, has made the negation of its short and sharp imperial past into the cornerstone of its modern political identity. The Germans were also latecomers to the imperial game, the nation having unified in 1871 from a myriad of principalities (which had once existed within the Holy Roman Empire).[30] The architect of unification, Prussia's 'Iron Chancellor' Otto von Bismarck, lived until the grand old age of eighty-three, dying in 1898. While Bismarck's statecraft had unified Germany *without* triggering a continent-wide war, his less-talented successor brought about precisely that calamity. Kaiser Wilhelm II wanted to create a German colonial empire – its own 'place in the sun' – but, in doing so, Germany ended up in a naval arms race with the British, which eventually contributed to triggering a full-scale European war in 1914.

Both world wars were very much imperial affairs because they pitted rival empires against each other. Germany was defeated in 1918, but dreams of a Germanic empire lived on in the fevered imagination of the Austrian Great War veteran, Corporal Adolf Hitler. He ended up promoting himself to high office by winning enough votes in 1933 for his Nazi Party, and eventually captured the German state wholesale under his authoritarian rule. Hitler dreamed up a 'Thousand Year Reich', replete with the conquest of Eastern Europe and the ethnic cleansing of Jews and Slavs, who were all to be killed or reduced to servitude. The Second World War remains the defining episode in modern Europe's development. For Germany, defeated and occupied in 1945, Nazism's legacy had to be painstakingly overcome. At first split between East and West by the war's outcome, and later reunified, Germany has benefited from a succession of temperate leaders. Its nation has recovered its dignity, in no small part due to the commitment of Germans to reject militarism, and to express their ingenuity and competence through economic performance instead.

Europe is a product of its many layers of imperial history. Its imperial traditions – of attempts to unify the continent, and of seeking glory and wealth outside Europe – are collectively its imperial inheritance. The former tradition is as old as antiquity. The latter stretches back around 500 years and ended only in the mid- and late twentieth century. These imperial histories are one reason why the different European national identities that we take for granted today – 'British', 'French', 'German', 'Italian', and so on – cohered as they did, and why Europe never properly unified.

It is also the story of how the more advanced parts of Europe developed a confidence in their political, scientific and technological systems (and sometimes an overconfidence in these, especially in their export through colonialism). The legacies of various imperial histories live on in modern jealousies. Today neither Greece nor Italy possesses anything of the influence and stature of the great civilizations of their ancestors. Mediterranean access, once so vital to the southward development of Europe's societies, has in the modern era instead been relegated by an unfairly prejudicial distinction between the economic powerhouses of 'northern Europe' and the often sluggish and patronage-based economies of 'southern Europe'.[31]

Imperial history also explains why it was far from inevitable that Europe's boundaries formed as they did. Modern Europe's notions of who may be deemed 'un-European' results partly from old imperial contests. There is little possibility of a cultural 'Europeanness' that wholeheartedly includes Russia or Turkey. What counts as 'Eastern' and 'Western' Europe flows from historical imperial experiences, and in cultural demarcations between the Protestant, Catholic and Orthodox Churches. Interdenominational theological divisions are one thing; it is how these religions were hitched to different imperial projects that contributed to the frontiers that persist today. The historical contest with Islam was even clearer. Turkey, the modern successor state to the Anatolian core of the Ottoman Empire, was never fully accommodated in Europe because of it.

As the architects of Europe's unity attempted to transcend the violent past of two world wars for a peaceful future, they were overcoming both wartime and imperial legacies, setting out to achieve this by attempting a task that no one in Europe had sustained for long – continental unity – just as the sun was setting on centuries of European colonial dominion.

After empire: Europe from 'community' to 'union'

Cognac, in western France, was a surprising birthplace for the ideas behind modern European unity. Jean Monnet was born there in 1888. His innocuous early life, as a salesman for the Monnet family-branded cognac, took a drastic turn because of the world wars. Monnet was horrified by Europe tearing itself apart, so after the end of the First World War he worked for the League of Nations in Geneva. When the Second World War broke out, he decided to use his skills in a different way to help Europe in its time of need. A behind-the-scenes wheeler-dealer extraordinaire, Monnet set to work by assembling networks of rich and influential people in Europe and across the Atlantic. After 1945 his great accomplishment was to have the bulk of American Marshall Aid (officially the European Recovery Program) channelled through what became known as the 'Monnet Plan', which funded France's post-war reconstruction.[32] But he was not going to limit his ambitions here: Monnet was a man who dared to dream a vision of European unity, and he had a cunning plan to achieve it.

Heavy industry was something the European economies of the day relied on, not least for the armaments that had been used in both world wars. Within the 'Monnet Plan' was an idea to manage cooperatively the coal and steel production between different countries. Monnet sold the idea to the supportive European politicians of six Western European states. In 1951 the Paris Treaty was signed, heralding the European Coal and Steel Community. Its signatories were the French host, foreign minister Robert Schuman, West German chancellor Konrad Adenauer, Italian aristocrat Count Carlo Sforza, Dutch politician Dirk Stikker, Belgian statesman Paul van Zeeland and the politician Joseph Bech of Luxembourg. Their robust negotiations led to last-minute changes to the draft text, and there were still many unresolved issues. Something had to be done to get past the diplomatic finishing line, so it was decided that the six representatives would sign a blank sheet of paper – something that symbolized a Europe restarting its history on a blank page.[33]

Other unity initiatives fell by the wayside, including a mooted European army. The 1950s initiative for the European Defence Community was stillborn, due to political opposition in Paris; and was less urgent, due to the presence of the American Army in Western Europe to keep the peace. Those who were committed to European unity continued their work, with Monnet's next venture being a cooperative agreement for pooling European atomic expertise (with the intention of offering the USA a single European focal point for cooperation on atomic energy). But the crucial step was the common economic market. When the Rome Treaty was signed on 25 March 1957, it established both 'Euratom' and the European Economic Community (EEC). From now on, thanks to the EEC, the original six members could cooperate in all economic matters, from industry to agriculture. The Rome Treaty text mentioned the vague aspiration of 'an ever closer union among the peoples' and came into force on 1 January 1958.[34]

With the birth of the EEC, European unity became much more tangible. The 'free movement of people' originated here when, in preparatory work for the EEC, an idea had been suggested that goods, services, capital *and* labour could flow openly across the common economic area. Italy's government seized on the idea, because it was struggling with unemployment at the time and so had a labour surplus. When other EEC members expressed concern regarding influxes of Italian labour, the Italian government got tough and threatened to block the free movement of capital, which would have disadvantaged Germany and the Netherlands, which wanted investment opportunities. In the end, free movement of both capital and labour were written into the Rome Treaty.[35]

The EEC caught on because it re-empowered European nations after 1945, rescuing them in their moment of need. Had the EEC failed to harness the post-war mood in participating capitals, Monnet's vision would have remained in his imagination. In short, the EEC was not a replacement of the various European nation-states, but a route to revitalizing them – as long as they were willing to pool some of their national sovereignty in Europe's new cooperative ventures.[36]

The EEC helped Western Europe find its feet during the decolonization period, both materially and intellectually. The two processes were unrelated, and the EEC was certainly not a replacement for the colonies. But it enabled countries like France, the Netherlands and Belgium to re-anchor their prosperity closer to home as their colonial flow of profits waned, to compensate for the loss of global influence that decolonization was ushering in.

Searching for a way to matter in a changing world, at a time of the US and USSR dictating the fate of the world, Western Europeans were keen not to be rendered insignificant. Monnet hence articulated a grandiose vision in 1954: 'Our countries have become too small for the present-day world, for the scale of modern technology and of America and Russia today, or China and India tomorrow. The union of European peoples in the United States of Europe is the way to raise their standard of living and preserve peace. It is the great hope and opportunity of our time.'[37]

Had the EEC remained a club of economic cooperation for a select number of Western European nations, the continent's history would have been different. Instead, European unity, and its accompanying set of institutions, became the vehicle for the ambitions of European politicians who had few other ways to assert their visions for the future, or to spread their values. Looking back on this period, the ex-Portuguese prime minister Barroso said: 'The great vision of the founding fathers of the European Community, from Schuman to Monnet to Adenauer, was a step by step approach to create a *solidariaie de fet* that brings people together.'[38] And the steps were continuing.

The Maastricht Treaty of 1992 heralded the metamorphosis of 'community' into 'union'. It came right after the end of the Cold War, as Europe once again searched for its place in the new world. The Maastricht Summit was held on 9–10 December and resulted in a treaty establishing a European Union. The treaty aspired to a common currency and a foreign policy. In other words, instead of simply opening up a shared economic space in which businesses, employers and workers could fish for opportunities, as the EEC had done, the EU was a deal between the states themselves and, consequently, was a huge step forward in the commitments it was suggesting for European countries.[39]

With monetary and perhaps political union beckoning, Maastricht had a polarizing impact. In 1999 the euro currency was launched. Member states were free to take it up if they chose, of course, since the EU was a voluntary organization. Those Europeans who backed such ideas wanted to consign European nationalism to the continent's darker past; those who opposed it were aghast at what they feared was an impending loss of national identity, and of 'union' leading to 'federation'.

High noon for the idea of a 'European federation' came in 2005. A draft EU constitution was put together but, in referendums in France and the Netherlands, voters convincingly rejected it. So the EU opted instead for another intergovernmental agreement: the Lisbon Treaty was signed by EU member states in 2007, and tried to bolster and harmonize a mixture of earlier treaties. There were by now many layers to European integration, including the single market, the euro and the 1985 Schengen Agreement on open borders. Each had its own strictures and its own participants (some member states opted out of certain mechanisms, for example, with the UK never adopting the euro). The EU was, collectively speaking, cumbersome, deliberative and slow to make decisions, which is why the Lisbon Treaty agreed to bolster the posts of the European Council president and the EU foreign-policy chief.[40]

Was this what Monnet envisaged, at the start of his journey in Cognac? 'Myself, I have always been convinced that the unification of Europe cannot be achieved by intergovernmental compromises,' he said.[41] Monnet died in 1979, but his ideas still influence those who advocate gradual steps towards a federation – a 'United States of Europe' – in which the continent transcends its various nationalisms. According to Monnet's biographer, 'The civilising role of institutions began to loom large in his utterances' and he wanted to neuter nationalism in European capitals, because 'The state had no romantic connotations for him, only uses and abuses.' Conversely, 'institutions could civilise men because, whereas every person is born afresh, supranational institutions can embody the principles for the common good from one generation to the next.'[42] These ideals are in evidence when EU officials address the European public collectively, with less attention being paid to national cultural differences, or to the different historical paths trodden by European nations.[43]

The EU: democracy's heir to empire

The EU is not an empire, but in its commitment to unification between its members, and to enlargement with new members, it has acquired quasi-imperial habits and characteristics. In this regard, it is a modern democratic inheritor of imperial legacies and, despite being intended as a vehicle with which to escape history, it still has to drive past the fallen masonry of the imperial age.

Voluntary association is the EU's lifeblood, with member states signing up willingly to its strictures. Once they have done so, the EU has limited tools with which to force them to abide by what they have signed up to. The European Court of Justice became the interpreter of its treaties, and a way for the EU to speak with authority to its member states, to citizens and to businesses operating in the single market. The Court has allowed the EU to influence life in its member states (or interfere, as Eurosceptics argue).[44] If the western Roman Empire's language was Latin, then the EU's has been legalese.

A great deal of interpretation is needed, not least because the EU's overlapping structures are as easy to trace as a bowl of spaghetti and bewilder many ordinary European citizens. At the top of the structure, the European Council was established in 1974 as a forum for Europe's elected heads of state or government. In principle, if they issue a joint communiqué, it reflects the will of all their populations. In practice, their equal standing in the Council has seen bigger countries lose their patience with smaller ones. For a while it was headed by a rotating presidency. On 1 January 2010 Herman Van Rompuy, an ex-Belgian prime minister, became the Council's first permanent president. He was succeeded by ex-Polish prime minister Donald Tusk. Rompuy and Tusk have boosted the notion of a 'European president' as the global face of the continent. Tusk's replacement was another ex-Belgian prime minister, Charles Michel.

What of the citizens of Europe? The European Parliament is their link to the EU. But the link is simply too stretched out for many citizens to really feel a connection. They can vote for an MEP (Member of the European Parliament) to represent their locality, something that has created the world's second-largest combined democratic exercise (behind India), enfranchising a total of 500 million people. But voter turnout has hovered around the 50 per cent mark, indicating only a limited buy-in to the idea of sending your local MEP to speak on your behalf in the EU.[45] Together, the

Council and the Parliament are key parts of the EU's legislature.

There is also the European Commission, which is the engine-room in charge of devising and implementing the EU's laws. A European Civil Service, if you will, divided into domains run by Commissioners, each with a portfolio (such as 'better regulation', 'digital single market', 'trade', 'development', 'external affairs', and so on). The Commissioners come from different member states and report to the Commission president. All of which seems a logical breakdown of responsibilities, even if the terms 'Council' and 'Commission' might get confused in some people's heads.

Instead of creating a superstate that directly controls territory, the EU has come to resemble a different type of imperial entity. As the academic Jan Zielonka has observed, 'The EU resembles an empire we know from many centuries earlier. Its multilevel governance system of concentric circles . . . resembles the system we knew in the Middle Ages, before the rise of nation states.'[46] This is why the EU has encountered the same age-old dilemmas that empires always faced: in striking a balance between central authority and the various regents who were nominally signed up to the imperial idea. Today the crown is worn by Brussels, and the regents who pledge their loyalty are the governments of its member states.

The EU is based around a 'ruling city' model, comprising Brussels, Luxembourg and Strasbourg, although Brussels has become more important than the others over time. Whereas Holy Roman or Byzantine rulers expected authority to emanate from the sanctity of their title, Brussels has recourse to no such legitimacy myth, aside from its core assertions that it makes good sense to band together to strengthen economies, live openly in Europe and avoid war.

Whereas historical empires may also have relied on military coercion, the EU does not; rather, it doles out fines for breaches of its regulations. Therefore the goodwill of the member states to partake is a basic determinant of the EU's ability to last into the future. Which, in turn, evokes the dilemma of empire: finding the biting point between central authority and constituent parts. When there is a revolt in one of the member states – as in Brexit Britain or Austerity Athens – the writ of the EU is shaken.

The outspoken ex-Greek finance minister, Yanis Varoufakis, offers one view from the receiving end of EU enforcement – of Brussels being robotic in its negotiations with Athens after the financial crisis. Greece needed bailouts, and the EU demanded that it (and other struggling EU members) adopt austerity measures. As Varoufakis recounts, he was once enamoured that 'diverse nations rather than an authoritarian empire might create a common land'. But he is scathing of how ahistorical the EU is: 'Europe is an ancient continent, and our debts to each other stretch decades, centuries and millennia into the past. Counting them vindictively and pointing moralising fingers at each other is precisely what we did not need in the midst of an economic crisis.'[47]

It may seem harsh on the EU to quote such a stern critic, but since Varoufakis has no need for diplomacy, he spots other obvious features of the EU that might be overlooked. For example, that the euro is quite literally a make-believe currency: 'Take a look at any euro banknote. What do you see? Pleasing arches and bridges. But these are fictitious arches and non-existent bridges. A continent replete with cultural treasures has unbelievably chosen to adorn its freshly minted common currency with none of them. Why? Because bureaucrats wanted to remove culture from our currency in the same way they craved the depoliticization of politics and the technocratization of money.'[48]

Technocracy is a term that sums up how the EU interprets the ideas of its founding fathers, who believed in the 1950s that a focus on technical processes can denationalize European politics. It is why the scaffolding of the EEC, and later the EU, has consisted of impersonal institutions and treaties between countries; and why, if there is a style and feel to the EU, it is one of a protracted exercise in process. This reflects the best and the worst of post-Enlightenment Europe. Technocracy focuses the mind on what is rational, scientific and proven in best practice. EU officials point to balance sheets, accession criteria and empirical facts as the impeccable logic of human progress – which would be fine, if humans were robots; but because they are not, populists have tried to hijack the reins of national histories, and stir people's hearts that have been left cold by the EU's technocracy.[49]

EU enlargement: a model for post-imperial expansion

Enlargement of the EU carries strong imperial connotations. It is an inheritor of the old tendency for Europeans to take such pride in their own systems that they need to replicate them elsewhere. Universalism has underpinned the EU's vision for expansion, and herein lies the genealogical link to past European habits. It is reminiscent of a civilizing mission, this time predicated on promoting peace, democracy and good economic practices by enlarging the single market. Expansion was a game-changer for the European project: it has been a model for post-imperial expansion by consent.

The EU has been an open project, willing to admit new members that sign its treaties and jump through the hoops of its Copenhagen criteria (which set out economic and political perquisites for a prospective member, and make technocracy the means of expansion). Enlarging the EU has been a controversial business. Former EU foreign-policy chief Catherine Ashton tried to head off the charge that the EU attempts to 'export' so-called European values to other countries: 'I reject that accusation. The rights to free speech, freedom of assembly, justice and equality are not European rights: they are universal rights.'[50] All of which is reflective of the EU as a post-Enlightenment project, imbued with a keen sense of knowing what amounts to human progress.

If there was some sense of shared history binding the original

EEC, this logic has been severely stretched by the EU's expansion. The turning point came after the USSR's collapse and its fragmentation into several successor states in 1991. This, and the collapse of the Berlin Wall in November 1989, offered a moment of real optimism for Europe's future. Long divided by the Cold War, the continent was divided no more. This added to the impetus behind the EU as a peace project. The principles of democracy, solidarity, economic recovery, and former enemies now cooperating for mutual gain were extended to former parts of the Soviet Bloc. For new inductees, accessing the single market has been the main lure, but joining the EU's club of democracies has also been hugely significant.

For the young Donald Tusk, born in Gdańsk in northern Poland, watching the protests against communist rule was crucial to his political upbringing. Gdańsk carried the scars of the Second World War, having been invaded by the German Army in 1939 and later by the retaliating Soviet Army. It was Poland's fate to have been trapped between these two warring countries, just as it had suffered at the hands of past European empires. So it was unsurprising that when Poland was finally free of Soviet influence, and the Iron Curtain had come down, someone with Tusk's life experiences would look enthusiastically to the EU for Poland's future.

There has been no greater assertion of the EU's post-imperial credentials than its inclusion of countries like Poland. The USSR was, after all, the world's last formal empire, and the EU was there to pick up the fragments when it shattered. Poland was officially admitted into the EU on 1 May 2004, after years of preparation. It was accompanied by a host of other Eastern European states, which joined alongside it and in a second tranche of expansion in 2007.

These enlargements fundamentally changed the EU by seemingly turning enlargement into a geopolitical tool through which to spread Western European values. Which state would be next? Turkey and Ukraine have been mooted in the past, as have the

Balkan states that came into existence after Yugoslavia's collapse. Croatia joined the EU in 2013, and talks around other prospective Balkan members have continued. Even if the EU thinks of itself as only widening the tent of democracy and solidarity, Russia has perceived the opposite; it even went to war in 2014 in Ukraine to stymie Kiev's EU membership prospects.

While the EU can attract member states into its common market, it cannot defend them since it has no army, and because its values have involved renouncing militarism, this has left the EU reliant on NATO and the US military. In other words, when it comes to the strategic and security implications of its enlargements, the EU has issued to its new members cheques that it cannot cash.

Eastern expansion has widened the range of cultural and economic identities that coexist within the shared spaces of open movement and commerce. The laudability of these developments has to be balanced against several uncomfortable facts. The larger the EU has become, the harder it is to imagine that smaller prospective member states have any leverage at all in accession negotiations, with newly admitted members effectively buttressing the periphery of Brussels' authority. Moreover, the flow of influence tends to be one-way. Eastern European culture is far less likely to influence the EU than the Western European ways of doing things, which have been influencing these newer members.[51]

This is clear in the way Eastern European economic migration has become a target for populist anger in the UK. However unfair and racist these sentiments may be, they point to real practical problems of maintaining a shared sense of community across an EU-wide population of more than 500 million people. The more the EU has expanded, the further it has eroded any clear sense of the EU harnessing a common cultural and historical identity. Aside from everyone wanting peace, it is hard to envisage what a credible story might look like to explain a union of nearly thirty countries.

With history in mind, it is important to note that Christianity has fallen away as offering a common cultural rootedness to modern European unity. Rather than being a Christian or even a post-Christian association, the EU has preferred to centre itself around a common democratic identity,[52] which reignites questions around what 'Europe' is, and the extent to which the EU can convincingly speak on the collective behalf of its members.

The future of post-imperial Europe

On the sixtieth anniversary of the Rome Treaty, Donald Tusk reflected on the future of European unity: 'We often hear the argument that the memory of the past tragedies of a divided Europe is no longer an argument [for having the EU], that new generations do not remember the sources of our inspirations. But amnesia does not invalidate these inspirations.'[53] The problem is that the EU has its own form of amnesia: it is fixated by the continent's immediate twentieth-century history, but largely ignores the broader patterns of imperial history that have shaped Europe. Signing treaties in Rome is a nod to this past, but only a symbolic one.

The EU cannot admit that the challenges it faces are analogous to the challenges of empires. 'Unity in diversity' was invoked by the European Commission,[54] which sounds like a quintessential conundrum of imperial politics – how to bind disparate communities together through a common vision so that they accept the edicts of a central authority, which in return promises to usher in an era of peace and prosperity.

The EU cannot call itself an imperial project, so it calls itself a peace project, and while this has been a fair observation, it is a selective one. As the implications of its eastern expansions play out, history remains our best guide to the art of the possible in further enlarging and unifying the EU because, no matter the dreams of its architects, it cannot transcend imperial history.

Nearly two millennia have passed since the Roman Empire

at its peak drew its frontier across Germania and Dacia (Romania). Since then, every putative heir to Rome's accomplishments has achieved only incomplete unity. Aspirations to create a 'new Rome' have resurfaced repeatedly over the centuries, and the EU ought to be understood as belonging to this pantheon.

Imperial legacies bear down on modern Europe in many ways. For instance, Charlemagne's medieval empire covered an area that roughly corresponded to the EEC's original six Western European members, giving these countries a common historical reference point as they began to pool their sovereignty in the 1950s.[55] Byzantium offers its own lessons for European unity. The EU's own bureaucracy is Byzantine in its complexity, and this remains a fitting description for such a tricky undertaking, of standardizing administrative practices across such differing European nations.[56]

Would a greater awareness of its imperial heritage help the EU to succeed? Imperial history offers insights into the durability of unity projects, with Byzantium and the Holy Roman Empire each lasting for around ten centuries. Empires of such long standing adapted to unforeseen events, coexisted with new rivals and adapted to their alternately expanding and shrinking realms. The EEC and the EU have existed for a mere fraction of this time, and it remains to be seen whether Brussels can demonstrate the flexibility of mind required to sustain its own pan-continental ambitions.

Unless Europe faces some major new existential catastrophe, it is difficult to foresee the EU taking the step to officially become a federation (formalizing the centralization of power in Brussels).[57] If a future crisis drastically panicked European countries into seeking to band together more tightly, they would probably look to NATO in the event of a widespread war, for example, rather than the EU. The common market remains the EU's calling card, rather than defence or foreign policy, which makes the EU better suited as a unity project for the good times of prosperity rather than the bad times of crisis.

Colonialism's legacies also still bear down on Europe's future. After European nations spent 500 years exporting their values, the global reality they now face is of a future that Europeans will not dictate. As the academic J. M. Blaut once explained, 'Eurocentrism' involved seeing the continent as the centre of its own universe, which it was in the colonial age. 'The really crucial part of Eurocentrism is not a matter of attitudes in the sense of values and prejudices, but rather a matter of science, and scholarship, and informed expert opinion.'[58] In other words, a 'Europeans know best' attitude was fostered over the centuries, which the EU has inherited in a modernized and benign form.

This has afforded the EU another imperial trait: of being sufficiently large and confident in its governing philosophies to want to influence events around the world, notably by embodying the old European tradition of telling others what to do. The peaceful exportation of Western European norms and values is part of the EU's style.[59] This is evident in how it tries to secure its frontiers, and how it deals with other world powers.

Consider the view of a former Indian Foreign Office minister: 'Indians have an allergy to being lectured to, and one of the great failings in the EU–India partnership has been the tendency of Europe to preach to India on matters it considers itself to be quite competent to handle on its own.'[60] This is not a good impression to create. The one-way traffic of Europeans dispensing wisdom will surely have the effect of annoying and irritating others.

Being democracy's heir to empire carries certain responsibilities, and peaceful democracy promotion has become part of the EU's tradition – for example, through statements of solidarity after the Arab Spring uprisings in 2011, or by sending election advisors and observers far and wide to help other countries' democratic processes. Having fostered democracy in the south, centre and east of Europe, the EU understandably believes itself to be a beacon of democratic wisdom.[61] This is a fair conclusion to draw, but the question is whether the rest of the world will care to listen in the future.

The trend lines suggest that Europe is now more likely to be influenced by the rest of the world than the other way round. Europe's population is ageing (the median age will reach forty-five by 2030, which will be the highest of any continent[62]). The EU's club of democracies abuts some troubled areas, and is impacted by events such as political instability in Turkey, wars in Ukraine and the Middle East, and the refugees and economic migrants risking their lives trying to enter Europe.

In the long run, the twin notions of 'civilization' and 'barbarism', which have an extended lineage in European imperial thought, may yet return to relevance. Ancient Athenians and Romans understood their civilizational accomplishments in these terms, as did later European colonialists, as they adventured and profiteered in Asia, Africa and the Middle East.[63] Modern Europe still gains confidence and comfort from its own notions of civilization, but it may feel increasingly isolated and embattled in protecting its civilization.

Whereas empires had frontiers that gradually petered out, the EU has fixed borders to police against the trends of the wider world. Even as the EU tries to be post-imperial, it cannot ignore its imperial DNA – and the variegated strains that different European countries possess. There is no way to escape the patterns, expectations and proclivities that history has bequeathed.

FOUR

RUSSIA'S EMBRACE OF ITS IMPERIAL LEGACY

I have conquered an empire; yet I have not been able to conquer myself.

Attributed to Peter the Great (1672–1725)

A Russian is self-assured just because he knows nothing and does not want to know anything, since he does not believe that anything can be known.

Leo Tolstoy (1828–1910), *War and Peace*[1]

... the collapse of the Soviet Union was a major geo-political disaster of the century ... Tens of millions of our co-citizens found themselves outside Russian territory.

Vladimir Putin, 'Annual Address', 2005[2]

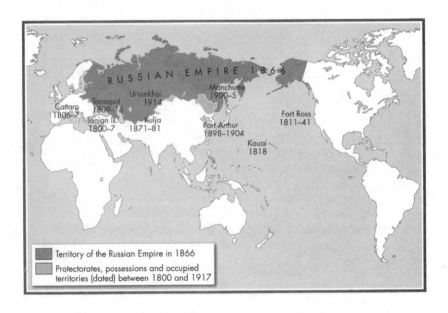

Map 5 The Russian Empire, 1866

Map 6 The Russian Federation and its successor states

The war in Ukraine was just a few months old when I deployed there as part of a diplomatic mission, which was tasked with monitoring a failing ceasefire between the belligerents. The mission was run by the OSCE (Organization for Security and Co-operation in Europe), a club of fifty-seven states with its origins in the East–West trust-building that had helped to end the Cold War. The OSCE's virtue was that its members included Russia *and* the Western states – countries otherwise at loggerheads over Russia's role in the war and its annexation of Crimea in March 2014.

Consequently the OSCE was the only organization that was palatable to Russia's government for deploying unarmed international monitors close to its border. My OSCE colleagues included Russians seconded by their government. Person-to-person, I got along well with most of them, which was essential to making our mixed teams work. Officially, relations between our respective governments were freezing over as rapidly as the winter climate, and it would take more than the passing of the seasons for there to be even the merest glimmer of a thaw.

Fighting between Ukraine's armed forces and Russian-backed separatists had intensified during 2014. On 17 July, Malaysia Airlines flight MH17 was shot down over east Ukraine as it flew high above the war zone. All 298 people on board had died, the unknowing victims of a war unfolding thousands of metres below them. To have perished in such a manner, blown out of the sky without warning, and with scant explanation for the bereaved, was beyond cruelty. Everyday in-flight paraphernalia littered the crash site, which was strewn over such a large area that we drove between clusters of wreckage. The OSCE was helping the recovery operation by facilitating access to the crash site with the gun-toting separatists who controlled the area.

My first job was to accompany the MH17 recovery team as they went about the grim task of repatriating bodies and recovering the twisted pieces of metal that had once been an airliner. I watched fuselage parts being loaded onto open-topped train carriages to begin the journey back to the Netherlands. The Dutch led the investigation, because MH17 had taken off from Amsterdam and 193 of their citizens had died. The recovery team worked hard to remove the debris before the ground froze, as the summer of 2014 turned to winter with scarcely an interregnum.

The aircraft had crashed close to the village of Hrabove, which was just thirty-five kilometres from Russia's border. The surrounding regions of Donetsk and Luhansk, former industrial heartlands, had been ravaged by war. Ordinary citizens were caught in the melee and many had fled, creating streams of displaced persons. Thousands of soldiers, civilians and separatists were losing their lives in what resembled the industrial wars of the prior century.

During my year in Ukraine I saw plenty of artillery being used by the belligerents to bombard each other over an increasingly static front line, which bisected Donetsk and Luhansk. Our monitoring patrols visited both sides, including Ukrainian soldiers digging trenches to shelter from the cold, and from shells being lobbed by weapons that looked like relics from a bygone war. One hundred years after the Great War's outbreak, it was being re-created in a corner of Europe.

I witnessed a fateful event on 10 February 2015, as cluster bombs rained down on the city of Kramatorsk, in an attempt by Russian-backed forces to bombard the Ukrainian armed forces' 'Anti-Terrorist Operations' HQ. The brutal reality of fighting over borders could not have been starker to me, as sixteen civilians died in this attack. As we drove to safety, we passed the bodies, and a tail fin of a rocket which, having disgorged its deadly payload, now protruded from the smashed pavement.

I had just returned from a patrol to a town called Debaltseve to meet a joint military body, comprising Ukrainian officers and – strikingly – uniformed Russian officers whom Ukraine had officially allowed into the war zone. As the OSCE had observed, this body was proving ineffectual in helping to maintain the ceasefire that both sides had signed up to. Indeed, when Debaltseve was overrun by the separatist side later in 2015, these Russian officers conveniently slipped away.

Nevertheless, at the height of the war, day in and day out, I would see these Ukrainian and Russian officers sitting in the same room. I looked at the generals heading each delegation and it struck me: given their seniority, they may well have campaigned together in Afghanistan during the Soviet Union's ill-fated war in that country in the 1980s. Now they stood at opposite sides of the geopolitical chess board. It may have seemed fratricidal to some; to others, Russia had simply invaded its neighbour. Each of us makes up our own mind on this matter, as we do regarding the extent to which imperial legacies can help to explain the calamity of Ukraine's ongoing war.

East Ukraine's current fate exemplifies the dilemmas that can haunt a post-imperial borderland, arising from histories that do not heed a line on the map. While we may take for granted that the world is demarcated into sovereign states with border lines, the historical reality was different: empires had frontiers, not borders. Influence used to emanate from centres of power, like city-states or imperial capitals, before petering out at the edges of authority, rather than stopping abruptly at a line on a map.

East Ukraine had for centuries been part of, or adjacent to, the Russian Empire. Its populace spoke Russian and many had extensive family ties in Russia (indeed, when the war began in 2014, many displaced people fled into Russia). West Ukraine, however, had a different imperial backstory, due to the abiding influence of the Austro-Hungarian Empire. Many of the people there spoke Ukrainian, and considered the prospect of their country forever being in Russia's orbit off-putting. However, there was no clear divide in the country, since Russian speakers lived in varying numbers in most parts of Ukraine. And no matter which language they spoke, many Ukrainians could agree that their government, sitting in Kiev, had tended to display rather corrupt, self-serving attitudes.

This is why, when in 2014 the Russian government decided to toss in a lighted match and start a war in Ukraine, there was ample kindling to catch fire. But why, in our post-imperial age, did Russia want to subject Ukraine to this treatment?

The landed colossus: Russia's experience of empire

Imperial history is essential to understanding modern Russia in terms of its size, ideals and idiosyncrasies. The evolution of Russia was inextricably linked to its expansion, so much so that it is unclear whether Russia created an empire or the process of imperialism created Russia. Both of these logics were at play: Russia's historical imperial character has contributed to its authoritarian political traditions, and to why it has coerced its neighbours, right till the present day.[3] So, whether looking at the emperor or the empire, there are imperial legacies to be spotted.

There is always the temptation to pen a diatribe against Russian imperialism. While I have little sympathy for Russia's actions in Ukraine, I am unconvinced that becoming red in the face about it makes much difference, since the Kremlin's occupants seemed impervious to criticism of their role in Ukraine's war. Hence, without trying to justify these actions, it is better to try and understand their mindsets and their evident compulsions, through the lens of imperial inheritances.

The territories that eventually became Russia developed as a hybrid of European and Asian influences. Amongst the early inhabitants were the nomadic Scythians, who were contemporaries of the ancient Greeks. The Scythians originated in Persia and later settled on Eurasia's steppe between around 900 and 200 BCE. This is an important part of Russia's prehistory, since it reflected migratory patterns that transcended modern notions of East and West.

The Europe-facing story starts in earnest with Kievan Rus,

a kingdom that existed from the ninth to the thirteenth centuries CE, and which consolidated the main Slavic tribes between the Baltic and Black Seas, up to the Vistula River (which lies in modern Poland). The peoples of Russia, Belarus and Ukraine can trace their heritage to Kievan Rus. Christianization overtook Kievan Rus in the ninth century, spreading from Byzantium, and this proselytizing spread is a legacy that has endured. Today the golden dome of St Volodymyr's Cathedral stands resplendent in Kiev, taking its name from Vladimir the Great, ruler of Kievan Rus from 980 to 1015, and under whose leadership Christianity supplanted idol worship amongst the Slavic peoples. Kievan Rus was essential to laying the early foundations of what, much later, became Russia.[4]

Kievan Rus fell to the Mongol invasion of 1240 by the khanate of the Golden Horde, descendants of Genghis Khan, who rode in from the east. The Slavs ended up subjugated and paying tribute to the Mongols to ensure their survival. This period further contributed to the blend of Eastern and Western influences. Kievan Rus had benefited from its Byzantine 'European' connections, which had connected it to the legacy of the eastern Roman Empire. This heritage was not erased by the Mongol occupation, but was subsumed under their control.[5] Nomadic conquerors, after all, tended to take over much of what they found, rather than having the wherewithal to establish their own extensive administrative structures.[6] Like the Scythians well before them, the Mongols contributed an Asiatic input to the people and their practices in these areas.

Centuries passed until the Slavs could fully reassert themselves. They did so from Muscovy, under the blood-stained banner of Ivan the Terrible. His army fought wars against the Poles and Swedes, and inflicted major defeats on the Mongols by conquering the Khanate territories of Kazan, Astrakhan and Sibir. Ivan's changing titles reflected his expanding realms: from Grand Prince of Moscow (1533–47), he became 'Tsar of All Russia' until his death in 1584. This was the start of the Russian Empire, according to the academic Dominic Lieven, who locates its origin in the 1550s.[7] As Ivan's armies aggressively expanded his realm, he kept the hereditary nobility on a tight autocratic leash, using violence and political oppression to hold sway.

Russia's boundaries expanded dramatically between the seventeenth and nineteenth centuries in three directions: a westerly push into Europe; a southerly push into Central Asia; and an easterly push into Siberia. In Europe, stiff competition awaited Russia in the guise of the Swedes, Poles, Finns, Germans and Lithuanians. Until the sixteenth century Moscovy was of no greater importance or strength than these rivals, and it would be some time before it eclipsed them. In Central Asia, Russia's expansion resembled other instances of Western European colonialism: of a Christian power pushing into Muslim lands. The difference with empires like the French and British was that Russia shared the same landmass with the places it annexed. This led the Russian writer Fyodor Dostoyevsky to quip that 'In Europe we are Tartars; in Asia we too are Europeans.'[8] In Siberia expansion was impelled by the fur trade, as bears, otters, minks and other members of the animal kingdom were hunted for pelts to be sold in Europe. Russian culture spread across the Asian steppe through its Christian settlers.[9]

Russia had expanded in many directions and absorbed different influences along the way. Geographically speaking, it became a hybrid of Eastern and Western lands, but the culture of its rulers remained anchored in the royalty and the Christianity of Europe. This is illustrated by two of Russia's most famous monarchs, both of whom were acutely aware of how their holdings stacked up next to the other European imperial powers of their day.

A crowning achievement during Peter the Great's reign (1682–1725) was his army's victory at the Battle of Poltava in 1709 against Sweden, which was a decisive battle in the Great Northern War and signalled the decline of Sweden as a major imperial power. War defined Peter's reign because, according to the historian Vasili Klyuchevsky: 'Peter had to solve inherited problems ... since at least half of the Russian people lived outside the political boundaries of his state, he had to find a way of uniting them.'[10] After Peter's army had vanquished the Swedes, east Ukraine and the Baltic areas were absorbed by Russia. St Petersburg, the city Peter founded in 1703 after seizing the area from the Swedes, served as Russia's imperial capital for two centuries. It remains a testament to Peter's Westernizing vision and (with its original name restored in 1991) a reminder to the Russian people of their imperial history.

During the reign of Catherine the Great (1762–96) – the wily Prussian usurper of Russia's throne, who achieved that by having her husband disposed of – expansion continued. Russia partitioned Poland in 1772, in combination with Prussian and Habsburg machinations. War with the Ottoman Empire (1768–74) consumed the energies of Catherine's army, which unfolded as these lumbering imperial behemoths clashed around the Black Sea.

The Hermitage Museum in St Petersburg remains a grand monument to Catherine's reign. Originally housing her private art collection, it now occupies the whole Winter Palace (which, from 1732, was Russia's official royal residence). A window into the golden age of the Russian Empire, the Hermitage's displays are a testament to the royal pomp underpinning Russia's expansion and the corresponding obsessions of its monarchs of the Romanov dynasty, which ruled Russia from 1613 until the revolutions of 1917.

The great contests of the nineteenth century involving Russia pitted it against the Ottoman and British Empires. The Crimean War of 1853–6 – which featured the ill-fated Charge of the Light Brigade, and the heroic Florence Nightingale – was waged by Britain, France and the Ottomans to stop Russia's expansion. If Russia controlled Crimea, then the areas around the Black Sea

would be vulnerable. The Crimean War was a thumping defeat for
Russia. Tsar Nicholas I, on the throne since 1825, dropped dead
at the height of the war in 1855. He did not live to see just how
creaky Russia now looked, next to its seafaring British rival.

Russia could still favourably face off similarly creaky empires,
and triumphed in a later war with the Ottomans (Russia won a slew
of Ottoman territories in the Caucasus, as confirmed at the Congress of Berlin in 1878).[11] However, Russia compared unfavour-
ably to a Britain that was now reaping the rewards of the Industrial
Revolution – by contrast, Russia remained an economic pigmy,
as its empire proved too cumbersome to reform. Ukraine became
known as 'Europe's breadbasket', and this emphasis on agriculture
was in turn dependent on slave labour. Serfdom was abolished in
1861 by Tsar Alexander II, who had begun a slow reform process.
What was his reward for this act of emancipation? Twenty years
later, in 1881, he was assassinated by anarchist terrorists in St
Petersburg, one of the first sparks of anti-monarchical revolution.

Cumbersome, too, was the official title of Alexander III, who
ruled from 1881 to 1894 as Emperor of Russia, King of Poland
and Grand Duke of Finland. He avoided major wars, but was
unable to arrest a moribund economy. The last tsar, Nicholas II,
reigned from 1894 until the Bolsheviks killed him in 1917. The
year of 1905 offered a premonition of the calamitous fate about
to befall Russia. Its navy having been sunk by Japan's in the Battle
of Tushima Straits, a blow was delivered to Russia's military prestige and eastern ambitions. Later in 1905 a domestic revolt broke
out against Romanov rule. Nicholas II began reforms under his
prime minister Pyotr Stolypin, who held office from 1906 until
his assassination in 1911. Such a brutal authoritarian was he that
the hangman's noose was nicknamed 'Stolypin's necktie'. Reforms
– whether economic, social or political – were too little and came
too late to arrest the relative decline of the Russian Empire against
up-and-coming rivals.

European power politics had changed dramatically in the decades after Germany unified in 1871. Before then, the German principalities were divided. Now Germany began to match and outstrip its rivals in military and industrial power. On the eve of the Great War, in July 1914, as Russia hastily mobilized its army, the die was cast for a domestic implosion so great that its consequences still reverberate today.

One hundred years since the Bolshevik Revolution of 1917, and looking back with the benefit of perspective, it is apparent that the end of imperial Russia was *not* the end of Russia's imperial story. At the time, however, no sharper ideological break with history could be imagined than between the arch-traditionalist lineage of the tsars and Vladimir Lenin's revolutionary vanguard.

Lenin's lifelong mission was to bring down the tsars and change the European order. In *Imperialism: The Highest Stage of Capitalism* he rightly spotted that Europe's empires had brought about the calamity of the Great War by competing with each other. His historical argument was categorically sweeping, as only a Bolshevik revolutionary could be: 'Colonial policy and imperialism existed before this latest stage of capitalism, and even before capitalism. Rome, founded on slavery, pursued a colonial policy and achieved imperialism.' Lenin was mainly aggrieved by the sharp spike in colonialism that began at the tail end of the 1800s. After criticizing the British in Egypt, he reminded his readers that 'the Russians are doing the same in *their* colony in Turkestan; and they are doing so because in this way they will be in a better position to defeat their foreign competitors'.[12]

Lenin and the Bolsheviks could not, however, rewrite Russia's imperial DNA, even if they tried to do things differently after inheriting it. Having seized power in 1917, Lenin immediately sued for peace with Germany, and in the Brest-Litovsk Treaty surrendered land in exchange for respite from a war that had been anything but great for Russia. The following year, in 1918, Germany's war effort collapsed.

Before Russia had a chance to recoup its lost European lands, civil war erupted between the Bolshevik Red Army, the counter-revolutionary White Armies and meddling foreigners who wanted the tsar rethroned. Several million more people died from fighting, disease and displacement, before the civil war ended in 1922 in a hard-fought victory for Lenin's Red Army.

Consolidating their victory, the new communist masters of Russia embraced once again the habits of empire. Just like the Russian Empire before it, the new Soviet Union operated by bringing smaller nations into its orbit, sometimes by offering to be their protector. For example, during the civil war, Georgia and Armenia sided with Russia to avoid Turkish domination. Georgia's position within the Soviet Union proved fatefully symbolic. When Lenin died in 1924, he was not to be succeeded by Leon Trotsky, the Bolshevik mastermind behind victory in the civil war and an exponent of world revolution. Instead Josef Stalin, the Georgian-born member of the Politburo, who favoured socialism in one country, took on the mantle. His brutal interpretation of the exigencies of power were exercised through purges and mass deportations against enemies both real and imagined, and included fostering a devastating famine in Ukraine in 1932–3 in order to stymie instincts there towards independence. His style of rule tainted the Soviet Union beyond his death in 1953, although no ruler after Stalin would be quite so tyrannical.

The USSR greatly expanded after 1945. Russia's Great Patriotic War (1941–5) began after Hitler broke the Molotov–Ribbentrop Pact, in which Russia and Germany had agreed to divide Poland between them in 1939. The Soviet Union's war effort against Nazi Germany was on a vast scale, such that one in nine Russians died in the Second World War – a higher percentage than in any other country – and yet its army still marched on to sack Berlin in 1945. No wonder Stalin felt Russia deserved its due, for doing so much to defeat the Nazis. And, correspondingly, that Russia both needed and deserved its post-1945 acquisition of a large buffer zone in Eastern Europe.

The imperial tradition had remained, even if the justifications for this control had changed. Despite its protestations at the time, the USSR was an empire that had subjugated a variety of surrounding territories. It provided a fresh instalment in Russia's imperial history. So powerful were these legacies that, after the last tsar had fallen, Russia had not become a nation-state, but had reinvented itself as another empire.[13] Whereas once its imperial mission had been Christianity, and the belief held by the tsars that they were the 'Third Rome', the next mission was communism.

Over time, the USSR's imperial character became more obvious in its dealings with its satellite states and its republics. Stalin's successor, Nikita Khrushchev, was born close to Ukraine. He gave Crimea back to Ukraine in 1954, but this was a mere administrative rearrangement within the USSR, because Moscow's authority remained supreme. The Hungarian Revolution of 1956, and the Prague Spring of 1968, were local uprisings that were snuffed out by the Soviet Army rolling in its tanks. Leonid Brezhnev, who led the USSR from 1964 until 1982, tightened Moscow's grip over the satellite states; and the Constitution of the USSR, adopted in 1977, further subordinated the USSR's republics under Moscow's rule.

At the same time, across the developing world, the Soviet Union was assisting as many Third World liberation movements as it could get its hands on, in its global competition with the USA, denouncing the old European colonialists along the way. This glaring contradiction – between the USSR's revolutionary rhetoric abroad, and the iron grip with which it held its own imperial sprawl – contributed to its final unravelling.

After Mikhail Gorbachev came to power in 1985 and addressed his first Communist Party Congress as leader in 1986, he explained that the USSR's different ethnic groups should not pursue their own interests, but must participate in the overall development of the USSR's single economic space.[14] In a manner not dissimilar to would-be reformist tsars, Gorbachev tried to balance the traditions of his forebears with the needs of the day, but found that the empire couldn't be reformed. His policies of *glasnost* (openness) and *perestroika* (restructuring) did not so much make things worse as expose how fragile the USSR had become. The pressures on it accumulated during the 1980s, as its economic sluggishness precluded it from competing with the USA, and as its soldiers in Afghanistan faced defeat, after a decade of trying to prop up a puppet communist government in Kabul.

Cracks were appearing, and Moscow's authority looked as if it was about to shatter, just as the Berlin Wall eventually did in 1989. A multitude of nations made their bids for freedom across the USSR, including in the Caucasus, Central Asia, Eastern and Central Europe. Each nation would have its own story to tell of the chaos of imperial collapse, from rioting against the Soviet authorities in Kazakhstan and Georgia, to outright war involving Armenia and Azerbaijan over disputed lands. In Central Asia there had for several years been protests against Russian immigration, which was seen as occurring at the expense of opportunities for the locals.[15] In the Baltic States, Belarus and Ukraine the cultural connections to Russia may have been closer, but independence was no less meaningful.

All told, the USSR's fragmentation led to the creation of fifteen countries, amongst them the Russian Federation – and to a world finally free of formal empires.

Russia's imperial legacies: geography, destiny, pride

Fathoming the sheer span of Russia is a beguiling task for any foreigner. Riding on the Trans-Siberian Railway was my own attempt to reduce Russia's vast expanse to manageable panoramas – and, even then, the scale of the country precludes it from ever being compressed into a single frame. Compounding the cliché,

I boarded the train clutching a worn copy of *War and Peace*. The parallel between the book's length and Russia's expanse was all too obvious.

The journey traversed Russia's multiple time zones, leaving St Petersburg and Moscow in the distant west. The changing topographies and ethnicities of the inhabitants became ever more apparent once I had travelled east of the Ural Mountains. Having reached Irkutsk, next to Lake Baikal, the 'European' feel of Russia was absent. Venturing further east, the proximity of Mongolia and China became apparent. How difficult must it be to govern this expanse? Aboard the rickety but robust carriages of the Trans-Siberian, it was clear to me how unwise it might be to squash all of Russia's diversity into a single thought.

Russia *still* positively reeks of its past imperial expansion in its shape. At its core, Russia is a European power, but the bulk of its territory exists in Asia. In the manner of a landed colossus, its experience of empire-building involved conquest through adjacency.

Russia's most obvious imperial legacy is therefore its political geography, which stops it from being pigeonholed as either an entirely European or Asian entity. There is a tradition of claiming that Russia's eastern anchorage has been its defining feature – an argument that has been made by Russia's Eurasian thinkers. Political scientist Marlene Laruelle has studied successive waves of Eurasian writers and observes how they have detected in the Scythians and Mongols the roots of Russian mastery of the steppe, while relegating the legacy of Kievan Rus as being excessively Eurocentric.[16] This is an important line of thinking: the Russian state has repeatedly faced the dilemma of just how far it ought to emulate and measure itself against its Western rivals, who have never really accepted Russia as part of their club.

Eurasian writers have tried to temper this, emphasizing Russia's authenticity as deriving from acting as a meeting point between Asian and European traditions. Indeed, Russia's traditions of political authority and loyalty may have stemmed in part from the hybridity of its East–West origins. An academic study on this subject observes how the Russian Empire, the Soviet Union and modern Russia have each based their politics primarily on loyalty to the ruler and not to the polity, resulting in patrimonial patterns of rule that may reflect the historical influence of Eurasian traditions.[17]

This sheds a different light on why Russia has been ruled by a lineage of strong rulers. Its default political setting has been a figurehead who sits atop the political tree and does not tolerate challengers. The Polish writer Ryszard Kapuscinski has reflected on this tradition: 'The era of Stalin, the era of Khrushchev, the era of Brezhnev. And before that: the era of Peter I, Catherine II, Alexander III. In what other country does the persona of the ruler, his character traits, his manias and phobias, leave such a profound stamp on the national history, its course, its ascents and downfalls?'[18] Rather than there being something 'wrong' with Russia, as some might conclude when considering why it has never become a pluralist democracy, its political traditions lean elsewhere.

This became increasingly apparent during the 1990s, the decade between the fall of the USSR and the rise of Vladimir Putin. It was a time during which the new Russian Federation lacked a strong leader and appeared to be chaotic and lost, and when Westernizing modernizers tried – and ultimately failed – to untether Russia from its autocratic imperial legacies.

Boris Yeltsin was the Russian Federation's first leader. His spiralling descent into a fumbling and alcohol-ridden persona mirrored Russia's post-Soviet descent into disrepair. Oligarchs had seized vast wealth from the privatization of former national industries. Russia's armed forces were a shadow of their former prowess, and were humbled in the Chechnya war in the 1990s, when Yeltsin was forced to sign a peace accord in 1996 with the separatists, who were trying to break away from Moscow's rule. In 2000 the tragic sinking of the nuclear submarine *Kursk*, after an on-board accident, with the loss of all hands, was another blow. It was made doubly ignominious given that the *Kursk* was named after the key tank battle of the Eastern Front in 1943, when the Wehrmacht was finally pushed into retreat by the Red Army, and was thus a deserved and enduring source of Russian martial pride.

In the 1990s Russia was weak, and the US was dominating geopolitical proceedings in places like the Balkans and the Middle East. This rankled with some of those who occupied the corridors of the Kremlin. Yevgeny Primakov, who served as Yeltsin's foreign minister (1996–8) and then as prime minister in 1999, thought an excessive desire to please and emulate the West was belittling, and that Russia should begin restating its independence as a geopolitical player.[19] But the conditions for realizing this vision were not present in his time in office. Other Russian politicians argued for a reinvention of Russia that was fit for the globalized world. And those who identified as Russian nationalists instead argued that the responsibility of the Russian government was to reassert a culturally stable orthodox community.[20] In short, Russia had lost its sense of direction.

However, there was little chance of Russia becoming an inward-looking country: it could no sooner deny its imperial heritage than deny its own history. Unrequited pride continued to pulsate in parts of the Russian psyche, in the mindsets of its elites in having to measure up to the past, and in the attitudes of many of its people, who had become accustomed to hearing about past Russian triumphs.[21] The Russian Empire was, after all, the second-biggest in the world in the early twentieth century, behind the British.[22] The USSR, at the Cold War's height in 1961, had launched the cosmonaut Yuri Gagarin into outer space. And so the list of accomplishments went on.

Nevertheless, its imperial past would have felt quite distant as Russia stood on the brink of acute decline in the 1990s. Its next generation of leaders would look to reverse the downward spiral, and to do so without surrendering Russia's destiny to emulate apologetically the Western world. In order to navigate Russia's future path, they would do so by harnessing its own imperial legacies.

Tragedy and triumph are woven together throughout Russian history, and this has hardened its people's spirit. 'Epic' hardly does justice to the cast of villains and victors that populate the pages of the saga, compressed into the preceding pages. This is why, when outsiders alarmed at Russia's modern behaviour (such as in Ukraine's war) fatuously implore it to behave as a 'normal' country, it is unclear what 'normal' means. Insiders, however, would find a host of imperial legacies to inspire and guide them – and there are no greater insiders in a political system than its spies.

Tradecraft as statecraft: thinking like a spy, acting like a president

The modern keepers of Russia's imperial legacies belong to the world's second-oldest profession: espionage. Enter Putin and the *siloviki*, a term that refers to the community of intelligence-officer colleagues from his KGB days and from other security bureaucracies, many of whom would assume powerful positions under Putin's patronage, in politics and in business.

Thinking like a spy – or, rather, as an intelligence case officer, to use more precise terminology – requires a rather peculiar mindset and employs some unusual skills. Case officer, or agent handler, was Putin's trade in the KGB, the Soviet intelligence organ that he served from a young age, starting in 1975. He had experienced the USSR's collapse from the vantage point of a KGB posting to East Germany, returning home amidst the chaos facing Russia in the 1990s.

Recruiting and running agents covertly, the case officer has a skillset that is quite divorced from the Hollywood presentation of spies as action heroes. Persuasion, emotional intelligence and political acumen are the real weapons of choice. Patience is essential to the profession, and the artistry of performance is also key. To be a skilled case officer is to appeal to multiple audiences in a convincing manner, without contradicting oneself, even when under pressure, and projecting a personal image that is completely convincing in the contexts in which it is deployed. Risks are embraced for the good of the mission and are not avoided. At the same time the case officer ought to be a pragmatist, willing to cut his or her losses and walk away from a failing endeavour.

'Tradecraft' is the term given to the skills of the intelligence officer as masters of dissimulation. What Putin brought to Russia is the turning of tradecraft into statecraft. This is how Putin's Russia picked up the various frayed threads of an imperial legacy and knotted them together for the new era: embracing the country's imperial legacies and infusing Russian statecraft with the spy's manoeuvrability.

This has been evident in Russia's domestic conduct, starting with Putin's rise to power. During Yevgeny Primakov's prime ministerial tenure in 1999, Putin headed the Federal Security Service (FSB), the domestic intelligence agency. The details of Putin's journey from chief spy to becoming Yeltsin's prime minister in 1999 are still shrouded in mystery. The emergence of the *siloviki* as self-professed custodians of the state, ruling the economy in a tense partnership with the oligarchs and carving up some profits for themselves, is more apparent. 'The spy agencies were largely left to their own devices during the "shock therapy" of 1991–93, with little supervision and insufficient funding.'[23]

The authors of this passage were Alex Goldfarb and Marina Litvinenko, the latter the wife of a murdered Russian spy. Conspiracy theories still abound around Alexander Litvinenko, who was a junior FSB officer serving at this time. He met an agonizing end in London in 2006, assassinated by polonium poisoning in what appeared to be revenge for his criticism of the Kremlin.

Litvinenko had suggested that Russia's state organs were complicit in the September 1999 bombings of apartment blocks in Moscow and other Russian cities that killed 293 people. The authorities attributed these bombings to Chechen terrorists, and used the resulting outrage to sustain public support for Russia's military to reinvade Chechnya. In 2000 Russian troops regained control of Grozny, killing and dispersing the rebels. It was a signature reversal of Yeltsin's prior humiliation over Chechnya, and it helped Putin build his early reputation.

Assassination has remained a feature of Russian political life. In 2006 the journalist Anna Politkovskaya, who also questioned the premise of the Second Chechen War, was killed on her way home in Moscow. In 2015 the charismatic opposition figure Boris Nemtsov was assassinated in view of the Kremlin. With allegations falling on Chechen assassins, their looming presence was felt as deliverers of violence who, whether or not at the Kremlin's behest, had silenced its critics.

This itself was a reflection of just how Chechnya was pacified. Putin picked a local warlord, Ramzan Kadyrov, to turn into a vassal. Kadyrov's security forces duly hunted the most extremist Islamist terrorists who had been involved in the war, while seemingly also hunting the Kremlin's political opponents. In return for Kadyrov's loyalty to Moscow, patronage was plentiful as Grozny, levelled during the war, was rebuilt with federal funds. The whole Chechen episode had involved a curious mix: part intelligence officer handling an agent (Putin to Kadyrov); part imperial capital (Moscow) managing a troublesome and rebellious periphery on the North Caucasus.

The traditions of autocracy were revived as Putin cemented his rule, guaranteeing himself power for two decades ... and counting (at the time of writing). Characteristics evident in Putin's public persona, and his approach to politics, have been redolent of his intelligence-officer past. Take his publicity photographs, much mocked by outsiders, which depicted Putin in a variety of manly sporting and military action poses. Biographers Fiona Hill and Clifford Gaddy have traced a line between Putin's case-officer days and the skills he has brought to bear as a statesmen, not least in being able to wear many hats in his public persona, ranging from 'father of the nation' to being its martial defender, and always alluding to his inheritance of Russia's lineage of strong rulers.[24]

No small measure of bravery would be required to challenge his regime, which proved able to see off all comers, maintaining only the veneer of democracy in the process. Veterans of the anti-Putin opposition include the chess grand master Garry Kasparov, who tried to stand in the 2008 election but was barred from doing so, and blamed official obstruction and harassment. Putin clearly had no interest in a fair contest: he had stepped aside in a stage-managed handover of the presidency to Dmitri Medvedev in 2008–12, biding his time as prime minister until he returned to the presidency. After this, Putin interpreted the constitution to mean that the two-term limit related only to *consecutive* terms, winning his third term in 2012, and his fourth in 2018.

After Nemtsov was killed in 2015, the next figurehead of the opposition was Alexei Navalny, who also found he couldn't get very far in challenging Putin without facing official harassment and jail terms. To democracy advocates, modernizers and Westernizers, Russian politics had become toxic. Judged on its own terms, however, Putin's manner of rule was consistent with history, offering a modernized version of how Russia was once ruled by tsars and Bolsheviks.

This is broadly how power has tended to be asserted in Russia for centuries, with a strong ruler holding together a vast polyglot country. Saying so is not an excuse for authoritarianism, but it does explain its roots and its persistence. As fresh generations of Russian democracy activists challenge these traditions, they will need to square their aspirations with the enduring hold that imperial history has over Russian politics.

Russia's post-imperial fightback goes global

To bolster Putin's reputation, his regime milked the Soviet victory over Nazi Germany as a staple of Kremlin ideology. Putin also spoke restoratively of aspects of the Romanov era. Allusions to the past can be symbolic but, in Russia's case, they have directly influenced its path, through the precedents they suggest for running Russia. One precedent is the link between domestic and foreign policy, which is as symbiotic as it ever was during the imperial age. Authoritarian politics at home remain joined at the hip with assertive and conquering actions abroad.

All foreign policy begins at home, and Putin's regime has mined an unrequited national pride that was diminished by Russia's loss of prestige in the 1990s. His messages and policies voice a desire for Russia never to be dictated to, and to forge its own destiny, free from Western hectoring and intervention. Putin famously explained that 'the collapse of the Soviet Union was a major geopolitical disaster of the century' because 'tens of millions of our co-citizens and compatriots found themselves outside Russian territory'. He also delivered this dictum: 'whoever does not regret the passing of the Soviet Union has no heart, whoever wants it back has no brain'.

To Putin's clique, the dissolution of the Soviet Union dealt a severe body-blow to Russian power and prestige. However, if placed against a timescale of centuries of periodically declining and ascending Russian power, 1991 did not mark the end of history, but the start of a period of shrunken Russian power. With Putin at the helm, Russia has sought to reverse this trajectory, rendering to the dustbin the notion of a diminished Russia that could be pushed around by the USA and hemmed in by NATO and the EU.

The fightback has been significant. Somehow Russia has manoeuvred itself back into becoming a big deal in world affairs, whether influencing politics in other countries or acting as a broker of war and peace on the world stage. It has deployed means both fair and foul – indeed, straddling the realm between the two has become Russia's forte.

As a good intelligence officer might, Putin has calculated that one way to seemingly manipulate fate involves waiting for events to take shape by their own momentum, before taking well-timed and decisive action in response. While you may never control the event itself, you retain mastery over your response. This is what it means to be cast as 'opportunistic'. The right pretext can stimulate all manner of useful, self-serving responses.

This use of pretexts to energize Russia's actions abroad ends up reducing every scenario to arguments of 'Who started it?', such as in Ukraine.

I had first visited Ukraine ten years before the war, in 2004, fresh out of university and volunteering as an OSCE election observer. Drama awaited in the 'Orange Revolution', so-called after the party colours of a pro-Western candidate, Viktor Yushchenko. Snow had draped Kiev's Independence Square as chants of 'Yush-chen-ko' kept up the spirits of his young supporters. They had camped out to protest at the electoral victory of his arch-rival, the pro-Russian candidate Viktor Yanukovich, who polled well in east Ukraine. This is where we spotted irregularities with voters' lists, and eventually the election was declared fraudulent by international observers. Adding to the drama, Yushchenko had emerged with a disfigured face and claimed that pro-Russian forces had poisoned him. In the end, a cocktail of street protests, irregularities reported by election observation and Western pressure forced a rerun of the vote on 26 December 2004. This time the Orange Revolutionaries won. Russia sat on its hands and watched as Yanukovich, its favoured candidate, lost the race.

A geopolitical tug of war was under way over Ukraine. Undermining Yushchenko from afar was all Russia could do, until Yanukovich recaptured the presidency in 2010. Even this was not all it seemed, and in 2017, during the FBI's investigation into Donald Trump's campaign links to Russia, it transpired that veteran US lobbyist Paul Manafort had been paid $12 million by Yanukovich's campaign to advise him on tactics to secure Ukraine's presidency.

These backroom machinations aside, it all fell apart for Yanukovich in the winter of 2013–14, when he refused to sign Ukraine up to an EU accession deal. Yanukovich (and Russia) had no desire for Ukraine to fall into the West's camp. Protesters again filled Independence Square, but were shot at by security forces loyal to Yanukovich. Kiev's makeshift ramparts resembled a war zone and, as the protests intensified, Yanukovich fled to Moscow – he was deposed by a coup, complained Putin, as Russia unleashed its military intervention in Ukraine.

Brazenly, the Russia of 2014 was a very different beast compared to 2004. Its ire having been kindled for years by what it saw as Western meddling in its sphere of influence, Russia interpreted the Orange Revolution as part of a pattern that included Georgia's Rose Revolution in 2003, which had swept modernizing president Mikheil Saakashvili to power in Tbilisi on a similar populist wave. Putin's regime blamed Western meddling for these so-called 'colour revolutions', and feared they could inspire youthful activists in Russia.

Putin saw the USA as feeding its triumphalist post-Cold War habit of fostering regime change by stealth, backing popular protests in former Soviet spaces, while the US military fought for regime changes further afield in Iraq and Afghanistan. On top of this, NATO and the EU had expanded into Russia's old sphere of influence, which was now being absorbed by Western economic and military alliances. This expansion seemed inexorable, as suggestions of NATO and EU membership were also made to Georgia and Ukraine.

Russia drew its red line here. In 2007 Putin voiced Russia's concern at the annual Munich Security Summit. In 2008 the Russian military waged a brief war with Georgia to censure and punish Saakashvili's apparent westwards drift. Finding a pretext, Russia inverted the norm of self-determination, announcing that it was fighting to protect the South Ossetian and Abkhazian people from 'Georgian aggression', but in fact waged a short, sharp military campaign to humiliate Georgia's armed forces and to entrench its hold on the disputed areas.

A variation of this logic was employed in Ukraine in 2014, as Russia announced that it was defending Russian-speaking communities, staging a referendum in Crimea to confirm the populace's supposed desire to join the Russian Federation. Russia's official line on Ukraine is fascinating. It has framed the problem as stemming from a Western obsession with preventing 'rapprochement' between Ukraine and Russia.

One of the more creative arguments I have heard, by a Russian academic toeing the official line, argued that just as Britain took centuries to find a peaceful balance in its relations with Ireland, leading to bloodshed along the way, so too Russia was exploring its own post-imperial balance with Ukraine. The Russian academic delivered this line not apologetically, but as a matter of fact.

The believability of these arguments is secondary to invoking language that has been used by the USA and EU countries since the 1990s around self-determination, humanitarian interventions and counter-terrorism. Putin's regime does not interpret these themes as Western countries do, but these terms offer up a smorgasbord of pretexts to exploit, spurious reasons to offset blame, and arcs of logic to be inverted in Russia's favour.

Russia's military intervention in Syria's civil war offers another example. The war had lasted close to half a decade by September 2015, when Russia's armed forces began a game-changing intervention, shoring up the embattled regime of their ally, Bashar al-Assad. Feeble US and UK demands for Syria's dictator to stand down in favour of democracy were outmatched by Russia's willingness to back the dictator with arms. Aleppo, a major city held by the rebellion against Assad, became a focal point of the war in 2016. Russian airpower delivered death from above, and Russian mercenaries assisted Assad's army on the ground, to inflict defeats on the rebels from which they could not recover. Russia had made sure to tar the rebel groups in Syria who fought Assad's regime as 'terrorists', thus creating verbal justifications for pummelling them in the broader name of fighting against ISIS. As the hostilities ebbed and flowed, Russia provided diplomatic cover to Assad, turning negotiations to end Syria's war into the imposition of a victor's peace and brokering talks involving Iran and Turkey.

Such a Russian power play in the Middle East would have been unthinkable just a few years before – for example, when President Obama dismissed Russia as being a mere 'regional power'. Syria's war galvanized Russia's military modernization programme, and served as a live-fire demonstration for its global arms sales. However, relying solely on the fire and steel of war is not a viable strategy in the post-imperial age. Russia's fightback involves other measures too.

An information war has granted the Kremlin a modern suite of capabilities with which to project power and influence. TV channels like Sputnik and RT (formerly Russia Today) propagate narratives that support its worldview. Online, however, is the domain where Russian information operations have whipped up the greatest storms. Troll farms (Internet research agencies with alleged connections a few steps removed from Russian officialdom) have planted online news stories and inflammatory user comments below existing coverage, to polarize factions of opinion in Western countries. Facebook and Twitter ended up investigating to just what extent fake profiles originating in Russia had proliferated on their platforms. Russia's hand was detected in alleged influence operations targeting US public opinion around the 2016 presidential election. Other Western countries have now battened down the information hatches, in expectation of Russian meddling in their own public debates.

Judo, Putin's beloved martial art, turns the strength of an opponent back against him. In this vein, Russia was using the very attributes of democracy – free speech, privilege of debate and accountability safeguards – to distract and disempower its international rivals. Democracy, the stick with which the West had bashed Putin's Russia, could also be the West's Achilles heel. Plurality of opinion in the media, and multi-party political systems, are all well and good, until competing perspectives are aggravated to such an extent that they paralyse the system itself. It is not of Moscow's making that there are divisions in the EU over the financial crisis, the migrant crisis and Brexit, or in the US between Democrats and Republicans; but with a malicious shove, Russia's inflammatory online activities can encourage a targeted public to adopt bitter and binary stances on divisive issues.

Had Rip Van Winkle fallen asleep in the mid-1980s and awoken three decades later, he might have been forgiven for thinking that the Cold War never ended.

During his interviews with Oliver Stone, broadcast in 2017, Putin told the US film-maker that framing Russia as imperialistic is self-serving: the West always needs a 'bad guy', an enemy, so as to give itself unity and purpose. In this regard he may have a point, although Putin's Russia is quite keen to play up to this role, turning its deteriorating relations with the West into a self-fulfilling prophecy. While the West lambasts Russia for its overbearing and aggressive neo-imperialist behaviour, this only validates Putin's observation that the 'weak get beaten', which in turn justifies his regime's domestic and regional stances. Unresolvable arguments over 'who started it' have featured in the deterioration of Russian relations with the US. Putin is adamant that at the USSR's dissolution, the US promised there would be no eastern expansion of NATO. The problem was, as Putin elaborated to Stone, that Gorbachev agreed to this verbally and did not secure a written assurance.

Another move interpreted as justifying a tough Russian response has been US missile-defence plans. In 2002, in order to build a missile-defence shield, President George W. Bush unilaterally withdrew the US from the Anti-Ballistic Missile (ABM) Treaty, which had been signed with Russia in 1972 as part of the Cold War's *détente*. Why, Putin argued, did the US persist with these plans, even deploying forward interceptor bases to countries like Poland and Romania, after Iran had signed a deal to limit its nuclear-weapons programme in 2015? Defensive ABM bases could turn into offensive attacking installations, warned Putin, who has argued that when the USA seeks advantages in its strategic weapons arsenal, Russia is imperilled.

International-relations theorists have long written of 'security dilemmas', in which spirals of insecurity result from perceptions and misperceptions between states. One side fears the intentions of the other and therefore acts to bolster and secure its position – these actions in turn stoke the insecurities of the other, which responds in kind.

By this logic, East and West each carries culpability: the US retained NATO after the Cold War and has subsequently expanded it; while Russia's paranoia and aggressive countermoves since then have worsened the situation. NATO and EU eastwards expansion was interpreted by Russia as Western neo-imperial expansion by consent. In this light, annexing Crimea was a response in kind.

NATO is now back in the business of defending Europe by deterring Russia (an undertaking that is more in NATO's comfort zone than its decade-plus attempted stabilization of Afghanistan after 9/11). After NATO's 2016 security summit in Warsaw, it set about deploying multinational battalions of soldiers to Poland and the Baltic States. At Romanian behest, NATO has also kept an eye on Russian naval activities in the Black Sea. NATO's warnings of Russian assertiveness in Europe are only novel because they have not been heard in a generation.

The Cold War demanded an assiduous managing of the security dilemma to ensure that it remained only a stand-off between its two biggest protagonists. Today the world is no longer bipolar (meaning dominated by the USA and the USSR). Enter Sergei Lavrov, who took on the role of foreign minister in 2004 (and whose time in office has since surpassed the record of his Soviet forebear Vyacheslav Molotov, who served Stalin in two stints as foreign minister for more than thirteen years). Lavrov has spoken of a 'polycentric world' in which many great powers interact, rather than a world in which Washington effectively dictates the terms of global affairs.[25]

Such a system seems comforting to Russia's strategists because it was in just such a world of many competitors that, several hundred years ago, Russia's empire thrived. Reaping the yields of a more pluralistic world order means, for Russia, finding common cause with kindred authoritarian regimes. Business can be conducted without lectures on democracy and human rights, or the West complaining about Russia's wars. For example, after Western sanctions were imposed on Russia due to its annexation of Crimea, Russia turned to China and concluded a thirty-year gas deal in May 2014. The deal enabled Russia's state-owned firm Gazprom to supply gas through a pipeline to eastern Russia and China, feeding the latter's energy needs. It was also an act of defiance to the West, showing the other options available to Russia in the widening geopolitical marketplace.

How China and Russia will interact in the future remains one of the foremost geopolitical questions of our time. US military fantasy writer Tom Clancy once imagined a future war between the countries he called *The Bear and the Dragon*. The reality, one hopes, will not be so cataclysmic. Both countries belong to the Shanghai Cooperation Organisation (SCO), a regional body that also has the Central Asian republics in tow, and which fosters cooperation on economic and security matters. It is far from being a non-Western EU or NATO, however, and it remains to be seen how Russia will adapt to it being cast in China's ever-growing shadow. There is no cultural commonality between these countries and, along their common border, there is a telling demographic mismatch between their populations. Next to 1.4 billion Chinese, there are fewer than 150 million Russians today, and their population density peters out the further east one travels.

Keeping Russia together as a polyglot entity will always be a task of the utmost importance to Russia's rulers. Reinterpreting and reinventing imperial traditions of statecraft does not mean re-creating the past. Restoring lost influence is not the same as rebuilding an empire, but imperial history looms large in the unfolding story of Russia's fightback to a position of global significance.

What Tolstoy can tell us about Russia after Putin

Seventy-four years of Soviet rule is akin to a small mark on the vast Siberian expanse, when placed against the four centuries of the tsars. Analogies of geography are highly appropriate, given the way in which Russia's imperial identity was forged by the duality of its Asian experiences plus its contest with European rivals. The durations of time involved are also important, because if imperial legacies have a half-life, then Russia will continue to be influenced and possibly even defined by them for a long time to come, especially if they are nourished by its leaders.

Russia's imperial mythos became a vehicle for nationalism, religion, leadership, ambition and its sense of standing in the world – it served these purposes for centuries and, in a modernized way, still serves them today in the way the past has deposited certain narratives, precedents and expectations deep in Russian national self-identity.

Aleksandr Dugin, the Russian political theorist, wrote the following in 1999: 'Every people moves through History according to its own trajectory, upholding its own understanding of the world. What is good for some people cannot be applied to others.'[26] It has been suggested that Dugin, who bears a passing resemblance to Rasputin, was an influence on Kremlin thinking, and there is some evidence of this. As Foreign Minister Lavrov wrote in 2016, the world needs a 'plurality of models' rather than a 'boring uniformity' in which the West lectures everyone else on democracy.[27] Or as conveyed rather more banally to me by a Russian to whom I chatted in the restaurant car of the Trans-Siberian Railway, who attempted to convey his thoughts in English by scribbling on a napkin: 'WASHINGTON = FASCHINGTON' – a clumsy allusion to 'fascism' and what he thought was unjust in the way America has judged his country.

There is a yearning inside Russia to play to its own tune, and this is a reflection of the imperial instinct – to want to be the influencer, not the influenced.

It is tempting to credit Russia's post-imperial fightback from the ropes to Putin, but no one person is bigger than an imperial legacy. Today's Russian soldiers and keyboard warriors fight for post-imperial pride, and for ideals and incentives that may not vanish after Putin passes from power.

There is an outdated tradition of writing about 'great men of history', with the past retold through the lives and experiences of certain towering figures. Russian literature offers a rejoinder.

Two centuries ago, in *War and Peace*, the Russian writer Leo Tolstoy penned a literary exposition of why the supposed 'great man of history' is in fact a fiction: 'History, that is the unconscious, general, swarm-life of mankind, uses every movement of the life of kings as a tool for its own purposes.'[28] He was quite clear as to the relative powerlessness of so-called great figures and their attempts to bestride the flow of events. What is power? In Tolstoy's mind, it was the aggregated activity of all the people who participate in events. Those taking on the largest burdens of command may in fact be taking the least responsibility, even if they act as conductors who guide the symphonies.

The philosopher and historian Isaiah Berlin, writing later in *The Hedgehog and the Fox*, was captivated by Tolstoy's diminished view of the free will of kings and generals and offered his own summary: 'What are great men? They are ordinary human beings who are ignorant and vain enough to accept responsibility for the life of society, individuals who would rather take the blame for all the cruelties, injustices, disasters justified in their name than recognise their own insignificance and impotence in the cosmic flow which pursues its course irrespective of their wills and ideals.'[29]

The message for today is this. It is unsatisfactory to overplay things and to assume that Putin alone is the malefactor: wait for him to go, remove the vestiges of his legacy from Russia's political and foreign-policy cultures, and Russia will be reborn without original sin. It is also unsatisfactory to underplay his role, only to argue that empire is Russia's original sin. Putin has been the vessel through which centuries of Russian great-power expectations have been channelled, and they will require new vessels after he exits the stage.

The gravitational pull of an imperial history that is just as illustrious as it is imposing will continue to define Russia's character and its conduct, both at home and abroad.

FIVE

CHINA'S JANUS FACES OF EMPIRE

All beneath Heaven is rooted in nation. Nation is rooted in family. And family is rooted in self.

> Mencius (*c.*371–289 BCE), 'second sage' of the Confucius tradition[1]

Empires arise from chaos and empires collapse back into chaos. This we have known since time began.

> Luo Guanzhong (*c.*1330–*c.*1400), *The Romance of the Three Kingdoms*[2]

History is our best teacher ... [Chinese] pioneers won their place in history not as conquerors with warships, guns or swords.

> President Xi Jinping, addressing the Belt and Road Forum for International Cooperation, 14 May 2017[3]

Map 7 The Qing Dynasty, 1765
Map 8 China's Belt and Road Initiative

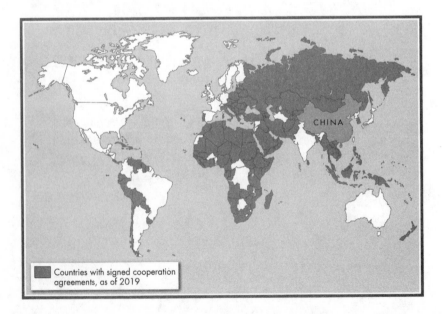

Countries with signed cooperation
agreements, as of 2019

Ostentation is par for the course in an Olympic Games opening ceremony. Beijing's in 2008 took this to a new level, delivering a spectacle of cultural self-confidence and a statement of future intent in China's National Stadium.

The performances took place on a giant unfolding scroll, a reference to the invention of paper in ancient China. On the scroll, a succession of troupes performed traditional dances, puppetry and synchronized Tai Chi. Drummers beat a thumping coordinated rhythm, ramming home a message of choreography and uniformity. An 'astronaut', suspended by cables, descended onto a giant globe, which later revealed itself to resemble a Chinese lantern.

Over a decade has elapsed since China delivered this statement to the world. Since then, a Chinese spacecraft landed on the dark side of the moon in January 2019, providing humankind with its first glimpse of this part of the surface, and indicating how seriously China wants a manned mission to the moon. For the Chinese propaganda machine, forever promulgating the country's achievements, this was gold dust.

China's economy offered its own headline achievements when, after the financial crisis in 2008, it became the largest contributor to global economic growth, according to the World Bank.[4] By 2018 its Gross Domestic Product (GDP) was 13.5 trillion US dollars – as counted by the International Monetary Fund (IMF) in the currency of a country whose economy China is poised to overtake.[5]

China's rise is now the subject of much fascination and concern. It prompts some Westerners to send their offspring to learn Mandarin at school, seeing this as the way the economic winds are blowing. Conversely, the apocalyptically minded warn of an impending Sino–US war over who sets the world's rules.[6] In recent years China has asserted its maritime power in the East and South China Seas, and disputes have broken out with its neighbours, some of which are US allies, over who owns certain islands.

Sensing that its size – let alone its behaviour – may be a source of alarm, China has been at pains, when on the world stage, to stress its 'peaceful rise', a phrase used repeatedly by Hu Jintao during his presidency (2003–13). This is a reasonable claim, since China can argue that, unlike the USA or Russia, modern China has not waged war on other countries.

All the while, however, China is building a new informal economic empire in the cleverest of ways: through trade, investment and by dispatching its companies and workers to the four corners of the globe. Some of this falls under the Belt and Road Initiative (BRI), known colloquially as the 'New Silk Road', which involves Chinese state-sponsored investment projects in dozens of countries. Beijing's government is already looking to a future in which China expands its influence through prosperity for itself and others, binding other countries through reciprocal arrangements.

China remains a one-party state under the Chinese Communist Party (CCP). So tight is CCP rule that while it has granted economic liberalization in order to power growth, this has not been accompanied by political liberalization. Censuring internal dissent, in particular by silencing the demands of its Muslim Uighur people who live in China's north-west, and by denouncing the protests of the inhabitants of Hong Kong who took to the streets in 2019, has remained part of the Chinese playbook. So has the role of a strong leader. Xi Jinping became president in 2013, and after a few years in power his two-term limit was scrapped by the CCP. Increasingly he has adopted the poise of a post-modern emperor, standing tall at the centre of an expanding web of Asian influence and an informal empire of Chinese economic dominance.

Consequently it is important to understand the roots of China's domestic political culture, its sources of self-confidence as a world power and its lingering insecurities.

Imperial legacies have been intrinsic in crafting China's view of itself and of the wider world. Depending on how far back in history one looks, China was either the centre of a vast inland empire or the victim of foreign domination.

Imperial China's history spans two millennia (from 221 BCE to 1911), connecting ancient and modern history. While its fortunes rose and fell over these centuries, including during periods of disunity and war, Imperial China endured with remarkable coherency. It even survived two bouts of foreign rule, by the Mongols in the fourteenth century, and by the Manchu who swept in from the north to take the throne in 1644. The 'Middle Kingdom', as Imperial China was known, absorbed these usurpers, taking in their cultural influence, but overawing both the Mongols and the Manchu to preserve the empire.[7] The modern map of China is a testament to its imperial heritage, taking in territories it acquired in the 1700s by expanding into Inner Mongolia, Xinjiang and Tibet.

And then, from its pedestal as a hub of regional power, China suffered a precipitous fall at the hands of nefarious foreign imperialists. British and French gunboats and traders forced their way in during the Opium Wars that began in 1839, marking the start of what the Chinese call their 'century of humiliation'. Worse, neighbours that once accepted subservience to China now broke free. Japan, unlike China, had chosen to modernize along Western lines, and it eventually colonized Manchuria. China's last emperor, Pu Yi, fled to Japan in 1924 amidst this chaos, having abdicated the throne twelve years earlier. Imperial China, a great power since ancient times, ceased to exist. Its failure to modernize had left it open to predatory Japanese and European imperialists.

Whether conqueror or conquered, there is ample historical evidence of China having played both roles in different periods of history. Whereas its own imperial saga is the far longer chapter in this story, its century of humiliation is much more recent. Both of these imperial experiences have deeply influenced the evolution of China under communist rule.

The communist revolution in 1949 brought Mao Zedong to

power, heralding the start of what was truly a brutal regime. Some of this brutality was spuriously justified by Mao as being necessary to protect China from foreign predation. Today the CCP considers 1949 to mark the end of the century of humiliation. Since Mao's death in 1976, China has steadily opened itself up to the world. But history does not disappear into thin air, and the CCP can at once lay claim to an imperial heritage of dominating its neighbours *and* a grievance at China having being plundered by others, a potentially toxic mix of historical narratives.

So has modern China overcome its era of subjugation, and the brutality of Mao's rule, to emerge peacefully, like a butterfly shedding its chrysalis? Or, taking a longer view of history, does it still experience post-imperial tics? Are notions of empire still relevant reference points for China's evolving aspirations?

All under heaven: Imperial China and the right to rule

Climbing the Great Wall's winding ramparts, or losing oneself amidst the Forbidden City's palatial layout, can feel like wandering into a labyrinthine imperial history. Notwithstanding the saturation of tourist traffic, most of the visitors are Chinese, reflecting a curiosity and fascination with their own history.[8] These attractions remain as relics of a bygone imperial age: the Great Wall was built to protect the central plains from periodic invasions by northerners; and the Forbidden City, located in the heart of Beijing, once served as the imperial palace. From here its emperors ruled 'all under heaven', which is how they distinguished their civilized world from the barbarian realms beyond.

With the cosmos in mind, Imperial China saw itself at the centre of a world that was ordered into concentric rings. Its sovereign emperor sat in the innermost ring, with power radiating first into areas of direct subordination, then into indirectly ruled tributary states, and finally fading away in its distant dependencies and over the known frontiers. What lay beyond these peripheries was of less interest. Chinese emperors ruled in the confidence that they had no worldly equal.[9]

China is amongst the world's oldest civilizations. The modern Chinese state took centuries to develop, and there have remained astonishing lines of continuity with the distant past. Language, borders and the ethnic make-up of the majority Han populace are tangibly rooted in history. Contemporary Chinese can take pride in this heritage, and in the cultural self-confidence it promotes. All of this is amplified by official state-sponsored narratives.

The National Museum of China occupies a gargantuan building close to the Forbidden City. The curators have divided its collection of artefacts into the eras of China's history. It explains how Imperial China was forged by various dynasties, and the vicissitudes of unity and disunity. Whenever there is a period of unity to celebrate, remarkably similar words are used in the accompanying captions, such as 'This gradually laid the foundation for unification and the centralized government that emerged in the Qin Dynasty.' Later: 'This laid the foundation for the establishment of a unified multi-ethnic country.' Some centuries on: 'Despite occasional conflicts, ethnic integration continued to strengthen the unified China as a multi-ethnic country.' And, in the early modern era: 'Upon founding the Ming (dynasty) ... Centralized authoritarian rule reached a new height.'[10]

Unashamedly teleological, the official narrative begins with its end in mind, ramming home the virtues of centralized rule and the reality of a multi-ethnic populace, all in harmony with present-day CCP concerns. In controlling the narrative, Chinese historians prefer to describe imperial expansion as involving 'unification' rather than 'conquest'.[11] However it is portrayed, the contours of modern China were undoubtedly traced by the country's long imperial saga. Moreover, claims of cultural continuity between the modern state and the ancient world are not altogether exaggerated. Chinese emperors thought they ruled 'all under heaven' for many centuries, right until European and Japanese imperialists began to undermine their sovereign rule around 180 years ago.

There are many layers in China's history, with each layer tending to be understood in terms of the relevant ruling dynasty. The mythical era of the 'Five Emperors' (Huangdi, Zhuan Xu, Yao, Shun and Yu) has left few traces of archaeological evidence. Firmer evidence exists from the 'Three Dynasties' era. The first was the Xia Dynasty (*c.*2100–1600 BCE). More akin to kings than emperors, they ruled over the people of the Yellow River basin, whom they named the 'Xia'. The Shang Dynasty followed (*c.*1600–1046 BCE). During this time a written script was developed that contains Chinese characters resembling those still used today.[12] According to China's National Museum, 'abundant written materials about the politics, economy, and culture of the Shang survive today'. The third of the Three Dynasties, the Zhou (1050–256 BCE), established a number of fiefdoms, and it was during this period that the Confucius and the Daoist classics emerged.[13]

In the West the best-known written document from this period is *The Art of War*, attributed to Sunzi (known as Sun Tzu by his modern readership). It is marketed in the West as an aide-memoire to boardroom battles and its oft-quoted aphorisms include: 'know yourself / know the enemy / and victory is never in doubt / not in a hundred battles'. The precise origin of these verses is lost in the mists of time. Bamboo strips dated to the second century BCE, with Sunzi's words written on them, have been unearthed in tomb excavations (bamboo was used as writing material before paper).[14]

Sunzi lived through turbulent times. The 'Spring and Autumn' period of Zhou rule (770–476 BCE) was followed by the 'Warring States' period (475–221 BCE). Order collapsed. Seven rival powers tried to overthrow each other and annex smaller communities. Disunity and conflict reigned supreme.

Whereas Sunzi contemplated how to triumph in war, not shirking to suggest devious ways to do so, the philosopher Confucius (551–479 BCE), who was also alive around this time, decided to address war's moral quandaries. Confucius was devoted to theorizing the moral superiority of Zhou rule. Compared to the human toll of the Warring States period, harmony was infinitely preferable.[15] An intellectual tradition evolved from these thoughts that proved profoundly influential. It understood morality as flowing from order, and order coming from unity. This is deeply ingrained in traditional Chinese thought. Analogies were drawn between a moral family life and moral government conduct.[16]

These were the ideas and historical contexts that preceded China's first empire. Emperor Qin conquered six of the seven warring states, uniting a large area stretching from north of Beijing to Sichuan in the west, down to Guangzhou in the south (this is the province above Hong Kong). The founding of the Qin Empire in 221 BCE represents the start of Imperial China.

The unity offered by Qin was a respite from the bloodshed of the Warring States era. Qin is a legendary figure: pronunciation of his name ('Chin') may be the etymological origin of 'China'.[17] The Terracotta Army, discovered in 1974 in Shaanxi province, was his burial mound. He died in 230 BCE, and although the Qin Dynasty outlasted his death by only fifteen years, it kicked off an imperial tradition that lasted until 1911.

Imperial China's history began in earnest with the Han Dynasty (202 BCE–220 CE), who were contemporaries of the Roman Empire. They were followed by the Tang Dynasty (618 CE–907 CE), who existed around the time of the Prophet Muhammad's Muslim empire; the Song Dynasty (960–1278), who spanned Europe's medieval period and the Crusades; the Ming Dynasty (1368–1644), who existed when the Ottoman and Mughal Empires rose; and the Qing Dynasty (1644–1912), who coexisted with, and ultimately succumbed to, Europe's colonial expansion.[18] Each bequeathed substantial influences to China's continual development.

The 'Han Chinese' – the country's majority ethnic group – retain the name given by the Han Dynasty, thus contributing to their sense of civilizational continuity. The Han Dynasty rose to power in the struggle that followed the collapse of the short-lived Qin Empire.

Schoolchildren commit these seminal events to memory, thanks to a rhyme that has been recited by groups of students throughout China for many centuries. The 'Three Character Classic' was written in the thirteenth century. It covers the Confucian ideas of valuing education and ritual, and lists key philosophers and dynasties. One of its verses summarizes the early imperial story, inculcating children with a keen sense of their historical origins:

> Ying of the Qin [The First Emperor] / Started to unify
> After two generations / Chu and Han battled
> Gaozu triumphed / Established the Han.[19]

How could such a large landmass ever be governed by a single emperor? This fundamental question has shaped Chinese political culture since the earliest days of its empires. A strictly legalistic set of arrangements and standardization of measurements, as pioneered by the first Emperor Qin, could never bind such a sprawling territory in perpetuity.

Imperial China also needed a binding philosophy. During the Han Dynasty, Confucianism became the official state philosophy and was widely propagated, to assert the emperor's moral legitimacy to reign.[20] However, even with its sense of Confucian moral legitimacy, the imperial edifice was prone to rupture.

In 220 CE the Han Empire suffered just such a rupture, resulting in several centuries of chaotic disunion. Conflict between rival fiefdoms became endemic. The mandate to govern all under heaven had been squandered by a motley cast of palace eunuchs, child emperors, conspiring warlords and barbarian hordes, whose machinations and endless conflicts failed to create a durable kingdom.[21]

This chaos later inspired a great work of literature, *The Romance of the Three Kingdoms*, which gives the modern *Game of Thrones* series a run for its money in its depictions of rival dynastic pretenders to a contested throne, and the intrigue, betrayals and vainglory that follow. Its enduring popularity, including TV and video-game adaptions, demonstrates how a jazzed-up version of history has inspired Chinese popular culture.[22] *Kingdoms* remains a parable of the perils of disunity.[23] As the book intones in its very first line: 'Empires arise from chaos and empires collapse back into chaos.' The closing of the book inverts this phrase: 'Empires collapse into chaos and empires arise from chaos.'[24] The need for unity reflects the fears of what might happen, should China ever fragment. And it duly validates the morality of strong central rule.

The Sui Dynasty re-established central control in 581 CE, but was soon overthrown by what became the second of the five great imperial dynasties. The Tang Dynasty's rule began in 618 CE and lasted for three centuries. It presided over Imperial China's golden age. Culture and artisanal craftsmanship flourished. The monetary system was further developed. More tribes were conquered and Confucianism was practised as a civic code. Tang territory eventually covered much of the map of modern China, minus Tibet and Manchuria.

However, in its later years, Tang power was steadily eroded, after repeated rebellions by tribes it had tried to conquer. The Tang Dynasty was finally overthrown by an uprising in 907 CE. China again split into warring kingdoms. Never missing the chance to convey a topical point, Beijing's National Museum depicts this era as a warning: 'The Tang reunified the country by abolishing regional separatist regimes', leading to a golden age; but later 'the empire continued to weaken as regional separatists gained power'.[25]

The message of this modern narrative is clear – separatism doesn't pay.

After fifty-three years of chaos, the third of the great dynasties came to the rescue. In 960 CE a general from the Song district reunited China, leading to three centuries of Song Dynasty rule. It presided over something of a renaissance era of innovation, including the 'Four Great Inventions': gunpowder, compasses, paper and printing. However, the Song Dynasty was also defined by what became a recurrent theme in Chinese history: the empire's vulnerability to northern invaders. Song rulers were forced to abandon their capital, Kaifeng (in the central Henan province), when it was overrun by the northern Jurchen people, who ruled as the Jin Dynasty. After the Jin–Song wars of the 1120s, the Song Dynasty relocated to a new capital in Hangzhou (in the eastern Zhejiang province), leading to a divided empire.

In the early 1200s the Mongols invaded from the north and ran rampant. The Great Wall had failed to protect the Chinese plains. Genghis Khan (1162–1227) attacked the Jin, reducing them to a vassalage. After more years of war, the Song were also forced to surrender. The Song Dynasty was brought to its end when Kublai Khan (1215–94) proclaimed himself emperor of the Yuan Dynasty in 1279.

The Mongol Yuan Dynasty (1279–1368) became the first foreign usurpers of China. Although eventually taking on local ways, the Mongols certainly influenced China, especially its map. Modern China extends far beyond the traditional Han Chinese heartland, as demarcated by the Great Wall. Its northern border now includes Inner Mongolia as an established Chinese province. This has stoked a tug-of-war over the legacies of Genghis and Kublai Khan. Some Chinese narratives claim they were not even outsiders. Conversely, the modern state of Mongolia venerates Genghis Khan as its forebear, having erected a gigantic silver statue of the horse-mounted warlord atop a museum, to make this point. Little love is lost between Mongolia and China today, each bristling at its conquest by the other at different times in history (including China's conquest of 'Outer Mongolia' in the 1700s), and each tussling with the other for the legacy of the Mongol Empire.[26]

*

China's fourth great dynasty, the Ming (1368–1644), took back control for the Han after Mongol rule waned. Founded by Zhu Yuanzhang, who ruled as Emperor Taizu from the capital of Nanjing (in modern Jiangsu province), the Ming reflected the resurgent impetus and durability of indigenous Han rule. After Taizu's death in 1398, the throne was usurped by his fourth son, Zhu Di. Calling himself the Yongle Emperor (ruled 1403–24), he moved the capital back to the Mongol city of Dadu, renaming it Beijing. Construction began on the Forbidden City in 1406 and it was completed in 1420. The Forbidden City would house twenty-four emperors in total: fourteen from the Ming Dynasty and ten from its successor, the Qing Dynasty.

For some people, Ming remains synonymous with the vases that were exported globally. While this does some injustice to the reputation of China's penultimate imperial dynasty, it does reflect Ming China's engagement with the wider world. The voyages of Admiral Zheng He (1371–1433), who reached the Persian Gulf, East Africa and India, are still much recounted today. But their significance remains disputed. On the one hand, they demonstrate China's naval mastery at the time, but on the other hand they also show the persistence of insularity. The voyages of Admiral Zheng did not spur further naval explorations, perhaps demonstrating a lack of vision on behalf of the Ming rulers. The Ming saw themselves as a continental and not a naval power. So their horizons remained fixed on their immediate universe and did not extend to what lay beyond the seas.[27]

The Ming Dynasty redoubled its efforts to secure its land frontiers by extending the Great Wall, and by reasserting its Confucian beliefs in the wake of Mongol rule. The Ming believed that the Mongols would always covet China's wealth and might reinvade, but the Ming ruled out taking the fight to the Mongols because of their unfamiliarity with the terrain that lay north of the Great Wall, and opted instead for a defensive strategy.[28] Ming rule was robust in the fifteenth and sixteenth centuries, but internal rot later set in. A series of less competent emperors, natural disasters and peasant uprisings all weakened its power. Poised to take advantage of this were the northern Jurchen people of Manchuria. They invaded and took over the empire in 1644, heralding the start of Manchu rule over the Chinese Empire.[29]

The Manchu ruled as the Qing Dynasty (1644–1911). This would be the last of the five great dynasties, ruling until the very end of Imperial China. At first the Qing ran the empire with great success and substantially expanded the geography of Chinese rule. Manchuria, from where they had originated, was brought into it. They invaded Tibet in 1720 and conquered Xinjiang (home of the Uighur Muslims) in the 1750s. In the late eighteenth century the Qing Empire reached a territorial apex, with an outline on the map looking very similar to contemporary China's.

The dynasty's sixth ruler, the Emperor Qianlong, reigned for an incredibly long time (1735–96) over a thriving empire. He happened to die not long after abdicating, in 1799. This is symbolic, since a new century was dawning that would prove much harsher to China.

China: at the mercy of the Europeans and Japanese

For all the dynamism displayed in building its vast and wealthy empire, and despite the cultural cohesion that had allowed it to adapt to Mongol and Manchu rule, Imperial China proved fatally vulnerable to new challenges from further afield. Things started to crumble in the latter half of the nineteenth century.[30]

Europeans had been arriving in small numbers since the mid-sixteenth century, including Jesuit missionaries and the Portuguese, who were allowed by the Ming to establish a trading post in Macau on the south coast of China.[31] Foreigners were now increasingly knocking on China's door, seeking access to its riches. Qing officials, keen to limit and dictate the terms of trade, constrained the foreigners to a southern port town called Canton, in Guangzhou province.

A diplomatic faux pas between the Qing Dynasty and a British delegation served as an early indication of what was about to go so badly wrong. In 1792 the British sent Lord Macartney to seek agreement with China to expand trading (and to meet the rising European demand for goods like vases). But a fiasco ensued in which Macartney did not bow to the Qing Emperor and failed to grasp why the Chinese would refuse to sign a trade deal with the British. For the Qing, to do so was tantamount to acknowledging equality with a far-away regent it had never seen, thus compromising its own mandate from heaven.[32] In Chinese eyes, the Europeans were barbarians from the sea.[33] It was a clash of imperial pride, and it foretold a disaster that was about to befall the Qing Dynasty.

Opium was the commodity over which misunderstandings escalated into war. Britain did not introduce opium to China, and the Dutch had already spread it to the islands of Java and Taiwan in the seventeenth century. Later the British developed a lucrative trade in which opium grown in India was shipped to China.[34] Without a hint of moral scruple, the British were prepared to use extreme violence to preserve this trade. In 1839 the Qing Dynasty refused flat out to legalize and tax opium (which was now being mixed with tobacco and smoked). An official called Lin Zexu was tasked with banning the opium trade in China. He enforced a blockade of Canton and ordered the seizure of opium chests. The Royal Navy retaliated in force, dispatching a fleet of ships to fire offshore coastal bombardments. Gunboat diplomacy had subdued Imperial China, which was forced to sign the Treaty of Nanjing in 1842 – a dire precedent, since this was the first treaty ever foisted on China.[35] A statue of Lin Zexu still stands tall in New York's Chinatown, but at the time his resolute actions to stamp out the awful opium trade had provoked a war that China could not win, due partly to the technological gap in military power.

Qing rule was also faltering domestically. The Taiping Rebellion began in the 1850s, as a nationalist insurrection with the intention of overthrowing the Qing for being Manchu. This rebellion was still simmering by the time of the Second Opium War in the late 1850s. Unhappy that the concessions forced on China last time round didn't go far enough, in 1860 British and French soldiers marched to the Emperor's Summer Palace, north of Beijing, looting and destroying it. The marauding Europeans now foisted the Treaty of Beijing onto China, which definitively opened it up to trade. The ruins of the Summer Palace remain viewable by the public, symbolizing the violent and terrible conjunction of Chinese civilization with Western barbarism.

Misery upon misery now compounded Qing China. A hallmark of its power was the regional tributary system. Neighbours like Korea, Japan and Vietnam accepted China's superiority and literally paid it tribute, engaging in ceremonial demonstrations of subservience that stoked Imperial China's ego as 'being at the very centre of the moral and political universe'.[36] Although the tributary system evolved considerably between China's various dynasties, its fundamentals had remained the same – China's civilization and its emperor were recognized by other Asians as being superior.[37]

It was shocking, therefore, for China to see its dependencies and vassal states annexed by outsiders. France established Annam, its protectorate over Vietnam, which China was forced to accept in 1885. Britain occupied northern Burma in 1886. China fought a disastrous war with Japan (1894–5), which resulted in Japanese control of Taiwan (known as Formosa) and the Pescadores Islands. Japan was, at the time, East Asia's rising power. It had existed in China's shadow for many centuries and had been heavily influenced by Chinese culture. It was not until Japan's Meiji Restoration in 1868 that Western ideals were adopted. Japan duly modernized its military along European lines. China, fixated by its own universe, had not done so, and was now paying the price.

Another domestic insurrection further weakened China. The Boxer Rebellion, which began in 1899, involved rampages by organized gangs against foreign influence and Christian missionaries. The Boxers marched on Beijing and laid siege to the Legation Quarter, to which several hundred foreigners and Chinese Christians had retreated. It looked as if they were about to be massacred. This prompted the Eight Power intervention in 1900, with troops from France, Britain, Japan, Russia, Austria–Hungary, Italy, Germany, and the US arriving in China and defeating the Boxers. The Qing were forced to accept yet another humiliating treaty, including paying reparations to the eight countries. Foreign troops heaped on further indignity by occupying the Forbidden Kingdom. Today in nearby Jingshan Park, a plaque at Jifang Pavilion still recounts the theft of a Buddha statue, 'robbed away by the Eight-power Allied Force in 1900'.[38]

After seven decades of clashes with technologically advanced foreign militaries, Qing rule was shattered. The end came as the child emperor Pu Yi faced ignominy in the Forbidden City, from where he abdicated in February 1912. By then imperial soldiers had started to rebel in what became known as the Wuchang Uprising. As their loyalties shifted, China became a republic.

Although foreigners had wrested control of its cities and ports, a silver lining for China was that no matter how bad things got, at least it had not been colonized wholesale, as India was by the British, or parts of the Middle East and Africa were by Europeans. It was a fleeting solace, however, as the Japanese Empire plunged China into an even deeper and darker pit of despair.

Mao, in a post-imperial light

After its empire had collapsed, chaos reigned in China. The Republic of China, founded in Nanjing in 1912 under Sun Yat-sen, struggled to assert its authority. Warlords built their own fiefdoms, as central rule waned. In the big cities, revolutionary sentiment was stoked by intense anger at how foreigners had torn away at China's sovereignty and pride. In 1919 'The May Fourth Movement' harnessed this anger in response to China receiving a raw deal at the Versailles Peace Conference, when Japan gained some old Chinese territories. Shocked at this continual bullying, China was at a low ebb.[39] And it sank to an even lower ebb when an emboldened Japanese military colonized Manchuria in 1932, turning it into the puppet government of 'Manchukuo'. By 1937 Japan and China were at war. Japanese soldiers descended with fury on Nanjing, the Republic of China's capital. The killing spree and sexual violence that ensued traumatized China and were referred to as the Rape of Nanjing; the 300,000 people estimated to have been killed by the Japanese are still memorialized.[40]

It became a three-way fight. The Republic of China, now led by Chiang Kai-shek, struggled to fight the Japanese; the other player comprised China's communists.

One man casts a shadow over modern China. Mao Zedong's face still stares out from renminbi bank notes, with his receded jet-black hair, simple suit and distinctive neutral expression. Underneath this portrait are his birth and death dates (1893–1976), provided in both Chinese characters and English numerals. Mao led the communists and, cunningly, let Chiang Kai-shek's forces take the strain against the Japanese.[41] When Japan's war effort collapsed in 1945 (after the USA dropped its atomic bombs to end the Second World War), China's struggle became a full-on civil war between the nationalists and the communists.

The nationalists, drained by fighting the Japanese, eventually fled offshore to Taiwan. Even today Taiwan's rulers still call their country the 'Republic of China' and some claim the lineage of Sun Yat-sen and Chiang Kai-shek. But mainland China was now under communist rule, becoming 'The People's Republic of China' (PRC).

The untrammelled brutality of Mao's rule, which reflected his pathologies, was also a reflection of the dire situation in which

China found itself when Mao took power. His legacy in China is itself a subject of interest for the way it is interpreted by the modern incarnation of the CCP. The official CCP narrative is that the start of communist rule in 1949 is also the start of the national renaissance, bringing to an end the century of humiliation.

The Chinese-born British writer Jung Chang remains an excellent guide to the harshness of this period. Her book *Wild Swans* recounts this era through the prism of her own family experiences: 'My grandmother had been the concubine of a warlord general, and my mother had joined the Communist underground . . . Both of them had eventful lives in a China that was tossed about by wars, foreign invasions, revolutions, and then a totalitarian tyranny.'[42] Jung Chang herself was born three years after Mao came to power and witnessed Mao's 'Cultural Revolution' with her own eyes.

Communism in China is very much a post-imperial phenomenon, coming after China's own imperial collapse, and as part of the fightback against predatory foreign imperialists. Between Pu Yi's abdication in 1912 and the communist revolution in 1949, there was an era of chaos and further national distress. It called to mind the ancient Warring States period, or the Five Dynasties and Ten Kingdoms period. Against this backdrop, communist rule effectively reunified China to its old imperial frontiers, kicking off its 'dynastic' legacy of one-party rule.

Upon closer examination, however, while communism at first seems a spasmodically violent break in historical continuity, it actually involved a radical refashioning of the nature of imperial rule in the Middle Kingdom. Mao restated China's borders and saw off external threats. His way of doing so killed millions of Chinese in a botched interpretation of modernity, by subjecting them to periods of forced industrialization and to purges – but the undercurrent of imperial rule remained.

*

Much has changed since Mao's death in 1976. In the decades that have elapsed, China's status has gradually metamorphosed from an isolated revolutionary pariah to becoming the next biggest thing in geo-economics. It began with the reforms of Deng Xiaoping in the late 1970s, which heralded China's entry into the international community of states. The US recognized the PRC gingerly at first, with its 'two-China policy' that included Taiwan, but in 1979 the US fully recognized the PRC.

Since then, the PRC has signed international agreements like the Nuclear Non-Proliferation Treaty, and is a member of bodies like the World Health Organization. China even stepped in to uphold the Paris Agreement on Climate Change after President Trump's administration withdrew the US in 2017. It has been quite the transformation, and suggests that the Chinese authorities have, to some extent, been willing pupils in learning how to participate in international forums that they had no hand in designing.[43] While China now accepts many of the world's legalistic norms and rules, it still vetoes the regulations and strictures that derive from Western notions of international humanitarian law. China remains on guard against separatism, individual liberties and any threats – whether domestic or foreign – to the CCP regime.

The return of Hong Kong in 1997 marked the final transition from the British Empire and an implicit recognition of the much older Imperial Chinese order. And in 1999 the Portuguese handed back Macau (which, with its casinos, has become China's equivalent of Las Vegas). Both Macau and Hong Kong now have the status of 'special administrative regions' (SARs). Hong Kong remains a financial gateway to the world for China and is the global centre for trading in renminbi.

In 2017, twenty years after its handover, I was attending an academic conference at Hong Kong university. Hong Kong's SAR minister addressed the gathered academics, reeling off impressive statistics about the island's connectivity to the mainland, stating that Beijing would be reachable by train in ten hours, Shanghai in eight and Guangzhou in one. Macau, Hong Kong and Guangzhou were also going to become an integrated area, he said.[44] Although 'Two Systems, One Country' had remained Beijing's official mantra on Hong Kong, and is supposed to remain so until 2047, ever since the handover, absorption into China has already been happening.

In 2019 Beijing's government tried to foist an extradition treaty on Hong Kong, resulting in its SAR becoming paralysed by angry protests. Hong Kong's youthful activists braved police batons and tear gas to assert their desire to remain apart from China's authoritarian state, and stormed the Hong Kong parliament building. When the British Foreign Office raised its objections around what was happening in its former colony, the Chinese Ambassador to London offered a curt response, telling the UK 'not to interfere in internal affairs', before reminding his audience that Hong Kong had returned to its 'motherland' and 'was not what it used to be under British colonial rule' when the British allowed no elections or right to protest.[45] Impatient and intransigent when being lectured by others, China will only become more confident in defending its own decisions and asserting its will.

New Silk Roads are the emperor's new clothes

China's highest-grossing movie in 2017 was *Wolf Warrior 2*. Alongside its endless action scenes, it was overflowing with patriotic swagger. Leng Feng (played by martial artist Wu Jing) is a former Chinese People's Liberation Army (PLA) special-forces soldier who is both muscular and moral. The plot saw him locked in battle with brutish, profit-hungry Western mercenaries in Africa. In 2018 *Operation Red Sea* topped the box office. In it, Chinese commandos save their country folk in a war-ravaged Middle Eastern country – a plot loosely inspired by the PLA's evacuation of Chinese nationals from Yemen's civil war.[46] Mainstream audiences flocked to watch films that channelled their nationalistic feelings, cultivating their pride in the PLA and helping them daydream about China's role in the wider world.

Popcorn fantasies aside, there are serious questions around China's growing international presence. It is far from inevitable that this century will 'belong' to China; but it is inevitable that China will play a huge role in setting the pace and tone of global affairs. Like a long-awaited development that the world can see coming from far off, we steady ourselves for the impact. Perhaps some singular future event will announce China's arrival as a dominant geopolitical force; or perhaps the existing trend lines of its steady rise will simply intensify.

It is impossible to predict with certainty how China's ambitions and abilities will develop. It is possible, though, to examine how its imperial legacies will shape this ascent – an ascent that might restore China to a grandeur it last enjoyed centuries ago, and which will make its nineteenth- and twentieth-century decline look like a short blip against a longer arc of historical progress.

The influence of imperial legacies is clear in Chinese domestic politics. What goes on in Beijing's halls of power is hardly a spectator sport. To outside eyes, the CCP seemingly comprises rows of serious-looking and unexpressive men in dark suits. And yet they did something quite astonishing on 11 March 2018. China's legislature, the National People's Congress, voted to scrap the two-term limit on the presidency, a rule that had existed since the 1990s. Just a handful of votes went against the motion, so the constitution was changed. Xi Jinping, president since 2013, now had no need to name a successor (which he would otherwise have done at a Communist Party Congress). Compared to his immediate predecessors, Jiang Zemin and Hu Jintao, who seemed more akin to party managers, President Xi has cut a rather more dynamic figure. The path was now open for him to rule beyond 2023. It seemed as if there was a new emperor in town.

The backroom manner in which the CCP has arranged its successions is utterly opaque. It bears the imprint of long-established Chinese political traditions, remodelled for the modern state. The decision could afford China's leadership a continuity in managing the country, and in pursuing its goals in the wider world, from which it hasn't been able to profit previously. This kind of continuity is inconceivable to democratic leaders elsewhere in the world, who have to contend with limited terms and their associated pressures. The absence of democracy and transparency has been deeply ingrained by China's immediate totalitarian past under Mao, but also through its inheritance of a centuries-long imperial tradition.

Zhao Tingyang, a somewhat hawkish Chinese academic, provides one explanation as to why democracy may be seen as an inferior form of government. In 2005 he wrote that democracy is an illegitimate way to represent political interests precisely because it is based on individual desires, which can be manipulated by advertising and clever campaigning.[47] Yan Xuetong, another Chinese scholar, explains why social hierarchies are more vital than equality: 'The early kings hated disorder and so they determined the distinctions of rites and norms so that there were classes of rich and poor, high and low status, sufficient so that there could be mutual oversight. This is the root of fostering all under heaven.' His conclusion is crisp: 'When distinctions are equal, then there is no sequence. When one grasps hold of equality, then there is no unity.'[48] This reads strangely to Western eyes, which are accustomed to favouring equality. In China, it is possible to come to the opposite conclusion.

Such talk has hammered a nail in the coffin of those hoping for some political representation in China. It also boxes in any aspirations for rights that China's ethnic minorities may have. Han Chinese by far outnumber other ethnicities, who exist within China's borders as a result of imperial-era campaigns. In the twentieth century Mao's China tightened its grip and inflicted great suffering in some of these regions. Today the narrative of 'unification' rather than 'conquest' is officially invoked. It is precisely because China was forged through the wars of imperial ambition that it has its present-day shape. To relinquish its grip over these regions would be to refute this legacy.

On 28 October 2013 there was a murderous backlash against this tight, centralized grip. A terrorist attack in Tiananmen Square mounted by Uighur separatists (as they were described) killed a total of five people (including the attackers). Striking right at the heart of Chinese power, prestige and history was seen as a terrible blow. Around this time a spate of stabbing attacks by disgruntled Uighurs were occurring both in the Xinjiang region, from which they came, and in other locations across China. The Chinese security response was expectedly tough, involving a saturation of police posts in Xinjiang, as well as the development of 're-education camps' to tame the local populace. It was 'de-radicalization', Chinese-style, and its workings were not visible to outsiders.

Metal detectors now surround Tiananmen Square, which tourists and others must pass through if they want to access the Forbidden City and the National Museum. The queues move quickly and security checks seem efficient, but they stand as an unofficial memorial to the threats faced by the Chinese state. When, in 1989, student protesters took to Tiananmen Square to agitate for democracy, the authorities used deadly force to disperse the protests, which came to an end on 4 June. A repeat of such scenes seems unthinkable three decades on, both in terms of such an unsophisticated state response and in there being any real wind behind the sails of mainland Chinese democracy. Hong Kong is another matter, however, although Beijing resisted any temptations it may have felt to deploy the PLA during the 2019 rioting against the attempted extradition bill.

Strong central rule over a multi-ethnic populace that is spread between disparate regions – this is the present-day Chinese model, and it was also the imperial model.[49]

China's cultural continuities also reflect the role of empires on the present. Dynastic empire was the vessel within which China's culture incubated for so long. China's transition from empire to state means that the vessel has changed, but its culture persists.

Just because China has strong imperial traditions and influences does not mean that it has to become a modern-day empire. President Xi has conveyed similar maxims in public pronouncements around his signature foreign policy, the 'New Silk Road'. He has tried to calm the nerves of foreigners concerning Chinese intentions: 'China does not subscribe to the outdated logic that a country will invariably seek hegemony when it grows in strength. Can the old practice of colonialism and hegemonism still work in today's world? Definitely no. It can only lead to a dead end, and those who stick to this beaten track will only hit a stone wall. The only alternative is peaceful development.'[50]

The contrast with the blood and thunder of historical European imperialism is a theme invoked from time to time. 'History is our best teacher,' Xi said in his opening address to the Belt and Road Forum for International Cooperation on 14 May 2017, making his point as follows:

> In the early fifteenth century, Zheng He, the famous Chinese navigator in the Ming Dynasty, made seven voyages to the Western Seas ... These pioneers won their place in history not as conquerors with warships, guns or swords. Rather, they are remembered as friendly emissaries leading camel caravans and sailing treasure-loaded ships. Generation after generation, the silk routes travellers have built a bridge for peace ... The ancient silk routes thrived in times of peace, but lost vigour in times of war.[51]

It is certainly a more heart-warming historical anecdote than the Opium Wars afford to the British. The marketing of Zheng He seems to be in full force, as I noticed in 2019 during a visit to

Malaysia, where a museum in the coastal trading town of Malacca proudly venerated his voyages. There was also a large advertisement for *Admiral Zheng He, the Peace Envoy of China and Malaysia*, replete with the tagline 'Sowing seeds of peace throughout the world', and featuring a heroic and youthful cartoon depiction of Zheng.[52] The illustration came from a fifty-two-episode animated series, *Zheng He's Voyages to the West Seas*, which retells these voyages as a series of fantastical adventures and is aimed at children in countries that China is keen to influence. From a Chinese perspective, this is a sensible message to aim at Malaysian children, for example, given the historical prevalence of the Peranakan (the Straits Chinese) on the Malay peninsula, their cultural ties to China and the overall importance of countries like Malaysia to China's ambitions for regional authority.

Nevertheless, there can be a vast gulf between such cosy rhetoric and the compulsions that come from inheriting an immense imperial tradition. So much so that immediately after the Second Belt and Road Forum in Beijing in April 2019, China's English-language national news magazine, *Beijing Review*, took out a two-page advert in *The Economist* newspaper to deliver the following message: 'Despite some governments and people in the West conjuring up arguments of "neocolonialism" or a "debt trap" to smear the Belt and Road Initiative, the China-proposed blueprint for common development of the world is becoming increasingly welcome.'[53]

China says that the Belt and Road Initiative is predicated on 'win–win' scenarios. It involves China investing in dozens of countries both in East Asia and far beyond, sending its workers and businessmen to make use of its abundant human resources, while getting the natural resources it needs to fuel its own economy. China's informal economic empire will consist of making the prosperity of other countries co-dependent on China's own economic advancement.[54]

In Pakistan, China has been building roads and other infrastructure stretching from their common border in the Himalayas and down to the Arabian Sea, where China has also renovated the port of Gwadar. Pakistan, a chronically unstable country, has been locked in competition with its bigger neighbour, India, since 1947; and since 9/11 it has been saddled with an unsatisfactory security partnership with the USA. So Pakistan welcomed the influx of Chinese money and attention, considering it a more predictable partner than the USA. China, for its part, gets a warm-water port, and another chip with which to bargain with India, its nearest potential regional competitor. So far, so good, in terms of the notion of 'win–win'.

The strategy involves using multilateral structures that exclude the USA, such as the Asian Infrastructure Investment Bank (AIIB), the regional body ASEAN and the Shanghai Cooperation Organisation (SCO), a club that links China and Russia. Russia has had concerns over the New Silk Road, but it has also tried to get in on the game by connecting its own initiative, the Eurasian Economic Union, to China's economic momentum. While the Sino-Russian partnership is never likely to be anything greater than a marriage of convenience, driven by proximity and overlapping concerns, it has evolved like a 'live and let live' arrangement between two large and adjacent countries. Russia has remained officially neutral over China's tussles in the South China Sea. Ditto, China did not officially condemn Russia's war in Ukraine. Neither country would want to end up fighting a war on behalf of the other, but each realizes that the other affords it some advantages. Central Asia is a case in point, because while Russia retains its linguistic connections there dating back to the USSR, it is China that now has far greater potential to invest in the region.[55]

Modern Chinese statecraft moves with a stately complacency. More the tortoise than the hare, it is not speed but scale that characterizes China's approach. In some ways, China's approach seems at once expansive and relatively risk-averse. Former US Secretary of State Henry Kissinger noted, in his interactions with Chinese statesmen, that they rarely risked everything on an all-or-nothing clash, preferring to patiently accumulate relative advantages. Kissinger explained this by contrasting the Western preference for playing chess, a game that teaches decisive victory, with the Chinese board game Weiqi, which teaches the encircling of rivals in a protracted campaign. He also mentions *The Art of War*: 'Sun Tzu addresses the means of building a dominant political and psychological position, such that the outcome of a conflict becomes a foregone conclusion ... a victory achieved indirectly through deception or manipulation is more humane (and surely more economical) than a triumph by superior forces.'[56]

However, assumptions concerning Chinese passivity should not be made from *The Art of War* and its oft-quoted dictum 'The skilful strategist/defeats the enemy/without doing battle'. US Sinologist Alastair Iain Johnston conducted a study of seven classic Chinese military texts, concluding that in China's historical military culture 'nonviolent means are not intrinsically better than violent strategies, but only under certain specific, limited conditions'.[57] He is careful not to fall into the stereotype of viewing Chinese strategic culture as 'sneaky'. Instead, he sees its preferences for avoiding all-out war as having developed in the Ming era, when China struggled to secure its frontiers against successions of barbarians. 'China has exhibited a tendency for the controlled, politically driven defensive and minimalist use of force that is deeply rooted in the statecraft of ancient strategists and a worldview of relatively complacent statecraft.'[58]

Decoding China's strategic intent is something that increasingly occupies political, media and academic minds around the world. Although the West likes to characterize Chinese investments in countries such as Malaysia and Pakistan as purely transactional, there is another side to this argument. In Chinese eyes, it is the West that seems transactional, because its business dealings relegate relationships to a means to attain ends, whereas Confucian beliefs put more value on relationships than on individuals, and on hierarchy determining how different parties should get along – by respecting the superior actor.[59]

When China looks out at the world, it sees clear hierarchies. Equality between radically different-sized countries can strike some Chinese as absurd. Especially because even if the US or the UN proclaims equality in statehood, the obvious disparities in size and coherency between different countries means that they end up being treated differently.[60] Perhaps a world run by China would embrace, rather than dress up, the power hierarchies that govern the world. As the scholar Yan Xuetong pointed out, 'having a single standard can only lead to conflict and is not helpful in reducing friction among states', and even 'boxing competitions are carried out according to different grades of weight'.[61]

What happens if China casts itself as the head of this family? The only country that could feasibly try to boss China around is the USA. Reflecting a hawkish Chinese attitude, the author Zhao Tingyang has conveyed his clear displeasure with America's 'hidden, yet totally dominating, world control'.[62] America's thinly-veiled imperialism and pursuit of capitalism have contributed to an unbalanced world system, he writes, explaining that globalization has facilitated America's new empire, succeeding the prior British imperial era. Zhao Tingyang thinks that ancient China became larger and larger not through imperial expansion, but through the 'vortex pattern' of Chinese history. 'Contrary to the outward spiral of imperialist adventure – the conquering of the seas and the domination of the world – the vortex pattern had the *effect of drawing inward* many nations to join and receive in the Chinese system by means of the *award attraction* of interests, power, honour, arts, knowledge . . . a true understanding of the uniqueness of China's past is the key to understanding of its present-day approach to politics.'[63]

Whether these views characterize mainstream Chinese thinking or not is less the point. More important is considering the range of lessons that Chinese intellectuals can draw from their historical legacies when thinking about the present era, and in particular the greater moral virtue that patriotic writers ascribe to China's means of enlarging its influence.

China seems to have no desire to take on the USA in a war. In its own back yard, however, it has boldly constructed artificial islands and pushed its claims to disputed islands in the East and South China Seas. In the East China Sea a dispute between China and Japan, over islands that the former calls Diaoyu and the latter Senkaku, flared up in 2010. After Japanese coastguards detained a Chinese fishing boat close to the islands, nationalistic impulses prevailed on both sides. China saw itself as a great power that no longer had to compromise with Japan. Conversely, Japan's President Shinzo Abe argued against Chinese domineering. In 2013 China began operating an air-defence zone over waters that included the disputed islands. That year in the South China Sea a dispute broke out with Vietnam when a state-owned Chinese firm placed an oil rig in water claimed by Vietnam. China has intensified its building of artificial islets around the Spratly Islands, moving ocean-floor sediment onto reefs to provide a foundation for airstrips, ports and military bases.[64]

Attempts to mediate and moderate these disputes have been weak or absent. In 2016 China refused to abide by a UN legal ruling against its claims over the Spratly Islands, after the Philippines brought the dispute to international arbitration. Chinese lawyers mounted a strong defence, arguing against the legality of the ruling, while the Chinese government incentivized the Philippines government to drop the case – which it promptly did. With so many overlapping historical enmities and interests involved, security of the South China Sea has played out as a high-stakes competition.[65] In 2017 the Chinese People's Liberation Navy (PLN) launched its second aircraft carrier, following on from its first, the *Liaoning*, which was launched in the 1980s. It is a reasonable bet that the PLN will not limit its ambitions to having just the two aircraft carriers, and that the naval contest for influence in the Pacific is only just beginning.

Gunboat diplomacy brought China to its knees in the nineteenth century. If China ever finds itself coming under Western and American sanctions concerning these maritime issues, then it can point to the fact that it was once a victim of international imperial aggression.

China is not out to seek wanton revenge for past injustices that it has faced, but it is seeking to compensate for its century of humiliation. Memories of China's previous fall at European and Japanese hands exist alongside memories of China's own imperial grandeur. The former serves for China as a warning, but the latter serves as inspiration.

Celebrating communism's centenary on the moon

Given the visual spectacular that was created at the Beijing Olympics, imagine what kind of party will be thrown for the centenary of communist rule in 2049. It will be the moment at which China can take stock of its rejuvenation at home and the immensity of its various roles abroad. By 2049 perhaps Chinese astronauts will celebrate the centenary from the vantage of a future moon base, their red flag with its yellow stars fixed and erect in the lunar vacuum.

By then, further technological advancements will no doubt have rendered China's remaining vestiges of agricultural labour even further into history than it already seems today. The Chinese peasantry is still vast, and in some provinces is still very much akin to those in a developing country – something that China has made reference to in its appeals for solidarity with its modern client states in Africa.

At the other end of the technological spectrum, in China's online presence – and in its attitude to the so-called 'great firewall of China', which blocks access to websites that are deemed to be inharmonious with CCP values – questions remain as to whether Chinese society will become more open to ideas and attitudes from elsewhere in the world by then.

Regardless, their past legacies of imperial success will remain a reference point for how the Chinese frame and rationalize their role in the modern world. History, culture and empire are far too interwoven for this not to be the case, no matter what the future has in store for China.

The Romance of the Three Kingdoms conveys how its characters feel the pressure of their lineage bearing down on them: 'They walk side by side through the imperial gallery, where the portraits of the former emperors hang. Walking from portrait to portrait, the emperor reflects upon the fortunes of the former rulers and bemoans his own weakness.'[66]

Weak no longer, the CCP has its eyes fixed firmly on its own position in the gallery. The CCP in 2049 may not look back to Mao so much as it looks back at the grander sweep of China's imperial history as the legacy to emulate.

SIX

INDIA'S OVERCOMING OF THE 'INTIMATE ENEMY'

I had hoped to improve my status and that of my people through the British Empire.

Mohandas Gandhi (1869–1948),
An Autobiography[1]

No people, no races remain unchanged. Continually they are mixing with others and slowly changing; they may appear to die almost and then rise again as a new people or just a variation of the old.

Jawaharlal Nehru (1889–1964),
The Discovery of India[2]

India does not want favours from the world, India wants equality.

Prime Minister Narendra Modi,
13 November 2015[3]

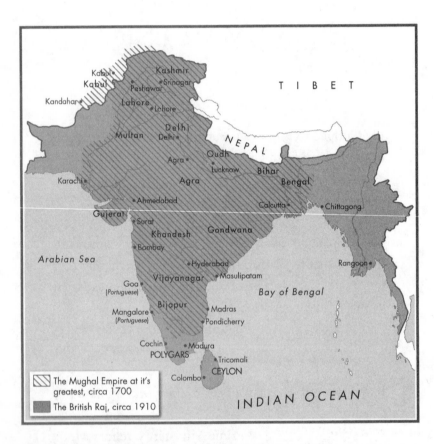

Map 9 The Mughal Empire and the British Raj compared

On a cold November evening in 2015 Narendra Modi packed out London's Wembley Stadium. His warm-up act was David Cameron, Britain's then prime minister. The tickets were free for Britain's Indian community. As my family love a freebie, we applied for tickets and, like many in the crowd, were intrigued by Modi, who had come to power in New Delhi the year before. Unlike his subdued predecessor, Manmohan Singh, who had been a bookish economist before he became prime minister, Modi had real fire in his belly.

Cameron was the first to speak, offering teamwork with India in trade and technology. For austerity-racked Britain, drumming up business in Asia was essential to its future prosperity. Cameron also promised to support India one day in a bid for a permanent seat on the UN Security Council, the top table of global diplomacy. The crowd cheered this idea, buoyed by the mental image of India taking on such an important position in world affairs. Modi now stepped up to the podium and addressed us in Hindi. He reflected on India's considerable domestic challenges, such as reducing poverty and providing electricity to the 18,000 villages that still manage without it. But the main thrust of his rhetoric was not to beg for help, from Britain or anyone else. Instead, his was a vision of India's self-assured ascent as a world power.

Bearing in mind the history between Britain and India, it was hard to stifle the thought that this was the Raj being reversed, rhetorically at least, ahead of India's seventieth anniversary of independence from British rule on 15 August 2017. Britain now seemed to have more to ask of India than the other way round. Meanwhile Modi could look out at a stadium full of Indians who were now citizens of the former colonizing power.

The extent of India's global ascent is not yet assured, and it remains to be seen just how energetic its economy and foreign policy can become. India's economy was the world's sixth-largest in 2017, just below Britain's and France's, but significantly behind China's. One record that India claims is in demographics: its population is projected to outstrip China's by the middle of this century. From 240 million people in 1901, India reached nearly 550 million in 1971.[4] Now its 1.3 billion people are set to expand even further, to become the most populous country on Earth.

Looking ahead to 2047, when the modern Indian state celebrates its centenary, this will be just two years shy of parallel celebrations in China for its own centenary of communist rule. Perhaps at this point India can rival China's modernization, not only in terms of GDP, but in lifting an ever greater share of its citizens out of poverty. Clearly India has great potential to be one of the major players in the post-imperial world, so long as it can harness and not be held back by its gargantuan population.

In another sense, India already has a source of informal global power, thanks to the twenty-five million or so people of Indian origin living around the world. From indentured labourers and taxi drivers to doctors and CEOs, they live in cities from New York to London, Dubai and beyond. Their spread is partly an imperial legacy, due to the forced migration created by the British Empire, and the displacement caused by Partition. Many others have since voluntarily left their motherland to join thriving Indian communities around the world where, in general, they seem to see no contradiction between loyalty to the country they live in and maintaining their cultural umbilical cord with India. This diffusion of its people affords India vast potential for projecting its cultural influence globally.

Modern India is the outcome of *many* imperial experiences intermingling with a grand old civilization. British rule was only the most recent, lasting from 1757 until 1947. Some of its abiding influences are clear, not least in having bequeathed institutions like parliament; practices such as Civil Service recruitment exams; street names like New Delhi's 'Connaught Place', named after Victoria's third son; and the English language. Today 'Hinglish' – a colloquial blend of Hindi and English – is pervasive in the chatter of the young and educated, and in newer Bollywood films, despite Hindi becoming the official language in 1965 of Bharat, the Sanskritic name India chose for itself.

But the British were only the latest occupiers. The Mughals – a dynasty of Muslim rulers who had swept into India via Afghanistan – ruled between the 1500s and 1700s. Their influence on India's evolution was vast, from culture to cuisine and that architectural icon of India, the Taj Mahal. The Mughal era also saw India's pre-existing Muslim populace expand further. Today, out of its 1.3 billion people, more than 170 million Indians practise Islam – a 'minority' larger than the entire populations of most other countries.

India's experience of moving beyond the imperial age can tell us much about its evolving identity as a global power. What will a jealous guarding of India's independence mean in the years ahead? Will India be biddable as an ally for countries like the US and UK, whose politicians are enamoured by India as the world's largest democracy and who are comparatively warier of China? Or will India avoid picking sides, just as it tried to do during the Cold War as a self-professed 'non-aligned power'? An India that is concerned with minding its own business is just as possible as an India that gets more stuck into the fray of world affairs.

India's evolving domestic politics, its regional identity and its great power potential will always be refracted through its identity as a survivor of colonialism, even if only subconsciously.

Mauryans, Mughals and Mountbatten: India's imperial experiences

While India is still a young country, it is an incredibly old civilization, and consequently the interplay between recent experiences and ancient history is crucial to any understanding of it.

This was instinctively grasped by its future president, Jawaharlal Nehru. His intellect, honed by an exceedingly British education at Harrow and then Cambridge University, flourished when he was later incarcerated in Her Majesty's Prison system for agitating against the Raj. Now, with time on his hands in jail, Nehru put pen to paper to deliver his interpretation of Indian history. The resulting book – *The Discovery of India* – presented India's history as comprising many layers, with the British merely adding the latest and Nehru convinced it would not endure.

People began to settle in the Indus Valley plain from around 4000 BCE. Dated to around 3000–1600 BCE, the Harappan civilization spread over what is now Punjab, straddling today's Indo-Pakistan border. Ruins of Harappan urban settlements suggest an advanced culture. After it went into decline, possibly due to the flooding of the Indus Valley, a new culture emerged, that of the Aryans.

The Aryans, known for the Sanskritic language and adherence to the rituals and teachings of the Vedas, emerged around 1200 BCE. They may have arrived as the result of migration from further afield; debate persists as to their origins.[5] What is clear is their immense influence on the Indus Valley, and their enduring cultural influence to this day. Vedic prayers and Sanskritic epic stories from the period remain integral to the lives of many Indians. The Mahabharata and the Ramayana are ancient India's great sagas, recounting the wars and expansion of the Indo-Aryans. These stories may have been passed orally between generations, likely taking shape hundreds of years later.[6] They are treated with a sanctity that is often reserved for a holy book. The Bhagavad Gita, which is one section of the Mahabharata, remains an enduring depiction of conflicting moral positions, between Arjuna's desire to avoid bad outcomes and Krishna's commitment to doing one's duty.[7] What we consider to be Indian culture grew from this cultural fusion between the Aryans and the people of the Indus Valley.[8]

Other influences swirled through the subcontinent. Buddhism emerged sometime around 500–400 BCE. It became a widely practised religion in India, and later spread across Asia and into

China. The Persians, under the kings Cyrus and Darius, arrived in 518 BCE, conquering the north-west (now Pakistan). Alexander the Great's head was turned by India, and he made his only foray there in 327 BCE. This was just four years before his death, after which the Greek presence did not endure. After Alexander's death, an indigenous empire formed.

Outside India, the fact that there were indigenous empires is less well known than the more famous Mughal and British eras. Perhaps this is because there was no single Indian empire, but several successive kingdoms.

One of the earliest and most important was the Maurya Empire, which lasted between 322 and 185 BCE and was founded by Chandragupta. Ashoka, the grandson of Chandragupta, was enthroned sometime around 268 BCE and ruled for nearly forty years. He is a key historical figure: his empire was huge and extended across much of today's India. Known for his magnanimity in victory, a trait attributable to his Buddhist beliefs, Ashoka unified the subcontinent, and his legacy as a local ruler who built such a unified empire lingers to this day.

From around the second century BCE until the third century CE, the Kushan Empire (from the Hindu Kush) expanded across much of north-west India and beyond, with ties to Persia and Rome in the West, and to China via the Silk Road routes.

Further, more localized empires followed, but the unity of the subcontinent as a whole was not to last, and the pattern thereafter was of smaller kingdoms. With indigenous kingdoms aplenty over the following centuries, no new unifying figure like Ashoka emerged to stitch the patchwork together.[9]

This is why, in the centuries that elapsed from this point in history until the present day, the subcontinent's destiny would be heavily determined by invaders.

Eventually India was overrun by Muslim conquerors. Right back to the seventh century, and the birth of the Islamic faith, the first phase of Muslim expansion had reached modern Afghanistan and Pakistan. In 1192 a crucial battle took place to decide who would control Delhi. Raja Govinda's Hindu army put up a strong fight, but Muhammad of Gor's Muslim army won. An Islamic sultanate was established in Delhi; but other Hindu kingdoms remained elsewhere. This unstable coexistence led to periodic wars between Muslim and Hindu armies. For example, the Vijayanagara kingdom in southern India held the line for Hindus against further expansion by the Islamic sultanate – until the Vijayanagara capital was overrun in 1565.[10]

The whole Indian subcontinent eventually fell to Muslim conquest and the Mughals. The Mughals derived their name from their Mongol ancestors. Babur, who established the Mughal Empire in 1504, was a distant descendant of Genghis Khan and, living up to this heritage, set out to capture his own empire. After Babur's death his eldest son, Humayun, took on the mantle, expanding Mughal rule across northern India. Reflecting their steppe traditions, the Mughals preferred to distribute power across their ruling families, creating numerous fiefdoms, rather than centralizing their control under the figurehead of one emperor.[11]

This changed as the Mughals went somewhat native. Akbar, who took the throne at the age of thirteen (after Humayun's death in 1556), later married his way into a position of greater authority amongst the Hindu princes. He married the Rajput princess Jodha, a smart move because it gave local Hindu rulers a stake in Mughal rule. In turn, the Mughal nobles took on Indian ways. Under Akbar's rule, the Mughals transitioned from being raiders from the steppes into a true empire. Akbar expanded Mughal rule at least halfway down India's territory, with annexations of Ahmadabad, Gujarat, Patna, Bengal, Bihar and Orissa, with his peripatetic court moving with him across his empire until his death in 1605.[12]

The Mughals contributed a legacy of architecture and art. Mughal painters produced numerous interpretations of scenes from sacred Hindu texts such as the Ramayana. The Taj Mahal in Agra remains the most globally famous icon of Mughal rule. Emperor Shah Jahan, who ruled between 1628 and 1658, commissioned its construction as a memorial to his wife, Mumtaz, who died giving birth to their fourteenth child. Old Delhi and the Red Fort, which served as a Mughal palace for 200 years, were also built at this time. The British later had the Red Fort partly restored, and Modi, speaking on India's seventy-second independence day, chose it as his backdrop.

In Mughal times a princely education started at a young age. Shah Jahan made his third son, Aurangzeb, the nominal commander of a military expedition to subdue a recalcitrant Rajput kingdom when he was just sixteen. Aurangzeb's later assignments spanned the empire, including stints governing the Deccan, Gujarat and Multan, and in battles over Kandahar, where the Mughals faced a Persian challenge. Aurangzeb eventually took the throne by deposing his father in 1658. Despite not being first in line to the throne, he outwitted his brothers in a war of succession.

Under Aurangzeb, the Mughal Empire reached the peak of its powers, while also sowing the seeds of its eventual decline through its overstretch. Dispensing with the plurality of his predecessors, Aurangzeb insisted that the Islamic faith anchor the empire. Under the influence of orthodox theologians, he decided that people of other faiths and kingly loyalties should bend the knee.[13]

Emperor Aurangzeb was especially aggrieved by word reaching him of Muslims converting to Sikhism. The Sikh faith was founded by Guru Nanak in the early 1500s and had expanded under his successors. The tenth Sikh guru, Guru Gobind Singh (1666–1708), fell afoul of Aurangzeb's drive to embed Islam in Punjab (where Sikhism is rooted). Guru Gobind Singh's two youngest sons were captured by a local Muslim governor and buried alive after refusing to convert to Islam. His two eldest sons died in a battle against a Mughal army in 1704.

The Mughal intolerance towards other religions continued.

Further south (near modern Mumbai), the disobedient Hindu Marathas posed an even bigger problem to Aurangzeb. The Maratha leader Shivaji (1627–80) ran a self-contained state that was undermining Mughal authority. Aurangzeb, now well into his seventies, personally led military campaigns into the Deccan, waging an inconclusive war against the Marathas.[14]

Aurangzeb's rule involved forced conversions to Islam, which reflected the imperial logic of quashing local loyalties in favour of central rule. But the population of the subcontinent was just too diverse for this to produce pacification. And it sullied the Mughals' legacy of uniting so much of India under a single emperor.

After Aurangzeb's death in 1707, aged eighty-eight, the Mughal line of succession never stabilized. Aurangzeb himself had weakened the claims of his own sons to his throne, partly to preclude his own murder by an ambitious son who might want to hasten the transition. The emperors after Aurangzeb ruled for shorter durations and with less authority. The power of the emperor and the dynasty faded as the power of its princes waned.[15] As Mughal authority began to be questioned by Sikhs, the Marathas and other groups, various local principalities began filling the void and, in the end, the Mughal dynasty remained only nominally in charge of India.[16]

They were completely blindsided by what came next.

The Raj and Partition

The fading Mughal dynasty handed out credentials to the East India Company to authorize its trading activities. It was during this era, in the 1700s, that the British laid the foundations for their eventual takeover of India. The ambitions of the East India Company had grown exponentially since its origins in the 1600s. It had begun by trading along the coast, in an effort to undercut its Portuguese, French and Dutch rivals, and its influence had not penetrated far inland.

The British breakthrough came at the Battle of Plassey in 1757, which took place north of Calcutta. Robert Clive led East India Company forces against the local regent, the Nawab of Bengal, and his French allies. The nawab's defences had been undermined by the British buying off some of his key lieutenants, making sure they didn't fight, by offering them future patronage. When battle was joined, the nawab's forces were routed. Bengal became a new source of Company profits and served as a base from which to expand its control across India in further military campaigns. The city of Calcutta was founded in Bengal as the centre of British rule in India, but there was still some way to go until British authority expanded.

The British faced stiff resistance and were beaten by a Maratha army in 1804. Since the time of Shivaji (the ruler who had fought the Mughals in the mid-1600s), a dynasty of Marathas had ruled the area as a major independent power. The Marathas offered resistance, but this couldn't last, and the British came back in 1818 to crush them. Again the British used their tactic of playing off the ambitions of rival Maratha chiefs against each other, thus weakening the opposition and dividing the locals, before stepping in to rule.

Skilfully loading the dice before the battle was one route to success; another was the massive build-up of arms. Back in its trading days, the East India Company's soldiers were there to guard its commerce. Now, in its conquering phase, the Company built up a private army, 250,000 strong, featuring well-trained and well-equipped British troops leading local sepoys. With British ambitions having grown insatiable after defeating France in Europe, the British could now concentrate on undermining the local resistance in India.

In Punjab the Sikh kingdom, led by Ranjit Singh, had hired European mercenaries to train his Khalsa army, which wanted to keep the British at arm's length. Singh's death in 1839 left the kingdom in the hands of less competent heirs, and the British sensed weakness. After defeating the Sikhs in 1846, the British cleaved off Kashmir, which the Sikhs had to surrender as part of their reparations to the British. These reparations helped to finance the next British campaign in 1848–9, after which Punjab was annexed into the British Empire. The Sikh kingdom was no more.

Victoria was crowned Empress of India in 1876, despite never setting foot there. What began as the East India Company's profit-seeking venture had culminated in the British Raj.[17]

British rule introduced to India things hitherto unseen: industrial modernity, and the ideals of a nation-state, in which a monarch acted as a figurehead for all kinds of commercial, military and missionary activities. British culture and ideas were so alien that they fundamentally challenged the way things were done in India. Ultimately, however, the Raj was a self-serving enterprise, conducted primarily for the colonizers' benefit.

Shimla, the hill station from which the Raj was ruled during the summer, illustrates how far apart the colonialists were, both physically and metaphorically, from the lives of ordinary Indians. Shimla appealed to the British because of its temperate climate and the stunning Himalayan vistas. Its faux-English buildings became resonant of the occupiers' vision of home and enabled British officials to largely insulate themselves from the daily realities of India. Down in the heat of the plains, and in the big cities, British rule was administered by the officialdom of the Indian Civil Service. This was accompanied by periodic coercion, with the British officers and sepoys of the Indian Army acting as final guarantors of the Raj's authority. Altogether, the number of British officials serving in India was relatively small in relation to the large territory and populace they governed. Nevertheless, India became the centrepiece of the British Empire, offering the possibilities of extensive profiteering and strategic command over Asia.

The edifice of British rule was shaken by the Indian Mutiny of 1857–8. It began when East India Company sepoys became frustrated with British rule and were moved to revolt, in the final instance because of rumours that the rifle cartridges they were expected to use were greased with animal fat from cows and pigs, and hence were offensive to them as Hindus and Muslims alike. The sepoy uprising was brutal, and the British only contained the revolt by reciprocating this brutality and because enough sepoys stayed loyal to them.

The final Mughal Emperor, Bahadur Shah Zafar (whose powerless title had left him stuck in Old Delhi), was thrust into becoming the nominal figurehead of the revolt. This prompted the British to exile him to Rangoon in Burma, getting him out of the way and finally terminating the Mughal line.

The next time the Raj was shaken, it faced an organized movement that was dedicated to undermining its authority. The Indian National Congress had formed in 1885 and later became the vanguard challenger to British rule. Gandhi and Nehru belonged to the Congress, and it helped to magnify their impact when the British made a tragic mess of things in 1919.

The colonial authorities had become extra-fearful of instability during the Great War. Elsewhere in the British Empire, the 1916 Easter Rising in Ireland had caught British authorities by surprise. To prevent this sort of thing happening in India, a new anti-terrorist law was promulgated, called the Rowlatt Act (named after the judge who passed it in 1919). It permitted a harsh range of measures that were intended to constrain revolutionary movements, such as allowing the detention of suspects without trial, stricter control of the press, and so on.

On 13 April 1919 a large crowd of civilians gathered at Jallianwala Bagh to demonstrate their opposition to the draconian Rowlatt Act and the detentions of leading national figures that had followed. British General Dyer interpreted this as a challenge to the Raj's authority, so he deployed his sepoys. Columns of soldiers lined up in front of the crowd, and Dyer ordered them to fire their rifles indiscriminately. In a matter of

minutes defenceless people were killed in their hundreds, with
thousands more injured. The site at Jallianwala Bagh where the
killing took place, and which became known as the Amritsar
Massacre, is today marked with testimonies to the suffering and
chaos that took place on that day, for example: 'To escape the
deadly firing, many people fell into this well. About 120 dead
bodies were found.'

The massacre galvanized the Indian National Congress. It
impacted on Gandhi, redoubling his faith in the protest method
of *satyagraha*, which meant peaceful, passive resistance. Gandhi
implored his supporters to abstain from violence, partly to wrest
the moral advantage from the British, and partly to employ tactics against which the British had no effective response. The
massacre also influenced Nehru, who was the younger of the
pair of nationalists, and who now embraced Gandhi's *satyagraha*
approach.[18] In a memorable passage from his book, Nehru conveyed his horror at the British:

> Which of these two Englands came to India? The England
> of Shakespeare and Milton, of noble speech and writing and
> brave deed, of political revolution and the struggle for free-
> dom, of science and technical progress, or the England of the
> savage penal code and brutal behaviours, of entrenched feu-
> dalism and reaction? For there were two Englands, just as in
> every country there are two aspects of national character and
> civilisation.[19]

Despite these tensions, when the Second World War came, the
British Indian Army still fought hard against the Japanese Empire
in Asia. Like the Roman Empire, the East India Company had
recruited among those it conquered. British officers had always
segregated combat units amongst different regional identities,
using their diverse cultural heritages as motivation in drill (such
as referencing Guru Gobind Singh's war against the Mughals

to motivate Sikh soldiers). 'The reasons why the Indian Army organised itself around the doctrine of the martial races had little to do with military excellence but rather with imperial politics,' writes the academic Tarak Barkawi. 'Troops were loyal, distinctive, and fierce because they were Sikhs, or Dogras, or Gurkhas, or Pathans.'[20]

Not all Indians wanted to fight for the British, or to heed Gandhi's pleas for peaceful protest at home. Subhas Chandra Bose was determined to kick the British out of India and wanted an army to do the job. A leading figure in the independence movement, he lost his job as president of the Indian National Congress after choosing a different path from Gandhi's. In 1939, with the advent of war, Bose looked to the Axis Powers to raise his army.

His life then unfolded like an adventure story: escaping from a British jail, he travelled via Italy and Germany to Japan. The Japanese helped Bose build the Indian National Army (INA). As the war in Asia unfolded, the INA fought with Japan against the British Indian Army.[21] Things looked bright for Bose when Japan forced the British garrison in Singapore to surrender in 1942. The INA even advanced far enough to hoist the Indian tricolour over Indian soil. But the run of advances couldn't continue when Japan lost the war. Sadly for Bose, he had picked the losing side. He died on 18 August 1945 after a suspicious plane crash over Taiwan.

The Raj survived the Second World War, but only just. The British had made concessions before and after the war, such as the 1935 Government of India Act, which differentiated how Burma and India were run and seemingly gave India's provinces self-rule, but was merely an attempt to undercut Nehru and India's nationalists.[22] For a growing number of Indians, the British no longer seemed to occupy a towering pedestal. After 1945 the British knew their grip was slipping.

Partition, when it happened two years later, was something the British were catastrophically unprepared for. The last viceroy,

Lord Mountbatten, faced competing demands concerning what kind of independent state to create, and whether there should be a single unified state or two states split along religious lines. Muslim leader and politician Muhammad Ali Jinnah politically exploited the fear amongst Muslims at the prospect of Hindu majoritarian rule. Jinnah advocated a Muslim state called Pakistan (a name devised by imaginative Muslim Indians studying at Cambridge University, who knew the Raj was fading). This insistence on a separate Muslim state came into shape in the 1930s, in time for independence.[23]

As independence approached in 1947, Gandhi tried to head off Jinnah's desire to create Pakistan by promising that Muslims would be safe in a unified India, and by suggesting to Viceroy Mountbatten that Jinnah become the first prime minister. Gandhi's reassurances did not work, and it looked increasingly as if the Raj would be replaced by two successor states. Britain's Radcliffe Boundary Commission hastily drew a new border on the basis of 'contiguous majority areas' of different communities, although its head, Sir Cyril Radcliffe, had no experience of India's demographics and geography before taking on this immense responsibility.[24]

A human catastrophe was not what the British wanted, but it was what they got. Bengal and Punjab, the provinces central to events in 1947, were cleaved in two. Each had a Muslim majority, so Pakistan claimed them, but each also contained millions of Hindus and, in Punjab, Sikhs too. In the end, some of Punjab was given to West Pakistan, and some of Bengal to East Pakistan.[25] The two parts of Pakistan didn't even join up.

Waves of panic rippled across the populace, and an exodus began as people fled to get into the 'right' country they were supposed to live in, based on their faith. Mobs began to ethnically cleanse certain areas, as law and order collapsed. It is hard to estimate the total number of people who died, let alone those who were raped, left injured and traumatized. 'Unquestionably the main victims of Partition were women,' writes the historian

Ramachandra Guha. 'Hindu, Sikh, and Muslim ... Women were killed, maimed, violated and abandoned. After independence the brothels of Delhi and Bombay came to be filled with refugee women, who had been thrown out by their families.'[26]

Even in their withdrawal, the colonizers were self-serving. Mountbatten pushed for an early withdrawal that did not allow the new independent governments to get ready, or enable a reconstituted Indian Army to prepare to keep the peace. Mountbatten even picked a date to end British rule that symbolically covered his own country's blushes. He chose 15 August 1947, the second anniversary of Imperial Japan's defeat – a date that boosted British pride. Nehru's Congress Party, which would now run India, wanted 26 January, which was a date they had celebrated since 1930 as an informal national day.[27] Mountbatten defended his decisions afterwards, but he had ignored Prime Minister Attlee's timetable for a slower British withdrawal.[28]

The causes of Partition still attract attention, but it is the consequences that matter most of all today.[29] After independence, India faced a future that would be quite different from the last 500 years of Mughal and British rule. How the accumulated weight of these imperial legacies shaped its independent future is a story that began in 1947 and has been unfolding ever since.

Layers of imperial legacies

If one is to say that India is 'post-imperial', to which empire are we referring? Experiences that are within living memory, like those involving Gandhi and the British, have directly led to the present. To pluck out only the last hundred years would be selective, however, as the interplay between recent experiences and the subcontinent's earlier history is crucial to any understanding of India.

The Mughal Empire has deposited significant legacies that, as time has passed, have become enmeshed with what seems to be indisputably Indian. However, certain interpretations of Mughal rule can still provoke polarizing interpretations in modern India. Were the Mughals Muslim usurpers of Indian territory, enslaving the Hindu masses? Or did the Mughals go native and evolve into an organic part of India's heritage?

On 6 December 1992 there was an ugly outbreak of religious violence as Hindu nationalists decided to reduce the Babri Masjid mosque in Uttar Pradesh to rubble. The mosque had been built in the 1520s and was named after Babur, the first Mughal emperor. In its place the nationalists wanted to build a temple dedicated to the Hindu Lord Rama, and a few of them were even filmed extolling that 'Babur's descendants go to Pakistan or to the graveyard'. It was an ugly misappropriation of imperial history, refashioned as ammunition for modern inter-communal anger. The controversy still bubbles away in the debate over building a temple for Lord Rama on the same site, and it remains to be seen whether Modi's government takes this step.

In 2008 Bollywood delivered a rather more glowing tribute to the Mughals in the film *Jodhaa Akbar* about Mughal Emperor Akbar. Artistic licence and historic accuracy notwithstanding, *Jodhaa Akbar* was an innocent journey into an imperial past for a modern audience and reflected the broadly positive image that Akbar has retained. Ruling over a largely Hindu realm, Akbar sensed there was no real prospect for conversions en masse to Islam and ruled by recognizing the diversity of the population.[30]

To say that India is 'multi-ethnic' or 'multilingual' scarcely does justice to its vast conglomerate of cultural and linguistic diversity. Hundreds of languages are spoken, religious sects worshipped and ethnicities logged in the Census. India is a continent unto itself, a vast social ecosystem of intermingling peoples.[31] Inter-community harmony is therefore essential to modern India, especially because of its substantial Muslim populace. The Mughal era's influence is by now deep-seated, generating narratives either of Muslim conquest of Hindus (if it is a lesson in antagonism) or of a shared historical experience (if it is a message of hope).

Was there something inherently more objectionable about British rule than Mughal rule? After all, both were outsiders when they invaded. Rabindranath Tagore (1861–1941), a Bengali poet and one of India's most revered literary figures, put the following thoughts on paper in 1917: 'We had known the hordes of Mughals and Pathans who invaded India, but we had known them as human races, with their own religions and customs, likes and dislikes – we had never known them as a nation ... But this time [with Britain] we had to deal, not with kings, not with human races, but with a nation – we, who are no nation ourselves.'[32]

The novelty of British ways was compounded by their arrogance towards Indians. Tagore also observed that in his time, Britain had 'produced the smallest number of scholars who have studied Indian literature and philosophy with any amount of sympathetic insight or thoroughness', complaining that 'this attitude of apathy and contempt is natural where the relationship is abnormal and founded upon selfishness and pride'.[33]

Nehru similarly complained that 'the British remained outsiders, aliens and misfits in India, and made no attempt to be otherwise. Above all, for the first time in India's history, her political control was exercised from outside and her economy was centred in a distant place.'[34]

And the novelist V. S. Naipaul was even pithier: 'the Raj was an expression of the English involvement with themselves rather than with the country they ruled'.[35]

At the time of the Raj, the British were quite convinced that only they could have 'created' India. Reflecting the British colonial consensus of the day, the scholar J. R. Seeley wrote in 1888 that there was 'no India in the political, and scarcely, in any other sense' before the British. Colonization was possible because, 'just as Italy and Germany fell as easy prey to Napoleon, because there was no Italy and Germany', so the British used similar methods by which 'Napoleon was able to set one German state against another'.[36] This was language that made sense to British imperialists.

Unsurprisingly, some Indians have taken real objection to this. Nehru had ruminated on this particular issue while writing in prison:

> The notion that the *Pax Britannica* brought peace and order for the first time to India is one of the most extraordinary of delusions. It is true that when British rule was established in India the country was at her lowest ebb and there was a break-up of the political and economic structure. [The Mughals] did not appreciate that a new and vital world was arising in the West ... the British represented that new world of which they were ignorant.[37]

Nursing an expectedly bruised pride at having been colonized has been an enduring way of rationalizing the British claim to having 'created' India. As the economist Amartya Sen has written, this British assumption reflected the colonizers' 'pride in alleged authorship, but also some bafflement about the possibility of accommodating so much heterogeneity within the coherent limits of what could be taken to be a pre-existing country'.[38] Writer and politician Shashi Tharoor is convinced that India would have united anyway, had the British never arrived, with the Marathas operating under a titular Mughal emperor.[39]

Fantasizing about a counterfactual history that never was might seem pointless, but it is also a reflection of the psychological contortions required to muster pride in India's own accomplishments and potential. It is a challenge facing those who were once conquered, and who are now looking to becoming more significant themselves.

Imperial legacies have deeply impacted upon India's self-confidence. Writer Ashis Nandy once called colonialism's legacy India's 'Intimate Enemy'. He argued that India had to escape not only the physical bonds, but also the mindset of subjugation –

something embodied by Gandhi in his non-violent resistance to British rule, according to Nandy.[40]

When several layers of imperial legacies accumulate over such long spans of history, they can become akin to abstract paintings – different contemporary observers can see in them different things. And they can reach back and pluck out almost any lesson they wish for the present day – all the way from the ameliorative to the chauvinistic, and from the insular to the extrovert.

Gandhi's and Nehru's post-imperial India

At independence, many Indians were in thrall to those who had spearheaded its struggle and their messages of healing and consolidation. Modern India's icons were Gandhi, the sage, and Nehru, the charismatic politician, who between them had successfully rejected the Raj. Their interpretations of India's imperial legacies remain influential. Between them, they set down political traditions that have defined modern India throughout much of the last eighty years.

Gandhi was an unlikely freedom fighter. His personification of stoic calm in the face of the chaos of Partition was enhanced by his wise, bespectacled appearance and his homespun white robes. His journey began as loyal subject of the British Empire, with his legal training in London, followed by his advocacy on behalf of Indians living in the Transvaal. In Gandhi's words from 1927, 'Hardly ever have I known anybody to cherish such loyalty as I did to the British Constitution.' Thinking of his homeland's plight, 'I held then that India could achieve her complete emancipation only within and through the British Empire.'[41] After twenty years in South Africa, he returned to India in 1915, aged forty-six, with his personality and outlook having been formed by a mix of Eastern and Western influences.[42]

Now immersed in India's independence struggle, Gandhi found that his views on the Raj's end had evolved. On one matter he remained fixated: that harmony between Hindus, Muslims and all faiths was sacrosanct. Gandhi described himself as a *sanatani* (an orthodox Hindu) but, symbolically, as a Sikh, a Muslim and a Christian too. He went on hunger strikes to persuade all Indians to work together. He was distraught after Partition, as Hindu–Muslim unity withered, but carried on preaching harmony and living up to his honorific Sanskrit title, 'Mahatma', meaning great soul.

Then, in the early evening of 30 January 1948, while walking to address a prayer meeting, his worldly journey ended. Three bullets fired from an assassin's pistol hit Gandhi at point-blank range, his white robe now blood-stained. The killer, Nathuram Godse, was a Hindu nationalist terrorist, who was convinced that Gandhi had appeased the Muslims. Godse's appalling act, for which he was tried and hanged in 1949, showed that the Mahatma was *not* universally venerated.

Keeping the Hindu radicals out of the way was an understandable priority for Nehru, who would serve as prime minister for seventeen years, until his death in 1964. India was too fragile, too unformed as a state, to run the risk of civil war erupting. Distraught at Gandhi's death, Nehru – and his fellow independence-movement stalwarts – set to work creating an independent India.

Nehru still had to contend with the vestiges of French and Portuguese colonialism, which persisted in India after the British left. The French hung on to their coastal colonial settlement of Pondicherry until 1952 (some French is still spoken there today). The Portuguese, whose first fort in India was built at Cochin in 1503, were unwilling to leave. In December 1961 the Indian Army moved into Goa and finally forced the Portuguese garrison to surrender. Five centuries of Portuguese designs on southern India, begun in the era of Vasco da Gama, had now ended.

Nehru went to work on accommodating some 500-plus princely states within the union of India in a vast act of nation-building. Although the Raj had ended in 1947, India remained a British dominion, and it was not until 26 January 1950 that India officially became a republic. Holding the election, and running India, relied on the inherited Indian Civil Service and the army (which retained some British officers). In a flash, India now had to develop a federal structure and a central government, after centuries of empires ruling over diverse pockets of local interests.[43]

Nehru needed to find a unifying vision for independent India. He had taken the helm of an India that had failed to meet Gandhi's forlorn hope: to keep India as one. Instead, Pakistan had been divided from India across religious lines, as well as by lines on the map.

Neither India nor Pakistan wanted to give up Kashmir. This beautiful valley state and its Muslim-majority populace had been bisected by Partition. The dispute over Kashmir brought India and Pakistan to war in 1948, 1965 and 1998; it remains a festering, unresolved matter today. In 1971 another violent schism tore the region further into pieces, as Pakistan's disconnected wings violently split apart to create Bangladesh. The 1971 war began when West Pakistan sent an army to repress a Bengali separatist movement in East Pakistan. This led to a huge refugee influx into India, and to India's military entering the war and inflicting a defeat on West Pakistan.

Indo-Pakistani tensions have sapped the energies of both countries, justifying an arms race that neither can afford, and offering each population a neighbourly target for their ire on all manner of issues. When tensions have risen between the countries, India's own harmonious relations with its Muslim citizens is put at risk. Muslim terrorists have also periodically targeted Indian cities. Overall, it is an awful imperial legacy.

Part of Nehru's post-imperial strategy was for India to declare itself a 'non-aligned' country, and this has cast another shadow over Indian foreign policy ever since. Non-alignment conveyed India's instinct to jealously guard its new-found sovereignty, which was understandable, given that the British had controlled India for so long. This legacy initially tilted India's foreign-policy sympathies towards anti-colonial struggles around the world, with India unwilling to be sucked into the Cold War by siding definitively either with the USA or the USSR.

This diplomatic balancing act was never going to be sustainable, given the complexities of world politics. India fought a short border war with China in 1962 and suffered defeat. The Sino-India War was an outcome of the old frontiers of the British Raj rubbing up next to where China was tightening its grip over Tibet.[44] India later got its own back, symbolically at least, when it offered refuge to the Dalai Lama in 1965, much to Chinese chagrin.

The unrelenting arms race with Pakistan created further pressures and by the 1970s prime minister Indira Gandhi was leaning towards the USSR for support. Russian military hardware would equip India's armed forces. There was commonality of interest, since both New Delhi and Moscow were wary of Beijing's intentions. In the end, Russia and India had drawn closer because China had drawn closer to Pakistan (the latter being a partnership that endures strongly today).

Nehru's vision was central to managing the chaos arising from Britain's haphazard departure, although he could never have extinguished all the fires. Such was his personification of India's destiny that his political lineage kept on winning elections. Nehru's daughter Indira, and his grandson Rajiv, ruled after him. The Nehru–Gandhi dynasty (as it is known, after Indira married Feroze Gandhi, no relation to Mohandas) was India's political establishment in the second half of the twentieth century.

It wasn't until Nehru's great-grandson, Rahul, was beaten at the polls by Modi in 2014 and again in 2019 that the Nehru–Gandhi dynasty – the original custodians of post-imperial India – were finally cast into the political wilderness.

How Modi and the Hindu nationalists
deal with imperial legacies

Narendra Modi belongs to the Bharatiya Janata Party (BJP), arch-rival of the Congress Party. One of the fundamental contrasts between them resides in their dramatically differing interpretations of the psychological legacies of empire.

Modi and the BJP are Hindu nationalists. Notice that the operative term is *Hindu*, not *Indian*, nationalism. Harking back to a mythical Hindu past – and one that is untainted by outside conquerors, known as 'Hindutva' – is a bedrock of Hindu nationalist thought. It has advanced a different post-imperial vision, reaching far back into history, to an ancient past that was untouched by Mughal or British rule. Hindutva offers its own recipe for overcoming the fact that for 500 years the dominant empires in India were not built by Hindus.

The Hindutva movement's beliefs, civil-society networks and electoral constituencies helped to propel Modi to the top. His Hindu majoritarian credentials are well established. He was chief minister of Gujarat in 2002 when inter-communal riots racked the state, leaving more than a thousand people dead. During this violence Modi's sympathies seemed to reside with Hindus and not Muslims. His alleged complicity in fanning the flames was never proven in court, but the USA and European countries conveyed their outrage at his apparent sectarianism by barring him entry.[45] In 2014, with Modi as prime minister and in charge of a growing economy, Western leaders were keen to turn the page. An older and apparently wiser Modi made sure to emphasize that Indians must live together in harmony and, when asked about his past, pointed to the economic boom that occurred in his twelve years running Gujarat.

However, the underlying influence of his Hindutva beliefs remained. Modi had been a member of a Hindu nationalist group called the RSS (its name, Rashtriya Swayamsevak Sangh, means

'National Patriotic Organization') since his childhood in the 1950s. Hindus of successive generations have found in the RSS what Modi found – a sense of purpose and identity. The RSS is still going strong today. Its members are of all ages, and belong to male and female wings in regional chapters across India. It is a perfectly legal entity (and there is even an online registration form to join).[46]

As a child, I recall being impressed and slightly intimidated by an RSS youth gathering that I watched while on holiday. Regimented lines of boys, each clutching a *lathi* (a wooden truncheon-like stick), were performing energetic synchronized callisthenic exercises. With all the paramilitary discipline on display, it was like a tougher version of the Boy Scouts. At the time I had no idea that behind the exercises lay a robust sense of patriotism.

The RSS was founded by a Maharashtrian doctor in 1925, but the ideas it channelled had a longer gestation period. Hindutva's key ideologue was Vinayak Damodar Savarkar (1883–1966). He lived through the Raj, was shaped by the independence struggle and in 1909 wrote a book entitled *The Indian War of Independence (1857)*. His 1923 book, *Hindutva*, set out his political ideology by explaining why Hinduism (the religion) ought to be understood as distinct from 'Hindutva' (the civilization). While he could not 'state definitively the period when the foremost band of the intrepid Aryans made it their home and lighted their first sacrificial fire on the banks of the Indus', Savarkar marked out the Aryans of India 'as a people destined to lay the foundations of a great and enduring civilisation'.[47]

Savarkar's pride in the Hindutva means that non-Hindu invaders were scorned. Regarding the Mughal period, the heroes were those Hindus resisting them. Referencing the Maratha ruler Shivaji, the interpretation in Savarkar's book is suitably dramatic: 'Shivaji thought to himself – We are Hindus. The Mohammedeans have subjugated the entire Deccan. They have defiled our sacred places! In fact they have desecrated our religion. We will, therefore, protect our religion and for that we would even lose our lives.'[48]

When it comes to later occupiers, Savarkar's venom resurfaces: 'Portuguese fanaticism at Goa was India's edition of the Inquisition in Europe.'[49] But his main effort was in exhorting the unity of the Hindutva civilization 'as a race bound together by the dearest of ties of blood'.[50]

Savarkar's writing made for a compelling alternative history that fused myth, religious faith and Hindu identity. Although his book is nearly a century old, Hindutva ideals still hold appeal for many Indians. This is because Hindutva conveys how an ancient civilization can reconnect with its past, and reclaim it from foreign conquerors and corruptors, by being true to its own early origins.

With these ideals in mind, the RSS set to work educating its flock. The group's leading figure for years was M. S. Golwalkar, who authored an article in 1952 arguing that it was 'necessary to wipe out all signs that reminded us of our past slavery and humiliation . . . Our present and future has to be well united with our glorious past. The broken chain has got to be re-linked. That alone will fire the youth of free India with a new spirit of service and devotion to our people.'[51] In other words, Hindus would be the primary owners of India. This was an unashamedly nativistic take, based on a particular interpretation of who the natives are.

This is why some Indians despise the RSS, warning that in its early years it was inspired by fascism and racial pride.[52] Controversies have dogged the RSS since Partition. Godse had a lapsed membership when he shot Gandhi; evidently the RSS had not been hardcore enough for him. The RSS was banned for a time by Indian authorities, since even if it did not order Gandhi's assassination, RSS cadres had participated in the violence during Partition. Some RSS members were privately pleased at the news of Gandhi's killing and may have shared Godse's worldview of the Hindus avoiding compromises with the Muslims.

Today the RSS, alongside the BJP and smaller parties like Shiv

Sena, fall under the political umbrella of the 'Hindu right', and as
a right-wing response to the Nehru–Gandhi establishment. Since
its initial electoral rise in the 1990s, the BJP has faced accusations of bias against India's Muslims. This has been compounded
by rumours of BJP sympathy with, or involvement in, bouts of
anti-Muslim violence, as when Hindu fundamentalists destroyed
the Babri Masjid in 1992, or during the 2002 Gujarat riots, which
landed Modi in hot water. By 2014, however, Modi had mod-
erated the BJP's tone and even tried to appeal to Muslim voters
by playing on disenchantment with the Congress Party, and on
nativist suspicions directed at Rahul Gandhi's mother, Sonia, for
being Italian-born.

A tame and passive India is not what Hindu nationalists want.
Rather, they want a prouder and tougher majoritarian India. The
fact that this appeals widely enough for Modi to win elections is
because it also serves to rehabilitate India from a history of occupation and colonization.

Shivaji is still venerated in Maharashtra. His legacy of resistance is important and there are traces of it in modern Indian
politics. Shiv Sena ('Shivaji's Army') is a far-right Hindu political party, founded in 1966 to defend the views of Maharashtrans.[53]
Illustrating the electoral appeal of its localized brand of Hindu
nationalism, Shiv Sena entered into a ruling coalition with Modi's
BJP in 2014 and again in 2018, winning seats in the Lok Sabha
(parliament).

The BJP has been keen to hitch itself to the tougher legacies of
resistance to occupation. To the wider world, Gandhi's pacifism
embodies the freedom struggle. But to many Indians the more
militant Subhas Chandra Bose, the independence figure who
broke with Gandhi, is an inspirational folk hero. In January 2019,
to mark 122 years since Bose's birth, a museum was dedicated to
him at the Red Fort. It was inaugurated by Modi, who offered
these words: 'Subhas Chandra Bose will always be remembered as
a heroic soldier. With his slogans like "Dilli chalo" [get to Delhi],

"Tum mujhe khoon do, main tumhen azadi dunga" [give me your blood, I give you your freedom], he created a special space for himself in every Indian's heart.' To mark seventy-five years since Bose's soldiers reached Indian soil, Modi (wearing a Bose-style army cap) led a chant of 'Subhas Chandra Bose zinda hai!' – Bose lives![54] All good historical fodder for a modern Hindu nationalist.

Modi has cultivated a devoutly spiritual side too, and has been photographed on pilgrimages and with his yoga-practising celebrity endorser, the saffron-robed Swami Ramdev. Yoga's origins lie in ancient India, with associations with Buddhism and Hinduism and references to it in the ancient Vedic texts. Yoga is one of India's great global cultural exports and, while it is now practised everywhere, its origins are authentically Indian, which is precisely why it fits into the package of associations that Modi has used to forge his electoral identity, as an authentically Hindu leader of India.

India's post-imperial ascent as a global power

Since independence, India has renamed several of its major cities. The names Bombay, Calcutta and Madras were heavily associated with the inauspicious colonial era, when Europeans used these coastal cities to ship goods out of India.[55] In 1996 Madras was renamed Chennai, and its state changed to Tamil Nadu, in reflection of the Tamil populace living on India's southern tip. 'Bombay' derived from the Portuguese boa Bahia or 'good bay', was renamed Mumbai. In 2001 Calcutta was renamed Kolkota, a name more in line with Bengali pronunciation. In some cases the changes have not stuck, as most people still refer to 'Bangalore', even after it was officially renamed 'Bengaluru' in 2014.

Names can be changed, but the essence of India's hybridity, comprising its many layers of imperial experience, will always be with it. Imperial legacies are intrinsic to India's being, but they only define India inasmuch as they have combined with its ancient culture. Whether actively or subconsciously, these mixed legacies are influencing India's ascent as a global power.

The themes and debate evident in its post-imperial rehabilitation will continue for some time, and will contribute to determining whether India remains a relatively outlying power in world affairs or moves to playing a more central role. Eventually India may be forced to make important choices around what role it plays in relation to China's growing influence in Asia. The late Indian strategist K. Subrahmanyam put it like this: 'If the US remains the world's predominant power, and China is second, India will be the swing power.'[56] Perhaps, though, an India that is still coming to terms with its imperial experiences is less likely to swing into action of any kind.

India was undoubtedly scarred by imperialism and by the manner of its independence. Some scars, like the persisting stand-off with Pakistan, and delicate inter-communal relations between Hindus and Muslims, will remain essential realities. Some of the scars were psychological, and have impacted on the self-confidence required to participate in a Western-designed world order and, increasingly, a Chinese-dominated regional economy. Doing so will require a further coming to terms with where India fits in the post-imperial world, and what it can bring to this world as a survivor of other people's imperial designs.

SEVEN

THE MIDDLE EAST'S POST-IMPERIAL INSTABILITY

The vanquished always want to imitate the victor in his distinctive mark(s), his dress, his occupation, and all his other conditions and customs. The reason for this is that the soul always sees perfection in the person who is superior to it and to whom it is subservient.

Ibn Khaldun (1332–1406),
Al Muqaddimah[1]

And my heart bled within me, for you can only be free when even the desire of seeking freedom becomes a harness to you, and when you cease to speak of freedom as a goal and a fulfilment.

Khalil Gibran (1883–1931),
'On Freedom', *The Prophet*[2]

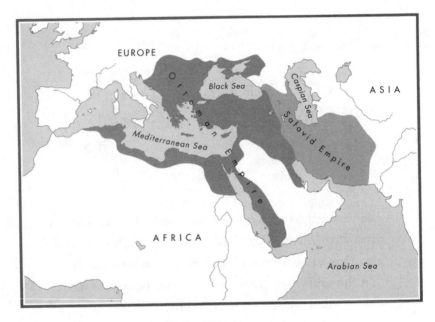

Map 10 The Ottoman and Safavid Empires, *c.* 1700
Map 11 The mandate system of European Control, 1920

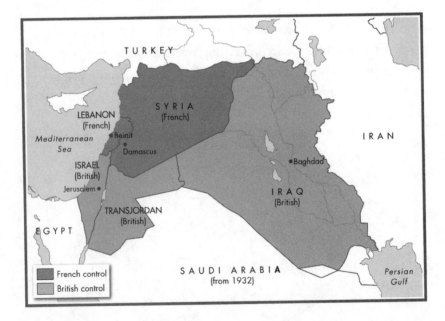

Nearly two-thirds of the population of the Middle East and North Africa is under thirty years old. There are 435 million people in the 'MENA' region, a term favoured by the World Bank and similar organizations.[3] Those of the millennial generation and younger have no memory of empires – only hopes for prosperity and security. Many of them also want a say in how their countries are run in the future.

In 2011 these aspirations spilled out in what became known as the 'Arab Spring', a series of street-protest uprisings against dictators and monarchies in countries across the region. Egypt experienced a momentous political change after activists had seen off Hosni Mubarak's rotting twenty-nine-year-old autocracy.

A year later I visited Egypt during what transpired to be an interregnum in the country's post-Arab Spring journey. Walking through Cairo's Tahrir Square, the focal point of the demonstrations, I found little to do except chat to locals and buy a souvenir T-shirt that marked 'a year of revolution'. I was there to visit various political parties ahead of the crucial June 2012 election that would set Egypt's next course.

Of these parties, the Muslim Brotherhood (MB) seemed the most buoyant. In its earlier incarnations, following its founding in 1928, the MB had been an underground revolutionary group, agitating for Egyptian politics to be more Islamic (hence the term 'political Islam' as describing this goal).

The MB had since gone mainstream and was on the cusp of electoral glory when I visited. I spoke to members of the Freedom and Justice Party (the besuited vote-winning face of the MB), meeting Dr Mahdi Akef, a genteel member of the MB's old guard who had been its 'Supreme Guide'. Born in 1928, Akef had lived through the early years of being an outlaw activist. Mindful of his foreign guests, Akef reassured us that the modern MB was nothing to do with rogues like Ayman al-Zawahiri (who was an MB member in the 1970s, left to form al-Qaeda and now has a $25 million bounty reward for his whereabouts, offered by the FBI).

Akef had inadvertently recalled the common heritage between political Islam's peaceful activists and its terrorists.

Electoral triumph awaited the MB in June 2012. President Mohamed Morsi duly took office – only for this result to be reversed a year later by an army coup in July 2013. The old order has now reasserted itself and General Abdel Fattah el-Sisi is in charge. Sisi promptly ordered the rounding up of the MB for allegedly leading Egypt to ruin during their year in power. MB activists, young and old, suffered in the crackdown. Some were killed and others, like Akef, were arrested.

According to press reports, Akef was put in solitary confinement and his health deteriorated until he died in 2017. In his lifetime he had seen political Islam emerge from the underground in post-colonial Egypt, only for it to be banished there again. In 2019 Morsi also died in captivity.

As this snapshot of Egypt's tumultuous recent past shows, today's burning questions are about opportunities for youthful populations; about the role of Islam in the state and in society; and about chasing away jihadists, some real and others imagined. Empire is far from the mind, and even decolonization is an inherited memory for the younger generation.

Yet, just as ancient Egypt's pyramids still gaze down over the country, so imperial histories cast their own shadows. These abiding influences are evident as one travels around the region, seeing its modern problems and contemplating their historical antecedents. Imperial history looms over much that happens in the region, and understanding this can help to enlighten us as to why a country like Egypt has suffered such instability. But this immediately poses another question: which imperial history?

As with much of the region, Egypt's history shows just how many layers there are.

The Pharaonic Kingdoms consolidated their rule over the Nile Valley in 3100 BCE. It wasn't 'Egyptian' as we understand it today, since neighbouring dynasties sometimes usurped control of the Nile Valley, only to adopt pharaonic customs as they took its throne.[4]

In later epochs invaders came and went, each leaving their influence. The Greek, Alexander the Great, marched into Egypt in 332 BCE. The Roman Empire expanded into North Africa (also called the Maghreb) in the later BCE and early CE periods. The Muslim conquests of the seventh century CE swept over the Maghreb, spreading the faith that is still practised today.

A later Muslim dynasty, the Abbasids, raised the Mamluk army to rule Egypt. The Mamluk era began in 1250, and was later absorbed by the Ottoman Empire and ruled from Istanbul.

Napoleon Bonaparte's brief conquest of Egypt (1798) shattered what remained of Mamluk rule, heralding a coming wave of European conquests. After the French, the British took Egypt into their empire. In the twentieth century, as the British Empire faded, Egypt became a subject of Russia's and America's competition during the Cold War, as each sought influence in Cairo.

As this snapshot illustrates, there is a long and layered history of empires. This makes the task of identifying imperial legacies anything but straightforward. While it can be easy to blame outsiders for some of the region's current woes, doing so *in isolation* is not terribly insightful. Against such a long history, the British, French, Russians and Americans were latecomers and, whether building empires of occupation or of influence, they did so on the foundations of past empires that were indigenous to the region.

Granted, the notion of 'indigenous' reflects a modern vantage point; to Arabs, Maghrebi Berbers, Persians and Turks, each may have looked foreign to the other. But their empires were built in accordance to adjacency, as neighbour conquered neighbour. Consequently the region's outline was never fixed. We may picture Arabia as the 'middle' of the Middle East, but in past centuries Turkey was a regional powerhouse, Egypt a centre of influence, and Iran an empire unto itself.

The tumultuous reality of the modern Middle East, the entanglement of war, terrorism and political revolution, means it is rarely out of world headlines, as another crisis always seems to be brewing. While we can never answer the question of 'who started it', when it comes to these abiding problems, we can approach them with the historical perspective they deserve. This requires an appreciation of the accumulated weight of imperial history, and how it has shaped different political, psychological and religious identities across the region. It is a complex imperial inheritance and untangling it requires absorbing a wide span of history.

Centuries of rising and falling empires

The historian Ibn Khaldun and the poet Khalil Gibran lived five centuries apart, and the strikingly different worlds they inhabited convey just how much the wider Middle East changed over this time, and how it inspired their creative works.

Ibn Khaldun's ancestors had touched the many corners of the Islamic world. His roots were in southern Arabia, in present-day Yemen. His family immigrated to Iberia at the time of the Muslim conquest of Andalusia in the eighth century, settling in a small city located between Cordoba, Grenada and Seville. By the thirteenth century Spanish reconquest threatened these cities, leading some Muslim families to flee as refugees to North Africa.

The Maghreb would become the theatre for Khaldun's life. Born in Tunis in 1332, he was educated in Fez and later made his name in Cairo, which is where he was buried when death took him in 1406. These cities hosted three great Islamic universities of the classic age, and some of the oldest in the world: al-Zaytunah in Tunis, founded in 737 CE; Karaouine in Fez, founded in 859 CE; and al-Azhar in Cairo, founded in 975 CE (which remains a bastion of Sunni Islamic learning to this day).

As befitted a scholar of his repute, Khaldun taught at al-Azhar later in his career. Before obtaining this prestigious post he had sailed alone to Alexandria, leaving his family in Tunis. But when he finally felt secure enough in Cairo to send for them, his wife and children perished during their voyage across the Mediterranean. Recovering from this tragedy, Khaldun saw his reputation grow. His book, *Al Muqaddimah*, is a magisterial depiction of a world in which Islam's expansion out of Arabia was well established. It presents the Islamic world's cycles of dynastic rise and decline, and the ebb and flow of its conquests, as part of the natural order of history. Crucially, the dynasties populating the pages of his work were mainly the products of the Muslim world.[5]

Five centuries later Khalil Gibran's surroundings conveyed a radically different reality. He was born in 1883 to a Christian Maronite family in Lebanon, a territory that then belonged to the Ottoman Empire. Back in the late fifteenth and sixteenth centuries the Ottoman Turks had swept out of Anatolia to conquer swathes of land, becoming the dominant face of power in the Muslim world. At its peak, the Ottoman Empire stretched from the Levant to the Gulf, and from south-east Europe to the Maghreb. As the twentieth century dawned, Ottoman control was looking vulnerable to European advances, while Ottoman subjects were agitating for freedom.

The expanding Western world was starting to grip the imagination of people across the region too. Gibran's Christian family may have thought the West offered better prospects, so they emigrated to the USA when Khalil was young. Gibran grew up in Boston, honing his poetic craft amidst a sense of cultural dislocation. His poems were written in Arabic, but the aching beauty with which they treated universal human themes has seen them translated and read the world over, long after his tragically young death in 1931. By then, Europeans had colonized much of the Middle East. Gibran's poetry in *The Prophet* is not about these themes, but contains his verses 'On Freedom', presaging the looming identity-split facing the region of his birth as it became torn between Middle Eastern and Western influences.

Two lives lived at different times in history, both offer a counterpoint for considering the changing meanings of empire in the wider Middle East: from the Islamic golden age to the region's eventual loss of competitiveness in the face of Western challenge.

Since ancient times, dynastic imperial rule has been a recurrent form of organizing politics in the region, and certain broad patterns of imperial history were established well before Islam. Mesopotamia (modern Iraq) hosted some of the earliest human settlements in the world, among them the Sumerians, forebears of the Akkadian Empire (2335–2154 BCE). On the same ground rose the Old Assyrian Empire (its foundational period is dated to 2600–2025 BCE). Its later incarnation, the Neo-Assyrian Empire (911–608 BCE), achieved a size and complexity unseen in any previous empire. Ultimately it was vanquished by an alliance between Medes (an ancient Persian people) and Babylon. Babylon later became a regional power in its own right.

And so on the story went. Throughout ancient history, power would pass from one empire to another, with the most enduring lasting for centuries. Duels between rival empires could last just as long, as was evident in the struggle between the Persians and the Greeks for regional mastery.

Persia had its own extensive pre-Islamic history, rooted in the Zoroastrian faith. At its peak, its easternmost provinces were in modern Pakistan and India, and its westernmost provinces in Egypt, Anatolia and some Greek islands. Persepolis, its capital city, featured grand palaces, the ruins of which remain near the city of Shiraz. The Persians' empire-building stoked the fears (and attracted the jealousies) of the Greeks, who defeated the Persians at Marathon in 490 BCE. So the Persians responded by invading Greece (resulting in the legendary Battle of Thermopylae in 480 BCE, when Leonidas' fabled 300 Spartans held off Persian attacks). Nearly 160 years later, Alexander the Great sacked

Persepolis in 323 BCE, sealing the end of the Persian Achaemenid Empire.[6] Alexander was captivated by the grandeurs of the East as he expanded his realm.[7] The boundaries of what we consider 'Europe' and the 'Middle East' didn't exist for him; instead, imperial frontiers were ever-changing.

Moving forward several hundred years, the superpowers of the immediate pre-Islamic era were the Sassanid and Byzantine Empires. The Sassanids had restored Persia's status. Modern Iran's sense of land, people and political culture has its roots in this period. The Sassanids fought over their frontiers with Byzantium, which had expanded into Asia Minor, Syria, Palestine, Egypt and the Balkans. Byzantium triumphed at the Battle of Nineveh in 627 CE, and temporarily restored the old Roman boundaries in the Middle East, but the path of history was about to change, as neither empire was aware of the epoch-altering developments brewing further south, deep in Arabia.[8]

The Prophet Muhammad was born in Mecca in 570 or 571 CE, and his Islamic revelation began when he was in his forties. He came from a noble tribe who were custodians of Mecca. Leading his devout followers out of the deserts, he (and his successors) built a sweeping religious-based empire, supplementing their small band of followers by forging local alliances, and by converting others to their faith. The Muslims evicted Byzantium from Palestine in 634 and from Damascus in 636. Whereas Byzantium survived for 700 years after losing these provinces, the Sassanid Empire met a definitive end. In 637, under Muslim attack, the Sassanid army was beaten. Its last king died in 651, and the Persian people eventually converted to Islam.[9]

The power and coherence of Islam as an empire was evident not least in its uptake by newly conquered peoples, whose religious conversions helped to solidify each expansion.

We can turn to Ibn Khaldun to make sense of the fate of the usurped and the conquered:

When politically ambitious men overcome the ruling dynasty and seize power, they inevitably have recourse to the customs of their predecessors and adopt most of them. At the same time, they do not neglect the customs of their own race ... The new power, in turn, is succeeded by another dynasty, and customs are further mixed with those of the new dynasty ... The eventual result is an altogether distinct [set of customs and institutions].

To Khaldun, this was the natural order of things. His reference points stretched far back in time, to the rising and falling dynasties and empires of the pre-Islamic and early Islamic ages.

With Islam's inception in the seventh century, empire-building acquired proselytizing power. A common religious vision, and the Arabic language, had diffused far and wide through conquest, but this did not usher in unity across the expanding Muslim world, as local identities and doctrinal differences stoked rivalries and led to wars between competing dynasties.

The permanent split between the Sunni and Shia branches of Islam occurred after the Prophet Muhammad's death in 632 CE. His first four successors had been his close companions, and Sunni Muslims address them as the 'Rightly Guided'. They ruled the First Islamic Caliphate (632–61 CE). Thereafter Ali, the Prophet Muhammad's cousin, was denied the leadership of the caliphate and assassinated in 661. Ali's followers carried on his struggle and his son Husayn staged a revolt in 680, only to be killed alongside his closest followers in Karbala (in southern Iraq). This seminal event gave birth to the Shia branch of Islam.[10]

There would be four caliphates altogether. The Umayyad Dynasty (661–750) was the second, and Islam's first hereditary dynasty. Its armies conquered land in the Caucasus, Sindh, North Africa and, in 711, Iberia, which paved the way for the Muslim conquest of Spain. In 732 CE Muslim armies were halted by a defeat at the Battle of Poitiers at the hands of the Franks, which stopped Islam from establishing further roots in Western Europe.

In 750 CE the third caliphate, the Abbasid Dynasty, overthrew the Umayyads. Abbasid rule endured for more than 500 years (750–1258). The Abbasids claimed legitimacy over Muslims through a line of descent from the Prophet Muhammad's uncle. This was disputed by the rival Fatimid Dynasty (909–1171), which was named after the Prophet Muhammad's daughter. Centred around Cairo, the Fatimid Dynasty captured North Africa and encroached on the Levant.

This lack of unity reflected quintessentially imperial themes: of rival dynastic claims; and of how difficult it is to maintain central authority over a patchwork of populations. While it is a sign of imperial success to have expanded the realm, doing so means ruling over more and more people, which brings its own challenges.

For Arabs, the spread of Islam and of their language – in which the Quran is written – is a proud and enduring legacy. So rapid and expansive had the Muslim conquests been that the Arabs alone could never have dominated the entire region. Whereas the Umayyad Dynasty had favoured Arabs, the Abbasid Dynasty had supplanted it partly because it had tapped into the sense of disempowerment felt by non-Arab Muslims. In the Abbasid era, former subject peoples who had converted to Islam increasingly took the mantle of steering the caliphate.

In particular the Turks edged their way into playing a role in the region's destiny. Islam arrived in Anatolia in the tenth century and was embraced by the Seljuk Turks, who traced their origin to their forebears' religious conversion in 980. The Seljuk Empire (1037–1194) brought the Fertile Crescent (an area that covers southern Turkey, the Nile Valley, the Levant and western Persia) under their control, ostensibly for the Abbasid Caliphate, to which the Seljuks had pledged their loyalty. They had snatched Syria and Palestine from the Fatimid Dynasty and, in their signature triumph, the Seljuk warrior Saladin captured Jerusalem in 1187.

Christendom poured its energies into the Crusades and tried to conquer Jerusalem. Its hostility was probably compounded by envy of the Muslim world's intellectual accomplishments during the Islamic Golden Age, which had begun in the eighth century when the sciences flourished, building on insights retained from their Greek roots and buried deep in the historical memory of the region, and uniting them with modern insights.[11]

Then, in 1258, the Mongols steamrollered a path through Baghdad, bringing the Abbasid Dynasty, and the Islamic Golden Age, to an end. The Mongols came as pagans, and those in medieval Christendom may have hoped this would subdue Islam. Instead the Mongols converted to Islam. And in 1261 the Mamluks reestablished the caliphate in Cairo. This weaker continuation of the Abbasid Dynasty lasted for centuries, but lacked both imperial power and religious legitimacy.

Ever since the First Caliphate, Islam had demonstrated its power to inspire grand conquests, and to impose an order that straddled different communities. Even when it was on the defensive, the power of its faith was demonstrated by the Mongols' religious conversion. But Islam's empires were also susceptible to succession struggles being exacerbated by rival claims of spiritual legitimacy. Moreover, the sheer extent of the Muslim world's expansion further hampered its unity.

Unbeknown to Ibn Khaldun, a new Muslim empire was starting to form during his lifetime, which, in the centuries after his death, brought a measure of coherence to this vast estate.

The Ottoman Empire's impact

Over its six centuries (1299–1923) the long existence of the Ottoman Empire brings us into modern history. From humble origins as just one of several minor Turkish principalities engaged in the war against Christian forces in the thirteenth century, the dynasty was named after its founder, Osman. Under his heirs, the Ottoman Empire steadily grew in importance. Over time it restored the caliphate to a position of security within an empire. It consolidated Muslim rule over an ever-widening myriad of territories, whilst engaging in rivalries with alternative centres of Muslim power in Egypt and Persia. Significantly, it also intensified Christendom's fears of a Muslim empire to an extent unseen since the height of the Crusades.

The Ottomans' most striking triumph was to shatter the Byzantine Empire once and for all. On 29 May 1453 Ottoman soldiers under Sultan Mehmed II had wrested control of Byzantium's capital city, Constantinople, and ransacked St Sophia church, a centrepiece of Byzantium for centuries. The sultan was apparently brought the severed head of the Byzantine emperor as assurance of victory being complete.[12]

Like all empires, the Ottoman Empire's vitality was demonstrated through conquest. Its next major triumph was to make the Arabs its subjects, conquering swathes of territory from the Arabian Peninsula to the Maghreb. Most Arabs reconciled themselves to living under the sultan's rule and accepted their place within the dominant Muslim empire of the age.[13] Those who resisted (as Mamluk Egypt attempted to) were summarily dispatched, thanks to the military might and technological sophistication of the Ottoman armies and their mastery of gunpowder weapons (the Mamluks were fighting back with swords). Sultan Selim the Grim absorbed the Mamluk Empire, which included Egypt, Syria, the Levant and the Hejaz – the site of Mecca and Medina – into the Ottoman Empire. Ottoman prestige was further enhanced by becoming the guardian of the Hejaz.

The Ottoman Empire reached the peak of its powers in the sixteenth century and, in doing so, established a number of precedents that have had an enduring impact on the region.

Starting in the 1500s, wars between the Ottoman Empire and its arch-rival, the Safavid Empire, hardened the schism between Sunni and Shia Islam. The Persian Safavid Empire lasted for almost 250 years (1501–1736), and its name was derived from an early founder, Sheikh Safi. The Safavids practised religious uniformity in Persia, bringing further coherence to its people's culture.[14] Shia Islam thrived in Persia, but this left some of its followers facing persecution elsewhere (for example, when Ottoman forces massacred Shias in Anatolia). Baghdad was a focal point of the wars between Ottoman and Safavid armies, and control over it changed hands several times. In 1638, when Ottoman armies captured Baghdad from the Persians, the resulting Treaty of Zuhab fixed the Ottoman/Safavid boundary more or less in line with present-day Iraq and Iran.[15]

Another precedent was established through the Ottoman contest with Christian Europe, changing their frontiers and influencing their perceptions of each other in ways that still resonate.

After the conquest of Constantinople, later sultans tried to top this accomplishment by conquering Vienna. This forever eluded the Ottoman armies, despite several attempts to do so, with the final failed push occurring in 1683. Nevertheless the sultans managed to hold territory in south-east Europe and in the Balkans. Christendom's fear was palpable – the Ottoman Empire seemed right on the doorstep and posed a genuine threat over many centuries through its expansion. The Ottomans became a bogeyman for several generations of Europeans, and these negative portrayals compounded views already held from the era of the Crusades: that Muslims represented the 'other', and that conquests by Muslim empires posed an existential threat.

The zenith of Ottoman power in the sixteenth century happened to coincide with Europe's Renaissance. Over time, the mercantile and military accomplishments of Europe's empires nibbled away at Ottoman territory.[16] There was no instant reversal of fortunes and, for a long time, the Ottoman Empire went toe-to-toe with Europe's upstarts, tussling and allying with them, right until the eighteenth century.[17]

In 1768 Sultan Mustafa III declared war on Catherine the

Great of Russia, but humiliation followed, as the once-mighty war craft of the Ottomans was shown to be outdated. The Russian Navy decisively defeated the Ottoman Navy in the Aegean Sea. In 1783 Russia annexed Crimea, and this spurred the Russian Empire to present itself as a protector of fellow Orthodox peoples in the Balkans, which further undermined the authority of Ottoman rule there.

Another sign of the regional balance of power tilting in Europe's favour was Napoleon Bonaparte's invasion of Egypt in 1798 and the resultant defeat of the Mamluks. After the French left, Ottoman sultans struggled to re-establish their control, and a strong independent ruler took power in Egypt. Muhammad Ali (1769–1849) wanted to build a mainly Arabic-speaking empire, and he raised an army that staved off the Ottomans at the battles of Konya in 1832 and Nezib in 1839.[18]

In a further indication of how the world was changing, it took a British intervention *on behalf* of the Ottomans to suppress Ali's revolt. This was a sensitive time for the Ottoman Empire. It had faced its first overtly nationalist uprising in Greece in 1821 (in that instance, too, British intervention was vital to Ottomans). In Egypt, the Ottoman sultans reluctantly accepted Ali's local authority. They even put Ali's warlike tendencies to use by commissioning him to suppress another revolt elsewhere in the empire. Ali's eventual successor, Said Pasha, led Egyptian troops against this new threat deep in the Arabian Desert, posed by the religiously devout Wahhabis, who practised an orthodox interpretation of Islam.

Such was the vast ecosystem of the Ottoman Empire: holding together so many different subject peoples was a tricky balancing act, and traces of the Ottoman approach still remain.

The 'exotic yurt arrangement called Ottomanism', as described by the journalist Christopher de Bellaigue, was prone to teetering.[19] This unique characteristic of Ottoman rule was the pragmatic devolving of power to subject peoples. Local Arab tribes would be made the protectors of certain regions, for example, while the *millet* system allowed communities like the Kurds, Jews and Albanians to live autonomously and be represented by their own leaders and theologians in everyday affairs (albeit pledging their ultimate loyalty to the sultan in Istanbul). There were no 'Ottoman people' as such, only the various subject communities.[20] This was how the empire survived for as long as it did – and, crucially, why local tribal and ethnic identities have survived for so long right across the region.

Arrangements like the *millet* system worked for quite some time, until the Ottoman Empire started to buckle under the pressures of competing with rival empires. The sultans were aware that they were losing authority and falling behind. They responded with the *Tanzimat* reforms of the nineteenth century, modernizing their military in line with European models and developing new administrative structures, which made the Ottoman Empire bureaucratically run and dynastically ruled (like the Austro-Hungarian and Russian Empires).[21] However, as the *Tanzimat* reforms imposed greater coherence and control over the empire, this created a backlash from subject peoples who had previously been happy to pay lip-service to Ottoman rule, but now preferred autonomy.

The straw that broke the camel's back was the Ottoman Empire's fateful decision to enter the Great War alongside the German and Austro-Hungarian empires. By the war's end they had all collapsed (as had the tsar's Russian Empire). During the war there had been Ottoman victories at Gallipoli and in Iraq, but the empire was rending itself apart, as Russia and Britain exploited its vulnerability across the sheer number of different places and peoples it ruled.

The Russians seized on the potential to support an Armenian revolt against the Ottomans, which ended in tragedy. Ottoman soldiers subjected the Armenian people to collective punishment, resulting in a genocide in which an estimated 1.5 million

Armenians were killed. The British fared better in backing the Arabs to revolt against Ottoman rule. British officers such as T. E. Lawrence (Lawrence of Arabia) promised the Arabs a state of their own after the war if they rebelled, which they did, opening up another front amidst the Ottomans' crumbling efforts to hold their empire together.

Having existed for six centuries, when the final collapse of the Ottoman Empire came after the Great War, it created a huge void. How it was filled has defined the Middle East ever since.

From indigenous imperialists to European colonizers

Circling like vultures, Britain and France tussled over the spoils of the former Ottoman Empire. The Sykes-Picot Agreement (1916), named after the officials who concluded it, placed Syria and Lebanon under French control and Mesopotamia (later named Iraq) under British control. It paid lip-service to British wartime promises to support an Arab state. Kingmakers in the most literal sense, Britain supported some Arab dynastic claims over others, for example proclaiming Faisal of the Hashemite Dynasty the King of Iraq in 1921.

Competing with Sykes-Picot for lasting notoriety was the Balfour Declaration (1917), which was a decision by Britain on how to rule Palestine.[22] Britain decided to sever Transjordan from Palestine in 1921, backing the Hashemite Dynasty's rule in Jordan (a royal line that continues today).

Seeing this European carve-up, a former Ottoman military officer took matters into his own hands to preserve the independence of Anatolia. In 1919 Mustafa Kemal (later known as 'Atatürk') led a Turkish army that fought to prevent a partition of Anatolia. This began the formation of modern Turkey. In 1923 the caliphate was abolished and, in a feat of condensed state-building, Turkey's language was changed from Ottoman Arabic to modern Turkish.

In Persia the Cossack officer Reza Kahn seized power in 1921 to become prime minister and, in 1925 secured the monarchy for himself and his Pahlavi dynasty. He stressed to the League of Nations that his country was breaking free from British and Russian influence, and encouraged foreigners to call his country Iran, rather than referring to it as Persia. Domestically, he expanded the army and strengthened the Iranian state. Turkey and Iran today are two of the most robust states in the region, having stabilised themselves independently in the 1920s.[23]

Countries that were able to immediately throw off the mantle of empire and adapt to being a new nation-state, without foreign interference, have shown themselves to be more stable than some that were forced to become vassals of other empires. Turkey and Iran were, of course, where the seats of power lay for previous empires. The Arabs, by contrast, were swallowed up by the 'mandates system', a 1920s version of 'empire-lite'.

The 1919 Paris Peace Conference, the influence of US President Wilson's 'fourteen points of peace' and the League of Nations (the Geneva-based precursor to the UN) had fostered the start of the end of colonization. Britain and France were given mandates to rule in the Middle East, which in practice dovetailed comfortably with their imperial habits. Former colonial governors sat on the Mandates Commission in Geneva, which operated by picking pliant local rulers, while allowing London and Paris to maintain effective control.[24]

It wasn't until April 1946, with France and Britain in no position to argue otherwise because of their exertions during the Second World War, that the brand-new UN wound up the Syria, Lebanon and Transjordan mandates. The Palestinian mandate was doomed from the start. British authorities could not please either side, and Jewish Zionists turned violently against Britain. No sooner had Britain left than the new state of Israel was fighting the Palestinians in 1948.

Elsewhere in the newly independent Arab world, military rulers were taking power in Syria (1949), Egypt (1952) and Iraq (1958).[25]

With the end of the imperial age and the start of the Cold War, these rulers tried to steer a new destiny. In Egypt, Colonel Nasser articulated a pan-Arabist vision that marked a concerted attempt to take control of the region's political future. Egypt tried to break out of the post-colonial state system by advocating a 'United Arab Republic', but Iraq decided to stay out, unwilling to accept Nasser's hegemony. Syria was the only participant, but it later found it hard to cohabit with Egypt in a single state.

Nasser's high point came elsewhere, with the nationalisation of the Suez Canal. This convinced Britain and France to ally with Israel and wage war on Egypt in 1956 – only for these countries to be rebuked by the USA and forced to withdraw in ignominy. Nasser's low point, and the war that broke him, came in 1967 when, in a self-declared action on behalf of the Palestinians, he took on Israel, and his Arab coalition army suffered a resounding defeat. The Six-Day War was the start of Israel's occupation of Palestinian lands. Three years later Nasser's health deteriorated and he died.

Oil had heightened the incentives for outsiders to retain influence in the region. Oil was discovered in Iran (1908), Iraq (1927), Saudi Arabia (1938), Algeria (1956) and Libya (1959). Initially Western companies enjoyed unfettered access. British Petroleum has its origins in the Anglo-Persian Oil Company, which kept a lion's share of the profits from the locals. It was Libya's ruler Colonel Qaddafi who struck a note of impertinence by arguing for a less inequitable split in profits between the foreign oilmen and the local government. And it was not until the 1970s that Arab states could transform their hold over the supply of oil into geopolitical power, by manipulating its supply and therefore its price, which impacted upon economies all over the world.[26]

Prying eyes from abroad have been attracted by the Middle East ever since ancient times, due to the wealth of its culture and its strategic positioning at the juncture between Asia, Africa and Europe. Now the prying eyes were accompanied by grabbing hands, as oil raised the stakes for influence and control. During the Cold War the superpowers competed for influence over newly independent oil-producing states, which only added to the sense of the Middle East being the subject of other nations' imperial schemes.

In a region so accustomed to producing its own past empires, adapting to these new realities proved difficult. It required a shifting mindset to accept that decisions made far away – whether in London, Paris, Moscow or Washington – could dramatically affect the Middle East. At first it was colonization by the European empires; next, it was the oppressive influence of the superpowers. To this day, parts of the Middle East flounder under a torrent of post-imperial pressures.

Orphaned lands and post-imperial instabilities

Of all the Middle East's enduring problems, that of the Palestinians and the Israelis has remained a crucible for tension, violence and distrust. There is tragedy not just in its duration and the suffering on all sides that has ensued, but in the fact that it has arisen through the relative success of Israel to adapt to the post-imperial world, and the comparative failure of the Palestinians and their supporters in the region.

This is evident today when passing from Israel's securitized cities into the West Bank and to the city of Ramallah, the de facto capital of the Palestinian state-in-waiting. It has been waiting for so long, in fact, that its folk hero and longtime resistance leader Yasser Arafat died in 2004 and was interred in a pristine white mausoleum in Ramallah. Since the 1960s Arafat had led the Palestinian Liberation Organization (PLO) in its guerrilla war against Israel, before switching tack in the 1990s to take part in failed peace talks with Israel. In doing so, Arafat ceded the terrorist mantle to a newer Palestinian armed group, Hamas, which inherited the war against Israel. During this time several generations of Palestinians have lived and died without seeing their hopes for a nation-state realized, with many Palestinians having fled to neighbouring countries such as Jordan, due to the incessant fighting with Israel.

The Palestinians have become the *cause célèbre* of post-imperial upset, both on the Arab street and in leftist Western political circles, because they are considered to have been the ultimate losers in the region during decolonization, and since then have been the victims of Israel's aggressive self-defence.

For its part, the creation of the state of Israel was a response to the sustained persecution suffered by Jews in Europe, notably the pogroms and murders that took place when Jews found themselves in other people's empires. Theodor Herzl (1860–1904), an intellectual proponent behind the idea of Jewish statehood, wrote of the Jews that 'wherever they live in perceptible numbers, they are more or less persecuted'. The example he gave was of Jewish persecution in the Russian Empire, and of German Jews 'receiving a good beating occasionally'.[27] He was writing this decades before the Holocaust, in which millions of Jews were the victims of a campaign of genocidal annihilation by the Nazis. Herzl's calls for the 'restoration of the Jewish state' gained new gravity in the 1940s. When he spoke of restoration, his reference point was the Hebrew kingdoms of Israel and Judah (contemporaries of the Assyrians in the ancient world).

This has imbued the State of Israel with a powerful sense of destiny, and a will to survive in a region where it has few natural friends. The European roots of many of its inhabitants, and the strategic alliance that its government has forged with the USA, has helped Israel to consolidate its position in the post-imperial Middle East as a country propagating a 'Don't mess with us' message. By contrast, the Palestinians became reliant on the Arab states to support their claims to statehood, but countries such as Egypt have not fared especially well in the modern world, let alone being able to fight successfully for Palestine.

Where the Israel–Palestine dispute is concerned, the dominant imperial legacies have been those of the British mandate, and of the competing claims for Jewish and Arab nationalism that began in the nineteenth century. In earlier empires, Jews and Muslims could coexist successfully. During the height of the Ottoman Empire, for example, Jews enjoyed freedom to practise their religion as subjects of the sultan. There is no inevitable hostility between Jews and Muslims but, while both communities may have been able to fit into an empire, clearly it has not been possible to fit them into a state.

Post-imperial Turkey's new sultan

The grandeur of old Ottoman imperial ambitions still radiates from modern Istanbul. The Hagia Sophia, once a great Christian basilica, was turned into a mosque after Mehmed II conquered Constantinople. The Blue Mosque, right opposite, was commissioned by Sultan Ahmet I in 1616, in order to leave a symbol of his rule.

When you take a boat ride around the Golden Horn into the Bosporus Strait, the Topkapi Palace's sprawling splendour is visible. This was the Ottoman Empire's hub of power, although later sultans preferred the Dolmabahce Palace, also visible further up the Bosporus. From here, Ottoman power extended into the Middle East, North Africa and Europe. The Bosporus Strait eventually opens up into the Black Sea, which is where the Ottoman armies fared so badly against Russia's.

Turkey, the Western world's bridge to the Middle East, is now at the edge of a region that its Anatolian predecessors once dominated. This has split Turkey's identity between two regions: the Middle East and Europe. The notion of Turkey joining the EU was floated in the early 2000s, but Germany and France were not keen and quashed the idea. Turkey was left to its own devices as its connections to Europe remained at an arm's length.

Since 2002 Turkey has been ruled by President Recep Tayyip

Erdogan, who took office and has kept on winning elections. A modern sultan for the democratic age, Erdogan has had no interest in giving up power. At first his political party, the moderately Islamic AKP, seemed a welcome break from years of military coups and military rule. In a turning point in 2013, Erdogan ordered a crackdown on peaceful protestors in Istanbul's Gezi Park. Three years later members of Turkey's military tried to get rid of him in a coup, but the plotters were thwarted by Erdogan's loyalists. After the 15 July 2016 coup attempt, his government jailed thousands of alleged conspirators from the military, Civil Service, academia and elsewhere. In 2019, when the AKP candidate lost the mayoral elections in Istanbul, Erdogan ignored the result and decreed that the election would be rerun (only for the AKP to lose again).

His dogged determination to monopolize power is a product both of Erdogan's personality and ambition and of a tradition of strong central rule reasserting itself, honed during the long imperial experience, during which time it became synonymous with authority. Now this aspect of Ottoman history has reared its head again.

Turkey has a diminished consciousness of its Ottoman legacies (aside from tourist attractions and soap operas featuring sultans). In order to make the jump from 'empire' to 'state', Turkey tried to jettison a lot of its past in one fell swoop. This is illustrated by its changing language: whereas a century ago an educated Turk would have a command of Ottoman Turkish, which was written with the Arabic script, the alphabet was changed in 1925 to the Latin script. The writer Elif Shafak observes that 'today the average Turkish citizen cannot read anything that dates from before that year: the text on an Ottoman grave, the inscription on a dry fountain or a poem carved in marble ... Every day millions of Istanbulites walk by the remnants of the past without seeing, without knowing. Somehow we have become a society that cannot read the tombstones of its ancestors. It's odd that a city so ancient now has the memory of an infant."[28]

Severing the bonds with the imperial past has also become a matter of life and death regarding the Kurdish problem. As we have already seen, back in Ottoman days the multi-ethnic empire was held together not by seeking to convert its subjects, but by creating the *millet* system of different autonomous communities, each with representation by its own leaders and theologians. The modern Turkish state has been far less accommodating, and for a while did not acknowledge that the Kurds even existed as a distinct people, arguing that they should adopt a Turkish civic identity (which is how Atatürk interpreted the model of the 'nation-state' when he founded Turkey in 1923).

Compared to Ankara or Istanbul, Turkey's south-east Kurdish heartlands feel like a different country. Diyarbakir, Turkish Kurdistan's unofficial capital, has a big-city feel, but when I travelled to the nearby city of Mardin, its architecture and narrow passageways felt far more Middle Eastern in flavour. I made the trip as part of my doctoral research into the Kurdish rebellion that had broken out in 1984. The PKK resistance group are still thought of as freedom fighters by some Kurds, but they are a violent group and are condemned as terrorists by the Turkish authorities. The war persists to this day, with neither side capable or willing of compromising with the other, despite more than 40,000 deaths.[29]

To resolve the war with the PKK also means addressing the issue of where Turkey's Kurds fit into the Turkish state. Clearly this is not a simple matter, given that the Kurds are spread between Iraq, Syria and Iran as well, and none of them were granted their own state during decolonization. Nevertheless, while Iraq's Kurds have gained de facto independence in recent decades, the Turkish state has been inflexible.

The Kurdish problem remains shrouded in an imperial shadow. In its golden age, the Ottoman Empire had contributed positively to relations between Turks and Kurds, thanks to the multicultural, multi-ethnic nature of the empire and its allowance of religious freedom. When the Ottoman Empire collapsed, Atatürk responded energetically to the demands of forging a modern state, bonded around a civic notion of nationality – but, in doing so, modern Turkey lost the feel for diversity that its Ottoman forebears possessed.

The Saudi and Iranian collision course

To a historian of empires, it would make complete sense that the Kingdom of Saudi Arabia and the Islamic Republic of Iran are vying for regional dominance. As the custodians of the Sunni and Shia branches of Islam respectively, an undercurrent of sectarianism has underpinned their power struggle. Unlike the imperial era, when armies clashed in great pitched battles, today's antagonists have instead opted for waging proxy wars and paying each other's enemies to fight for their interests in the region. The current rulers of Riyadh and Tehran both reflect certain older imperial antiquities, and have tussled with the other as much for reasons of domestic posturing as they have to conquer the region.

The Kingdom of Saudi Arabia was established in 1932 under the leadership of Ibn Saud. The Ottomans had tried to place Arabia under greater control, occupying it in 1818 and 1871. Ibn Saud sided with the British during the Great War, benefiting considerably from British subsidies.[30] After the war, Ibn Saud took over the Hejaz in 1925. His personality and his alliances still define Saudi Arabia.[31] He fathered his first four successors and, to give his progenies hegemony over Arabia, partnered with a puritanical Islamic reform movement founded by 'Abd al-Wahhab.

Wahhabism is the official faith of Saudi Arabia, but its influence has been felt far and wide across the region and around the globe. As they looked across the Middle East, the Wahhabis were concerned that post-colonial modernity was leading to secularization and Westernization. So they took action, contributing to an Islamist counter-reformation, funding movements elsewhere that reflected their staunchly Islamic principles. As the custodian of Mecca, Islam's holiest site, and through its propagation of Wahhabism, Saudi Arabia has staked a claim for regional leadership.

None of this influence would have been possible without money. Thanks to its oil wealth, the Saudis have attracted an underclass of South Asian labourers and an elite of Western consultants to supplement the workforce. Saudi Arabia's warm relationship with the USA, a customer of its oil, has become a fulcrum of global politics. But it is not only about money: unlike the Iranians, the Saudi state has always accepted the Western world's dominant role in the Middle East's post-imperial transitions.

Dynastic rule remains in Saudi Arabia, and it is still run by descendants of Ibn Saud. In 2017 the ageing King Salman placed the young Crown Prince Mohammed bin Salman (or 'MBS', as he is dubbed) in effective control. Under MBS, the kingdom has more actively staked out its claim as a regional powerhouse, notably in opposition to Iran's regional role by, for example, embroiling itself in Yemen's civil war, where Saudi Arabia and Iran have backed opposite sides.

The contest between Iran and Saudi Arabia has a clear imperial heritage, in how the doctrinal split between Shia and Sunni became entrenched in the clash between the Ottoman and Safavid Empires. In the modern incarnation of this contest, Iran seeks influence from Mesopotamia to the Mediterranean. And, thanks to the wars of 1982 in Lebanon, 2003 in Iraq and 2011 in Syria, Iran has steadily extended its reach through the involvements of its Revolutionary Guard military forces, and through its sponsorship of the Lebanese armed group Hezbollah.

Whether Iran can become a regional leader is, above all, the issue that has energized Israel, Saudi Arabia and the USA, each of which has displayed its own obsessions to try and hem Iran in.

Iran stands for everything the Saudis do not. Opposition to Western empires of influence has become Iran's political creed since the 1979 revolution threw off the rule of the Western-backed shah. Since then, rather than cosying up to America, as the Saudis have done, Iran has been defiantly anti-American.[32]

Iran's revolution in 1979 was a revolt against foreign influence, notably after the 1953 coup masterminded by the American CIA and British SIS intelligence services. The coup involved the removal of Iran's elected prime minister in order to elevate the status of its monarch, Shah Reza Pahlavi, who was more compliant with the West. In the years afterwards, Iran hosted thousands of US workers and bought US arms. Every action has a counter-action and, in the 1960s, the Shia cleric Ayatollah Ruhollah Khomeini began to preach against the shah's corrupting US influences. In 1979 Khomeini returned to Tehran from Paris to a rapturous welcome, and to a revolution that set Iran in an antagonistic stance with America and the West that persists today. Pahlavi's regime was overthrown, the USA and the UK bitterly denounced, and Iran became a Shia theocracy.

Denunciations of Western colonialism are still occasionally invoked. Iran's current Supreme Leader, Ayatollah Khamaeni, said in a 2007 TV address: 'Why, may you ask, should we adopt an offensive stance? Are we at war with the world? No, this is not the meaning. We believe the world owes us something. Over the issue of the colonial policies of the colonial world, we are owed something.'[33]

The theme resurfaced in an open letter published online in January 2015 and addressed 'To the Youth in Europe and North America': 'The histories of the US and Europe are ashamed of slavery, embarrassed by the colonial period ... I would like to ask [Western] intellectuals as to why the public conscience in the West awakens and comes to its senses after a delay of several decades or centuries. Why should the revision of collective conscience apply to the distant past and not to current problems?'[34]

The 'Great Satan' of the American bogeyman and the 'Little Satan' of its British ally have become a perennial feature of the way the Iranian government perceives its own history, as a proud bastion of resistance against Western imperialism past and present.

Imperial history remains an active reference point and even rears its head in Twitter disputes. When in 2019 Donald Trump directed his sabre-rattling against Iran, by building up US forces in the region, Iran's foreign minister tweeted the following response: Trump 'hopes to achieve what Alexander, Genghis & other aggressors failed to do. Iranians have stood tall for millennia while aggressors all gone'.[35] It is a matter of post-imperial pride for Iran to stand up to the USA.

Which makes it all the more ironic that the US military did Iran a favour in 2003, through the destruction of Iran's arch-rival, former Iraqi dictator Saddam Hussein. Iran and Iraq had fought a terrible war for much of the 1980s (incidentally, across the fault lines of the old wars that involved the Safavid Empire). In 2003 the US invasion of Iraq removed Iran's biggest local enemy, despite George W. Bush's administration having also named Iran in its 'Axis of Evil' of rogue states.

Amongst other things, this outcome illustrated just how ignorant the USA was of Middle Eastern imperial history, and why, in a region of such historical complexity, there are plenty of hornets' nests that should only be poked with extreme caution; or, better still, left well alone.

Al-Qaeda and ISIS, the new barbarians at the gates

Back in the age of empires, the caliphates safeguarded the Islamic order. With modern Turkey's decision to end the caliphate in 1924, Sunni Islam was left to find its place in the new world of post-colonial states. Whereas in the imperial age the relationship between politics and religion had been a co-dependent one, Middle Eastern governments seemed now to have other concerns. Modernity had ruptured long-established traditions.[36]

Over the last hundred years the struggles across the Muslim world waged in the name of religion were largely defensive: to preserve an Islamic heritage and gain independence from Western ideas. Political Islam (or 'Islamism') reflected a number of these post-imperial concerns. First, it filled the vacuum created by the absence of the caliphate. Second, it allowed pious Muslims to influence their newly independent countries.

This is the void that Egypt's Muslim Brotherhood wanted to fill. In 1951 the Egyptian writer Sayyid Qutb joined the Brotherhood, and tried to use it as a revolutionary vehicle through which to return Islamic principles to prominence in Egypt, instead of the rule of posturing generals like Nasser. According to Qutb: '... the Islamic world was comprised of a number of provinces with widely differing races and cultures and ruled from a single centre. This is a mark of empire! But it is merely an outward mark ... It is more appropriate to say that [Islam] was worldwide in its tendency because of its ... goal of gathering all humanity under its banner of equality.'[37]

His revolutionary activities earned Qutb a decade of torture and imprisonment, followed by his execution in 1966 – but not before his writings, and his dedication to his mission, had forged a connection between Islam and martyrdom that inspired many after him to stage acts of terrorism.

This included the Islamist militant who in 1981 killed President Anwar Sadat (Nasser's successor). The assassin, who belonged to the 'Egyptian Islamic Jihad' group, knew he was on a suicide mission, although he survived the attack and was arrested and only later executed by the Egyptian authorities. In de Bellaigue's words, 'Qutb and his fellow martyrs set a standard for defiance in the face of tyranny ... Victory doesn't go to the last man standing, but he who dies last.'[38] Sadat's death was a seminal moment that announced the arrival of modern militant Islam.

The path to the formation of al-Qaeda began here. Egyptian doctor Ayman al-Zawahiri formed al-Qaeda with Osama bin Laden, who came from Saudi Arabia. In the 1980s and 1990s al-Zawahiri and bin Laden constructed their diagnosis of what was going wrong in the region: foreign empires were taking over and corrupting Muslim lands. The first empire they took on was the USSR, which had occupied Afghanistan throughout the 1980s. Al-Qaeda assembled a band of volunteers to fight the Soviets. Bin Laden's contribution to this guerrilla war was primarily financial, drawing on his family's Saudi wealth. When the USSR withdrew from Afghanistan, bin Laden and al-Zawahiri felt confident that their efforts had helped to expel an empire.

Their next concern became the USA, which, in the 1990s, had dramatically increased its military presence in Saudi Arabia (initially to wage the 1991 Gulf War against Iraq after it had annexed Kuwait, but afterwards staying on and retaining its military influence over the Gulf region). Bin Laden was incensed that a Western army seemed in no rush to leave the country where Islam's holy cities of Mecca and Medina were located.

In al-Qaeda's worldview, the malign influence of the Americans and Israel had corrupted the Middle East. The solution was a violent Islamist revolution: 'The masters in Washington and Tel Aviv are using the [Arab] regimes to protect their interests and to fight battles against the Muslims on their behalf . . . Therefore, we must move the battle to the enemy's grounds to burn the hands of those who ignite fire in our countries.'[39] Al-Qaeda fervently believed in a fightback against America's informal empire. This motivated its attacks against US embassies in East Africa in 1998; against the USS *Cole* warship in a Yemeni port in 2000; and, ultimately, the 9/11 attacks.

The scale of the jihadist problem has since developed into one of the world's major challenges, with numerous countries across the world suffering terrorist attacks perpetrated by al-Qaeda and, more recently, by ISIS. The perversion of the Islamic faith that these movements draw on has tended to capture most attention in the West, leading to a distinctly distorted view of the religion as a whole. The underlying post-imperial discontent that lies behind their terrorism garners less attention. The jihadists are waging an open-ended war against what they perceive to be a corrupting Western influence that has spread right across the Muslim world and is inherent in the post-colonial state system itself.

This was brought into sharp relief by ISIS during its short and incredibly violent existence. ISIS managed an embryonic empire-building project. In 2014 the group made great stock of abrogating the Sykes-Picot border between Syria and Iraq, when it mounted a spectacular military offensive that cut across both countries. The jihadists wanted to erase these lines on the map and return the Muslim lands to a pre-colonial state, where the Islamic religion and culture could predominate. An ISIS propaganda video called *The Breaking of the Borders* proclaimed: 'This is not the first border we will break. Inshallah, we break other borders also, but we start with this one.' The ISIS leader Abu Bakr al-Baghdadi said that 'this blessed advance will not stop until we hit the last nail in the coffin of the Sykes-Picot conspiracy'.

There were more proximate factors behind the rise of ISIS, notably the instability gripping the Middle East ever since the US invasion of Iraq in 2003, and the Arab Spring in 2011. The motivations of the foreign fighters who flocked from across the world to join ISIS varied, from the romantic associations that some saw in becoming a revolutionary holy warrior, to adventure-seekers with violent tendencies, and young people who had fallen for the online propaganda put out by ISIS that promised some sort of religious paradise. Behind all the events and individuals associated with the rise of ISIS were great historical forces that gave its followers the sense that they were doing God's will to remake the region and to re-establish the caliphate.

The iconography of ISIS laid claim to a distant Islamic imperial past, to when the Prophet Muhammad first conquered the region. Capturing the Syrian town of Dabiq in 2015 was of great significance to ISIS members, since Dabiq had featured in an ancient prophecy as the location of an apocalyptical final battle between Muslims and 'Romans' (which is interpreted as relating to the armies of outsiders). *Dabiq* was also adopted as the title of the ISIS propaganda magazine.

ISIS ended up inspiring so many attacks of terrorism in countries all over the world that the jihadists effectively became today's barbarians at the gates of statehood. Dozens of countries sent their armed forces to contribute to its defeat, including the USA and its Western allies, and regional countries like Jordan and Saudi Arabia, while Russia mounted its own anti-ISIS military campaign in Syria. By 2019 there was little of ISIS left in the territorial sense, its ground having been retaken after years of fighting, but its millenarian ideas are still relevant, in the minds of its supporters, and those who are still trying to connect to these ideas online.

The jihadists' perversion of religion only explains so much, and as the contemporary philosopher prince Ghazi bin Muhammad writes, 'every religion has a ghoul that follows it around, misquoting and misusing its texts for its own purposes'.[40] In the context of imperial history, the rise of the jihadists has shown just how conjoined notions of religion and empire were in the Middle East's history and how, in the absence of an empire, it could become an obsession for the jihadists to rebuild it.

Breaking the imperial habits of past generations

The Middle East came to exist in a world of empires and caliphates; one hundred years ago it faced a difficult transition into a world of European colonization; and in recent decades it has subsequently faced another transition, this time into the post-imperial world. The legacies of such a long imperial past can only ever be managed, never negated entirely. Moreover, various problems facing the region today somehow entangle with each other and with the distant past, making them seem unresolvable.

To make sense of this knotty collection of ongoing problems, it is instructive to contemplate what the absence of formal empires has wrought for the wider Middle East. And, dare one say it, to consider whether some form of *indigenous* empire might historically have been the route to a relative balance between the region's competing interests.

The scholar Efraim Karsh runs with this argument, highlighting 'the region's millenarian imperial tradition', which is conflicted 'between the reality of state nationalism and the dream of an empire packaged as a unified "Arab nation" or the worldwide "Islamic umma" [community of Muslims]'.[41] The Middle East's adaption to the post-imperial world has been a troubled one, because empire has been part of the region's historical DNA for so long.

As one travels across the region, vestiges of an imperial past are visible in the ruins and in the museums, and in the nature of today's problems. The question, therefore, revolves around these lingering effects, and how to reference history responsibly when grappling with contemporary problems. The Middle East is not riven with primordial 'ancient hatreds', but by a long, complex and layered dynastic imperial past which resonates differently depending on where in the region one is standing.

It can be intellectually and emotionally comforting – or simply politically convenient – to blame mainly the oil-hungry influences of Americans, Russians and Europeans for creating a mess in the region. There is historical evidence to back up such beliefs, in terms of the colonial legacies that haunt the problems of places such as Palestine and Iraq. And there is recent evidence of neo-imperial action, like the US military invasion of Iraq in 2003 and Russia's military intervention in Syria in 2015. However, these episodes are only a part of the historical puzzle.

Nor is it possible to understand the modern Middle East with sole reference to the end of the Ottoman Empire. To do so would neglect the incredibly long imperial heritage of the region, which is as long as recorded history itself. Present and future rulers in Baghdad, Cairo, Damascus, Ankara, Riyadh and Tehran are unlikely to gaze upon their region through anything other than historically tinted glasses – as will future generations of jihadists. Power hierarchies in the region will develop in ways that reflect these varied imperial histories.

The only way to take in the full picture is to grasp this layered history, these different stages of empire, and the multiple perspectives it has generated. Western interventions have created and scarred the modern Middle East in certain ways, but the region's own patterns of conquest, control, domination and submission have had far deeper foundations.

EIGHT

AFRICA'S SCRAMBLE BEYOND COLONIALISM

Does the white man understand our custom about land? How can he when he does not even speak our tongue? But he says that our customs are bad; and our own brothers who have taken up his religion also say that our customs are bad.

Chinua Achebe (1930–2013), *Things Fall Apart*[1]

Colonies were meant to be exploited both for the mother country and for those who came to settle in our area . . . when you assess the achievements and failures of Africa you must always keep this background in mind.

Nelson Mandela (1918–2013), 'Africa and Its Position in the World Today'[2]

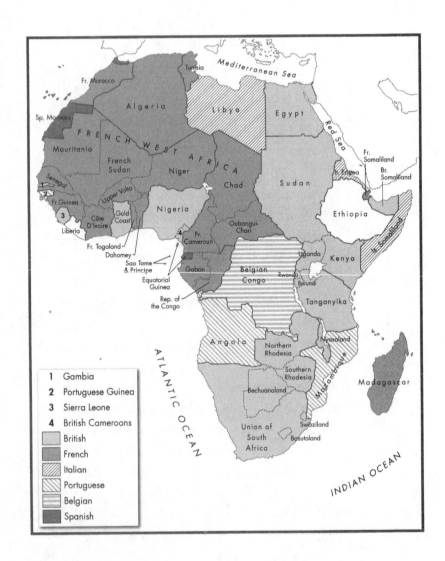

Map 12 The Scramble for Africa, c. 1920

The cool evening air of the outdoor polling station offered no hint of the burning tyres and tear gas soon to come. The Kenya that I recalled from long stays during my youth was often unsettled around polling day and a little unrest was always to be expected, but this time the descent into violence was to be genuinely hellish.

It was 27 December 2007, the evening of the presidential election. I was serving as an election observer for the EU, alongside a young Hungarian diplomat, and we were posted to Nakuru in the Rift Valley province, north-west of the capital, Nairobi. Our day had been spent patrolling remote polling stations in an EU-emblazoned Land Rover, traversing our appointed 'area of responsibility', just as dozens of other observers were doing across Kenya to see whether the voting process was fair.

To little avail; as the final results from the regions were tallied back in Nairobi, allegations of electoral fraud were flung between the candidates. Neither Mwai Kibaki nor Raila Odinga could afford to concede defeat. Each politician represented a different ethnic constituency. Kibaki, the incumbent and Kenya's third president since independence, flew the flag for the Gikuyu people. Odinga did the same for the Luo. His father, a Luo chief, had been a key figure in Kenya's independence struggle and later vice-president. The top job had never yet gone to a Luo candidate, and Odinga was not going to let his chance slip away. In the course of their mutual intransigence, a thousand people were to die.

No longer playing for votes, Luo and Gikuyu militias were now playing for blood. Kenya went up like a lighted match after election day. Riots consumed Nairobi and death squads stalked the Rift Valley, retaliating blindly against members of other communities. Law and order broke down, and looting compounded the chaos. Our powerlessness made me uneasy. It was not in the EU's remit to do more than point out where the cheating had occurred (which was in the central tallying process). So, alongside my colleagues, we set out on the main road from Nakuru to Nairobi.

Along the way I received a warning from a roadside seller, whose oddly relaxed tone suggested that none of this was taking him by surprise: 'Don't drive up *that* road,' he said, pointing, 'there are Luo and they are very angry people.' We followed his advice. As so many foreigners have done in the past, we returned to our safe compound as the violence that some people choose to call 'tribal' kicked off.

Machete-wielding gangs; displaced people; corruption; politicians refusing to surrender power – in the example of one sorry episode, several themes converged that have surfaced across the continent ever since independence. Even Kenya, one of Africa's more prosperous and stable states, was not immune. It eventually needed Kofi Annan, the former UN Secretary-General, to mediate between Kibaki and Odinga and ease them into a power-sharing agreement.

Later, both men were called to The Hague for their alleged culpability in having encouraged the militias. However, the cases against them were eventually dropped, perhaps because the International Criminal Court was being criticized in some quarters for its Western moralizing on Africa. And perhaps also because Kenya was a Western commercial partner and a vital ally against the region's growing problem of Islamist terrorists.

Independence from European colonial rule came only a generation or two ago. My mother, born in Nairobi when it was under British rule, vividly recalls independence day in 1963. My father was raised in Dar es Salaam in neighbouring Tanzania. And my long school holidays were often spent in East Africa, staying with grandparents. Having arrived from India, my maternal grandfather had worked his way up from laying railway lines to becoming the headmaster of a state school in Nairobi. He, and successive generations of his Kenyan students, lived through the giddy optimism of independence, and the promise it suggested of a new path opening for the continent. But they also saw how difficult it was to traverse this path while saddled with colonialism's baggage.

Each African country has a unique post-colonial story to tell. Their very shapes on the map – some with unerringly straight lines – is an outcome of European rule. Direct colonialism had lasted for about eighty years, starting in around the 1880s. This was when European interest had exploded into a competitive burst of colonizing known as the 'Scramble for Africa'. The real competition was between Europe's empires; against the native kingdoms, the technologically superior European armies wrought havoc, and there was no real competition at all. Annexation of subdued peoples followed, and the partition of the continent between rival European empires was the result.

But the story goes further back than this. Long before the scramble, Europeans had coveted the continent's riches, but had contented themselves with claiming preferential rights over what ought to have belonged to native kingdoms – including kith and kin. European slavers abducted Africans to work in their colonies in the New World, and the Atlantic slave trade predated colonization. There were also Arabian slavers at work in Africa, and while they have left their own abiding influences on parts of the continent, they eventually lost out to the Europeans.

One of the main legacies arising from European imperialism is the undeclared war of blame that still simmers over where the line should be drawn between past injustices and modernity. Slavery and colonization involved the self-centred pillaging of the continent. In its later stages this was predicated on a notion of 'civilizing' the Africans. All of this flowed from the essential fact that Europeans had first encountered African populations when they were at a radically different stage of socioeconomic development.

In the 1960s the sociologist Immanuel Wallerstein wrote that 'European colonial rule abetted the process of modernisation and nurtured nationalism'.[3] This rationalization reflected what is still a fairly conventional Western opinion: that despite its clear and abhorrent injustices, the colonial era catalysed a form of modernity that would otherwise have arisen more slowly, or not at all, in Africa.

Conversely there is a totally different opinion, which a Cameroonian professor pointed out to me at a conference on Africa's present-day security problems: 'the initiation of the state in Africa was shrouded in corruption, so how can one accuse African states of being corrupt? The problems are the conditions within which the state in Africa was born and is evolving.'[4] The 'gift' of modernity was poisoned by the giver, held in the chalice of colonialism.

When we consider the ways in which the colonial past has contributed to the challenges facing African countries today, binary arguments are clearly unhelpful. Colonialism is not the only cause of Africa's contemporary problems, and to argue this turns a blind eye to failures within the continent since independence. Equally negligent is downplaying colonialism's troubling legacies. Accommodating both perspectives is the only intellectually responsible position to take, and this requires a balanced consideration of how imperial legacies continue to influence Africa's realities.

Africa's kingdoms before Europe's colonizing scramble

An old colonial-era trope was that Africa had no history before the Europeans arrived. White explorers duly cast themselves as a shining light over the 'Dark Continent' – to invoke the patronizing parlance of the day. David Livingstone, the Victorian-era British explorer, is commemorated by a statue and a plaque at the spot of his 'discovery of the Victoria Falls' in 1855, which he duly named after his regent. Livingstone was apparently reliant on locals who long knew of the immense waterfall (which is situated between modern Zambia and Zimbabwe). But, as the tale was retold with embellishment by other Europeans, long after Livingstone had died in 1872, he had somehow 'discovered' the falls.[5] The novelist

V. S. Naipaul poked fun at this mentality in a dialogue between fictional British characters, as they traversed newly independent Africa:

> 'It's funny,' Linda whispered, 'how you can forget the houses and feel that the lake hasn't even been discovered.'
>
> 'I don't know what you mean discovered,' Bobby said, not whispering. 'The people here knew about it all the time.'
>
> 'I've heard that one. I just wish they'd managed to let the rest of us know.'[6]

There is an accidental irony in colonial perceptions of Africa as being backward and undiscovered because, as we now know, human life itself began in Africa. Our early ancestors have been found, fossilized some two million years ago, in the Rift Valley. Our species' first 'colonizations' involved our ancestors spreading across and out of Africa when, after several million years of evolutionary development, a set of primates diverged from apes and began to walk upright.

Far more meritorious of the 'discovery' epithet were the fossils found in Olduvai Gorge, named by local Masai people and located close to the Serengeti plain in northern Tanzania. Today the area lies in a national park, overshadowed by the awesome Ngorongoro Crater. The discoveries were made in 1955 by the paleoanthropologists Mary and Louis Leakey, who came from Britain. Their discoveries were a gift of knowledge to the world and were enabled by importing European scientific insight into Africa. Inadvertently, this was facilitated by empire. Some of what we have learned about Africa has come from outsiders, and this sits awkwardly with the modern reality of Africa's independence.[7]

Although Africa was at a different stage of development when European explorers arrived, it did not present a blank slate. African societies experienced their early stages of development similar to elsewhere in the world. Advanced food production and ironworking techniques spread to central and southern Africa, replacing Stone Age working and creating steadily more complex societies and kingdoms.[8] Latterly, however, African and European societies developed in dramatically diverging ways. When they encountered one another in the colonial era, this divergence had a momentous impact on Africa's development. It led to racist attitudes that were based on the convenience of portraying Africa as a land of savages, rife for exploitation and in need of salvation.

Such attitudes were evident, for instance, in the suspicion that ancient Egypt's sophistication could not have had African roots. When Napoleon invaded Egypt in 1798, his soldiers were accompanied by scholars who set out to study ancient Egypt; they concluded that the Egyptians were the precursors to Mediterranean and Greek civilization. Such sentiments may have influenced the German philosopher Friedrich Hegel, who in 1826 felt confident enough to ignore the Pyramids and opine that 'Africa may be classed as belonging to the phase which precedes culture and development in the proper sense.'[9] Just as Napoleon's scholars had downplayed ancient Egypt's role in Africa's development, so Hegel discounted Africa from his understanding of world history.

Having none of this, the Senegalese scholar Cheikh Anta Diop advanced a counter-thesis: that ancient Egypt comprised black Africans. Diop pointed out that Nubia (in Sudan) had its own civilizational history dating back to the 2000 BCE period, and that the Nubian Kingdom of Kush had in fact conquered Egypt in the eighth century BCE.[10] Ancient Egypt could, of course, have influenced both Europe and Africa, but the dispute concerned the alleged European appropriation of our knowledge and assumptions about Africa.

North Africa had been a gateway to outside influences since ancient times. It became part of Europe's domain when the Roman Empire conquered Egypt in 30 BCE. Later, Byzantine Romans helped to spread Christianity to Africa, and by the fourth century CE it had reached Nubia and Ethiopia. The Kingdom of

Axum (100–940 CE) ruled what is now northern Ethiopia, and its well-developed society adopted Christianity. Elsewhere in Africa the Islamic faith became dominant, after the Arab conquest of the Maghreb in the seventh century CE.

Indigenous African kingdoms were no mere passive players at this time. Ghana's empire, one of the oldest for which historical evidence exists, spanned the third century CE and lasted until 1240. It was supplanted by Mali's kingdom, which (unlike Ghana's) adopted Islam to cohere its society. Mali's kingdom lasted until 1464, when it was defeated by the Songhai Empire, which came to dominate the Sahel (the area between the Sahara and the Savanna) and became one of the largest states on the continent. Zimbabwe also became a great trading centre from the eleventh to the fifteenth centuries, before it withered when the business of mining picked up further north.[11]

Topography, such as arid land and desert, may have prevented these kingdoms from growing larger, as the kingdoms in other continents did around this time. Be that as it may, it doesn't negate the political and cultural sophistication of these societies. Kingships were established, loyalties forged, wars fought, captives taken and (topography willing) interior trade lines opened.[12]

Thus, when the Portuguese and the Dutch arrived on West Africa's coast in the late fifteenth century, they encountered not savages but Benin's long-standing kingdom (located in present-day southern Nigeria). It emerged around the twelfth century CE, and had probably peaked in its territorial expanse about a century before the arrival of Europeans. Its kingly rituals and well-ordered society were impressive to the visitors: the Dutch wanted to trade with the locals and the Portuguese to build churches. Benin still enjoyed its independence for some time after these early encounters.[13]

So what went wrong – what was the tipping point after which European contact spiralled into predation? Historians face the challenge of often only having one side of the story, given the oral traditions of African societies and the absence of written records from pre-colonial kingdoms.[14] What is clear is that Africa's kingdoms faced the challenge of predation from multiple directions, from Europe and Arabia alike. This competition seems to have spurred on the Europeans ('to break Africa's chain and subdue the cruel Arab' was the refrain of a later Belgian colonist[15]).

The Europeans had to contend with an established Arabic influence in North Africa (which the Portuguese circumnavigated by sailing to the kingdom of Benin). Arab influence had also increased in East Africa. For example, the Sultanate of Zanzibar was run from Oman and, to this day, Arabic influences in Zanzibar's culture and architecture are evident. There was an Arab slave trade, and Arabs tended to take slaves to perform such roles as family servants and soldiers.[16] The situation at this time was far from being in Europe's favour. Fort Jesus (which remains a tourist attraction in Mombasa) is illustrative of the competition. It was built by the Portuguese in 1593, and fifty years later it was raided by Omani seafarers. In 1700 the Arabs managed to kick out the Portuguese.[17]

Africa in Europe's dominion

For Portuguese explorers, it ultimately came down to profit. Vasco da Gama found that plundering parts of Africa's coast, as he passed in 1498, earned him many times the amount of money that the King of Portugal had invested in the voyage. Francisco d'Almeida's fleet did the same in 1505, storming the Kilwa Sultanate (off modern Tanzania's coast) and Mombasa. D'Almeida was already famed for his exploits as a soldier in the campaign to evict Muslim Moors from Granada in 1492; now the rival imperialisms of Christendom and Islam had come to Africa.

The Portuguese, and other Europeans who came afterwards, possessed clear advantages in naval and gunpowder technology, but literacy, although more developed in Europe, was hardly universal, and many Europeans were entirely illiterate. Politically, the Europeans came from feudal monarchies riven by sectarian fighting between the various wings of Christianity. The more advanced indigenous African kingdoms may have been comparatively politically sophisticated and stable, at least for the needs of local governance.[18] In an alternative version of history, partnerships in trade may have flourished between the Europeans and these African kingdoms.

The Americas, however, were calling. After Columbus made his discoveries in 1492, European voyages reached the Caribbean islands and the southern Americas. Columbus, who came from Genoa, was bankrolled by the Spanish kingdom of Castile. Mercantilism was the governing principle, and there was a huge impulse to turn a profit from sugar and other plantations in the New World. The Portuguese began shipping African slaves to work on these plantations. English, French, Dutch and other Europeans piled in as well, turning their colonies in the Americas into destinations for slaves. From the sale of the captives to their transportation, and on to their forced labour in the plantations, the whole sorry enterprise became a web of interlocking profiteering.

The slave trade compounded the racism of Europeans, who viewed Africans as subhuman. Africa was literally plundered for its people. The slavers even paid some willing African kingdoms to take captives specifically to be shipped to the New World. Captivity has existed everywhere in some form, such is the grim reality of war; but the industrial scale of slavery inflicted on Africa, and its interlocking system of profiteering, was unprecedented; and by the 1790s it was occurring on a sufficient scale to seriously reduce the populations of the regions being preyed upon.[19]

For maritime slavers, though, there was little incentive to head inland from the safety of coastal forts and enclaves and, until around the 1870s, much of the continent's interior was still in African hands.[20]

The British outlawed the slave trade after an advocacy campaign by the politician William Wilberforce brought greater attention to the untrammelled inhumanities it had begotten. The Royal Navy duly fought those who failed to follow suit, from the Arabs to the Portuguese. In America the outcome of the Civil War and the defeat of the Confederacy in 1865 added to the sense that a page would be turned. From an African perspective, however, one evil was simply replaced by another, and different types of slavery persisted. Mahmood Mamdani, a Ugandan scholar, has noted cynically that the slave trade was replaced by colonialism 'so that Africans who yesterday were transported to the New World could now stay at home – to produce cotton for "the Satanic mills"', as well as other crops such as sugar and rubber, all required to propel European economies and societies during industrialization.[21]

What was it that set off the Europeans on their colonizing scramble? Much of the answer lies in changing balances of power in Europe. The established imperial powers (Portugal, Spain, Britain and France) long had privileged rights to African labour and resources. The new kids on Europe's block – Belgium (unified in 1830), Germany and Italy (both unified in 1871) – now entered the imperial race, staking claims to their own empires. These ambitions accelerated the competitive dynamic in Europe to secure spheres of influence. 'The most remarkable aspect of the first ten years of the scramble for Africa,' wrote the academics Roland Oliver and J. D. Fage, 'was the extent to which almost everything of importance happened in Europe. Statesmen and diplomats met in offices or country houses and drew lines across maps which themselves were usually inaccurate.'[22]

The Berlin Conference of 1884–5 was a key event in such European machinations. It was a triumph for Germany's Chancellor Bismarck, who had presided over Africa's partition without triggering war in Europe – in other words, using Africa as a pressure valve for tensions between rival European nations. This conveys just how Eurocentric world power was at the time. And it will come as no surprise that the Berlin Conference is considered the ultimate sin by critics of colonization – 'The curse of Berlin', as the contemporary academics Sabelo Ndlovu-Gatsheni and Brilliant Mhlanga described it.[23]

Within the annals of colonization, the tale of the Belgian Congo still stands apart in its sheer gruesomeness. One of the big winners at Bismarck's Berlin Conference was Belgian king, Leopold II. He had secured German backing for his 'Congo Free State'. The Portuguese had traversed the Congo basin in 1491, but Portugal's imperial power had later waned. Leopold II saw an opening, having long coveted a colony to magnify little Belgium's significance in the world, and to multiply his bank account. Belgium relied on volunteers for its colonial army from across Europe. Slavery, mutilation and disease ravaged Congo during the Leopold period and immediately afterwards. The colonizers engaged in systematic acts of mutilation and murder in the course of running their rubber plantations. Overall, due to colonization, the Congolese population is estimated to have fallen by around some ten million.[24]

Joseph Conrad's novel, *Heart of Darkness*, remains controversial not for what it recounts, but for how it is recounted. A merchant sailor, Conrad passed through Leopoldville in 1890. He captured something of the sense of chaos behind colonialism, and its sheer precariousness for the Europeans who sought adventure and profit. For that, *Heart of Darkness* remains an important reference point. But it is not universally regarded. Chinua Achebe, the Nigerian novelist, does not pull his punches: 'Conrad was a thoroughgoing racist,' he argues, because Conrad revelled in presenting an image of Africa that is the 'antithesis of Europe and therefore of civilisation, a place where man's vaunted intelligence and refinement are finally mocked by triumphant bestiality'.[25]

Although each European power approached colonization in its own way, the whole enterprise ended up being propelled by the twin rotors of commerce and Christianity. Quests for profit intermingled with a misguided idealism around civilizing supposedly 'savage' peoples – all the while backed by superior military force.

Back home, Europe's politicians and regents expected their colonists at least to break even financially and, ideally, to make huge profits. Initially small colonial armies formed around African coastlines and cities, trading and stealing to try and recoup the costs of occupation. Raw materials were extracted from Africa and turned into manufactured goods in European factories, for European profit. Colonial officials and traders had no patience in allowing African entrepreneurs to become wealthy.[26]

In bringing 'civilization', the Europeans thought Africans would require their tutelage for centuries. The impetus of the missionaries increasingly came to the forefront of imperial expansion at the end of the nineteenth century, which also served the purpose of dignifying the idea of colonization and rulership.[27] The European Church therefore served colonialism, not least by judging what would be considered culturally permissible. 'African ancestral beliefs were equated with the devil (who was black anyway),' wrote the activist Walter Rodney.[28]

Some colonies were run by the 'direct rule' of European settler communities; others by 'indirect rule', which required cultivating a pliant political class amongst the locals. This in turn compounded the creation of 'tribal identity'. Europeans, who may have been perplexed by African sociopolitical arrangements, felt they had to equate them with nationalities, grouping together nearby villages under administrative districts. 'Chief' became a manufactured title to be awarded to those locals who would run things on behalf of the colonists. In the end the word 'tribal' cut both ways, as the Ugandan scholar Mamdani observed: 'tribalism signified both the form of rule and the revolt against it'.[29] Such was the social engineering taking place during colonization.

In settler colonies, land was stolen. Natives were turfed off the best land, which had also been synonymous with social prestige and status. Kenya was just such a case. Jomo Kenyatta, who became

Kenya's first president in 1964, had earlier studied in London and wrote an anthropology on his kin, the Gikuyu. Of the arrival of the *muzungu* (European): 'When the Europeans first came into the Gikuyuland the Gikuyu looked upon them as wanderers who had deserted from their homes ... As such the Europeans were allowed to pitch their tents and to have a temporary right of occupation on the land.' Over time, however, it became clear that the visitors had no intention of leaving and had exploited their hosts' naivety. 'These early Empire builders, knowing what they were after, played on the ignorance of the people.'[30]

Kenyatta was also cynical of the Europeans' claims to being more civilized. 'The European prides himself on having done a great service to the Africans by stopping the "tribal warfares" ... [but consider] the modern warfare waged by the "civilised" tribes of Europe, and in which the Africans who have no part in the quarrels are forced to fight to defend so-called democracy.' Tens of thousands of Africans were fated to die in the Great War, and 'the reward for this was taking away the best lands from the African'. And it did not stop with the war's finale in 1918: 'the Italian invasion of Ethiopia, where the wholesale massacre of the defenceless population took place to demonstrate European civilisation.'[31]

The Italian conquest of Ethiopia came late in the colonial era, in 1935, and attracted great criticism from African voices, like Kenyatta's, which were now able to write in Europe's languages to make their case. Italy's war in Ethiopia was important in catalysing this chorus of disapproval, but it was not until the exhaustion and destruction inflicted by Europe upon itself in the Second World War that independence movements across Africa came into their own. The colonial powers, drained by both world wars, at first tried to tighten their grip, before it loosened of its own accord.

Quickly European rule ended before Africa's independence movements could really cohere. Astonishment greeted Congo's independence in 1960, for instance, as the writer Ilunga Kabongo captures: 'I was twenty years old when, at the end of January 1960, we learned in the Congo that the country was to become independent on 30 June of that year. We were so surprised by the sudden Belgian decision that we did not believe the story.' An atmosphere of frantic energy gripped the Congolese, who had no time to prepare and no idea what to expect. 'It was simply beyond words. "Independence" was wrapped in an atmosphere of religious, almost mystical, joy and apocalyptic expectation but at the same time of the most tragicomic mis-understanding and fears.'[32]

European colonization at once made and unmade Africa. The word 'legacy' almost seems inadequate, because the path away from colonialism is the path that Africa still treads. The next port of call is decolonization, and how the transitions out of colonial-ism lead us to the present day.

Distorted modernity: Africa's colonial inheritance

In a continent of fifty-four recognized sovereign states today, colonialism's legacies will have had varying impacts, depending on where one looks. Each African country has had a unique post-colonial story. To take specific examples is clearly selective, since some countries have fared better than others. There were all sorts of reasons for this, often to do with the wisdom (or lack thereof) of the departing colonizers and of the new local rulers. Intractable problems often arose that compounded the failures of both. The fate of southern Africa illustrates just how badly things could go, and just how distorting the so-called path to modernity may have been.[33]

Colonialism's legacy in South Africa is inseparable from the life and ambitions of Cecil Rhodes (1853–1902), who went to Africa to work on the diamond mines as a young man. His ruth-lessness in the trade saw him become a mining baron and then Cape Colony's prime minister (1890–6). The arch imperialist,

Rhodes bought into the notion of the white race as intrinsically superior to black Africans. His career typified how to profiteer personally from public work in a way that today would be called corruption, but within its colonial context had served the British crown's needs.

In 1652 the Dutch East India Company established a shipping station at the Cape of Good Hope. Later settlers (more Dutch, plus other Europeans, including some refugees) called themselves 'Afrikaners' (people of Africa). Among them developed a class of wandering farmers called Boers, who went off in search of better land deeper in Africa. In 1806 Britain took control of the colony, ostensibly to act as a naval base in the Napoleonic Wars. Later it began to meddle in colony affairs. In 1834 Britain decreed that slaves should be set free across its empire.

Resisting this idea, the Boers upped sticks to set up their own republics: the Transvaal and the Orange Free State. Initially Britain recognized the independence of the Boers. But in 1877 Britain annexed the Transvaal, hoping to federate South Africa. This provoked the First Boer War (1880–1). Seeing all this transpire, Rhodes set out to take over the Transvaal for the British Empire, and for himself, all to be paid for by its diamond wealth. He also established another colony north of the Transvaal, immodestly called Rhodesia. In the end, ambition got the better of him. Rhodes ordered the botched Jameson Raid into the Transvaal in 1896; it went so badly that it brought down his government and eventually triggered the Second Boer War (1899–1902).[34]

Black Africans were trapped in the disputes between different bands of Europeans, whose arguments seemed only to land them in further trouble. The roots of what became apartheid were planted in the colonial era. The Afrikaners had maintained a system of racial hierarchy from the eighteenth century. The British Cape Colony was not much better, following rigid racial laws during the height of its profiteering in the nineteenth century. Apartheid officially came into being in 1948 with the election of

Afrikaner nationalists, who were bent on protecting white rule through legalized segregation. It was the ultimate expression of settler logic, and it lasted for decades.

Nelson Mandela, who was born in 1918, grew up amidst a racial hierarchy that, as a boy, he understood to be entirely natural. His father was a chief in the Thembu tribe (although the British had to ratify his chiefship before delegating local authority to him). 'I came across few whites as a boy at Qunu,' recalled Mandela. 'The local magistrate, of course, was white, as was the nearest shopkeeper. Occasionally white travellers or policemen passed through our area. These whites appeared as grand as gods to me.'[35] As a man, Mandela took on the system that had made them gods. His resistance to apartheid earned him a twenty-seven-year incarceration, after he was sentenced in 1962 for armed revolutionary activities against the apartheid state. Mandela's release, when apartheid was flailing under world criticism, and his election as South Africa's first black president in 1994, transformed him into the very embodiment of the overcoming of imperial legacy.

Apartheid had been a mutation of white settler logic, which had cut off its bonds from Europe. In 1965 Rhodesia's white government under Ian Smith declared independence from Britain in order to defend the status of its 200,000-strong white settler minority. 'I don't believe in black majority rule over Rhodesia, not in a thousand years,' said Smith. A Royal Air Force veteran, he ardently believed that Rhodesian volunteers had done so much for Britain in wartime as to deserve protection. London did not answer his call. Left alone, Smith's security forces became locked in a fifteen-year war with black guerrilla movements (which received military aid from the USSR, turning Rhodesia into a Cold War theatre).

Robert Mugabe's Zimbabwe African National Union (ZANU) was one of Smith's opponents. Britain brokered a ceasefire with the 1979 Lancaster House Agreement. Mugabe was told to wait a decade for land reform, but the deal fell apart. Mugabe came to power in 1980 and over the years, as Zimbabwe's economy ground to a halt due to his inept rule, he ordered the violent repossession of the remaining white farms. Mugabe defied old age and was president until 2017.

The colonial era has bled into the modern era across Africa, sometimes through war. The Portuguese, who were amongst the first Europeans to explore and plunder Africa, were also among the last to leave. Angola and Mozambique, two of their colonies, both suffered as a result. Portugal did not want to leave and hung on right until 1975. Both countries suffered bitter wars of independence. The Mozambican War (1964–74) involved Samora Machel, a freedom fighter who later became Mozambique's first president. In Angola, Portugal refused to allow self-rule, which contributed to an independence war (1961–75). After independence, Angola suffered a civil war between the two main liberation movements, and fighting did not end until 2002.

At the time of independence, the immediate problem was the speed at which it came, and this contributed to why some transitions from colony to sovereign state were so violent. It was easier for independence movements to agitate against colonization than it was to build nations, especially when the colonial inheritance involved borders drawn by others.[36]

These borders bear an enduring testimony to the designs of colonialism. 'The fact that state borders on the African continent were and are artificial is not unique to Africa, but what is problematic is their arbitrariness which has an impact on issues of nation building and identity politics,' wrote the academics Ndlovu-Gatsheni and Mhlanga.[37] During colonial times, the borders mainly mattered to colonial administrators. The implications of packing different ethnic groups, and uneven economies, into different administrative units was felt by Africa after independence came.

Why did Africa's new leaders become possessive about these borders and not tear them up? One answer lies in the ultimate failure of the Pan-African movement, which could have offered

an ideology to rethink the political organization of the continent. Over time, it inadvertently played a role in doing precisely
the opposite. Pan-Africanism had initially gained momentum as
a way of building solidarity for independence. It attracted celebrity endorsements, from the African American writer W. E. B.
Du Bois, to the political activist Marcus Garvey and the boxer
Muhammad Ali. It was eventually institutionalized in the Organization of African Unity (OAU), which was founded by thirty-two
African governments in 1963. The OAU's opening meeting was
chaired by Haile Selassie, Emperor of Ethiopia, in Addis Ababa,
a symbolic place due to lingering anger over Italy's 1935 invasion.

Anger in the OAU at this time was directed at then-con-
temporary issues, such as Portugal's colonies and the situations in
South Africa and South Rhodesia. After the independence era,
the significance of the OAU changed. It became a club for sovereign states, and whatever initial spark there might have been
for different kinds of pan-continental solidarities was replaced by
horse-trading between the African governments. With the new
millennium beckoning, the OAU's anti-colonial slant seemed outdated, so it was replaced by a new body, the African Union (AU),
created to reflect African responses to current concerns, such as
the enduring problem of civil wars and the changing nature of
neoliberal globalization. Part of the AU's ten principles, adopted
in 1999, was 'To defend the sovereignty, territorial integrity and
independence of its Member States'. In other words, the AU is a
statist body – it accepts and defends the arrangement of the continent into states that, with some notable changes, have remained
largely unchanged since independence.

Another reason for the prevalence of these states is that African politicians became wedded to their new thrones. Sometimes,
as Mugabe's egregious example shows, they simply did not want
to leave their kingship. Perhaps such reluctance is simply a case of
power attracting megalomaniacs. The other explanation resides in
the corruption underpinning their systems. To what extent were

the seeds of these problems with democracy and corruption sown by imperial legacies?

For European colonialism to have worked as pervasively as it did, African elites had to be brought over to the European side. 'Collaboration' is the wrong word; in some cases, Europeans made treaties with local African kingdoms that were interpreted by the locals as pacts of friendship, but were understood by the Europeans as a prelude to occupation. These treaties may have been the least-bad choice for the African kingdoms, which thought they were guarding their territories by working with the Europeans.[38] Whatever the motivations, colonialism involved cooperation with local elites, some of whom would become Africa's post-independence rulers. As Oliver and Fage recount: 'The new black leaders had stepped into the positions formerly occupied by the colonial officials in the most literal sense. They moved into the offices and houses occupied by their predecessors, were driven by the same chauffeurs in the same or larger cars, and had the same servants, administrative and technical officials, policemen and soldiers at their command.'[39]

Democracy faced an uphill struggle. Colonialism had left a legacy of authoritarian rule, and of economic dependency on the former colonizers. Predatory practices endured from the colonial era. This contributed to the rise of a motley cast of 'big men' who dominated politics from the 1960s to the 1980s. For example: Mobutu Sese Seko in Congo, Idi Amin in Uganda, Jean-Bédel Bokassa in the Central African Republic, Jomo Kenyatta and Daniel arap Moi in Kenya, Jerry Rawlings in Ghana, Hastings Banda in Malawi.

Some pursued socialism, such as Milton Obote in Uganda and Julius Nyerere in Tanzania. Nyerere was also prone to delivering fine words, such as these from 1969: 'We are making this attempt as Africans and as Tanzanians; as people who have been shaped by a history which goes back further than a century or so of colonialism. Further, we look at the world as people who believe they have something to contribute to mankind, as well as something to gain from it.'[40]

Other leaders did not even bother paying lip-service to the responsibilities of independence. A notorious example was Mobutu in Congo (which he renamed Zaire). While responsibility for his misrule clearly rests with his own indulgences, Mobutu was also a product of colonial legacies. Although it is an oversimplification to offload the blame to Belgium, Mobutu seemed to mimic the behaviour of King Leopold through his one-man rule, his appropriation of the country's wealth and the evident ego of naming a lake after himself.[41] Mobutu's rule was so bad that neighbouring countries at first ganged up on him to remove him from power in the 1990s, and then fell into fighting each other on Congolese territory for its natural resources. The Congolese Wars contributed to millions of deaths through fighting, displacement and disease and ended only in 2002.

In several parts of Africa one-party political systems were dismantled in favour of multi-party systems during the 1990s, but this did not stop the predatory politics of ruling elites that wanted to dominate the polls through means both fair and foul, to cling on to power and the profits it construed.[42] This returns us to the example of Kenya's disastrous 2007 election, in which the leaders have been reluctant to accept the results and loath to step down.

This reluctance has often been underpinned by the profiteering and patronage afforded by high office. How is one to apportion blame for endemic corruption? Africa inherited European forms of government, but the temptation for rulers to seize and hold power was sometimes fed by European businessmen and by foreign aid in the immediate post-independence period.

Nevertheless, the prevalence of the problem means that it is not purely a colonial legacy. Achebe, the Nigerian novelist, wrote in the 1980s of his country's corruption: 'certainly [it] was not created by the post-military civilian administration. It might even be called one of the legacies of colonialism. If so we have had more than two decades to correct it; we have failed to do so but rather chosen to multiply the evil ten fold. We have no excuse whatsoever.' He goes on to rebuke the Nigerians' own failure to improve: 'We have turned out to be like a bunch of stage clowns who bump their heads into the same heavy obstacles again and again because they are too stupid to remember what hit them only a short while ago.'[43] Blame for the outcome clearly goes both ways.

However, the laws, institutions and values of colonial and apartheid governments offered up poor inheritances, which continually disadvantaged those African citizens and leaders who want to confront it today. The NGO Transparency International has ranked sub-Saharan Africa as the worst-scoring region in its 2018 global study of how corruption weakens democracy.[44]

Corruption has also held back economic growth, and so have the legacies of empire. Africa's post-colonial borders compounded all kinds of problems, with map lines seemingly blind to the ethnic groups they bisected, to the history of pre-colonial kingdoms and to natural geography and resources. Looking at the political map, the very shape of some African countries, and the absence or presence of a coast, remains a permanent legacy of the ambitions of their former rulers to extract their resources.

After independence, many African countries rushed to implement modernizing state-building reforms, encouraged and funded by international donors. Sub-Saharan African states were forced to take on structural adjustment loans from the IMF and the World Bank. Ghana's first president, Kwame Nkrumah, was withering about this, writing in 1965: 'Still another neocolonialist trap on the economic front has come to be known as "multilateral aid" through: the IMF, the International Bank for Reconstruction and Development (World Bank) . . . These agencies have the habit of forcing would-be borrowers to submit to various offensive conditions.'[45]

Nor was the solution to be found in offering aid. Donor

expectations were often not met, debts accumulated and money was misspent by the recipients. The economists Daron Acemoglu and James A. Robinson trace some of these problems to imperial legacies. 'Many expected the worst practices of colonial rule in Sub Saharan Africa to stop after independence', but 'post-independence African politicians were only too happy to take up the baton themselves'.[46]

Looking at the 2018 rankings in terms of GDP for all the world's economies, there are no sub-Saharan African countries in the top thirty. The highest-ranking sub-Saharan African economy is Nigeria (thanks to its size and oil wealth), followed by South Africa, Sudan, Ethiopia, Kenya, Tanzania, Ghana, the Democratic Republic of the Congo, Ivory Coast and Cameroon. These economies each have their own workings, but commodity dependencies have held some of them back.

Across these various issues there is the temptation to dispense blame, even if only in the assumptions that underpin our attitudes. In the West, opinions can still surface that suggest African countries could not handle the 'gift' of independence.

The legacy of empire affects how we interpret Africa's journey into the modern world, and what modernity means. How people *feel* about this situation is just as important as what can be proven by statistics. Regaining a sense of dignity has also been part of Africa's independence journey, even if some feelings of inferiority to the former colonizers may remain.[47]

Mandela, speaking to a UK audience two years after he had left office, tried to make sense of the 'sometimes contradictory' relationship of South Africa with its former colonial ruler:

Britain was the main colonial power in our history, with all of the attendant problems and consequences of such a relationship. Much of our traditional systems and institutions still carry the scars of the distortions inflicted by colonial rule. At the same time, so much of what we have to build on in the competitive modern world is also the result of what we could gain from that interaction.[48]

Such a delicate handling of colonial legacies will be required for the foreseeable future. The big challenges facing African countries today have moved well beyond the immediate ones of independence, but their map lines will remain imprinted by colonialism's indelible ink, while their people's imperial inheritances remain defined by the inequalities of imperialism.

Modern problems, imperial legacies

Amongst the most serious issues facing Africa today are civil wars, terrorism, enduring poverty, the departure of its people as migrants to Europe, and the opportunities and risks posed by the Chinese and other outsiders interested in African markets.[49] There is not enough space to examine all these themes in detail, so what follows are examples of how imperial legacies can assist in understanding the underlying structural problems. An example of civil war is discussed, followed by the migrant crisis, and concluding on China.

Civil wars have been a scourge in parts of Africa. The term 'state failure' has become popular with Western journalists and policymakers in summing up the moment when the anarchy and killing indicate a complete lack of effective governance (to be fair, state failure is a term used to describe such situations across the world). It is a curious piece of jargon: how can a state 'fail' if it has only existed for a few decades and was a colonial construction in the first place?

Sudan offers an example. Britain had ruled it in a nominal partnership with Egypt and, on 1 January 1956, Anglo-Egyptian Sudan became the independent state of Sudan. Since then it has been blighted by a series of wars, partly driven by Sudan including a majority Muslim population in the north and Christian in the south, all squeezed together in a single state. Two civil wars (1955–72 and 1983–2005) wrecked the country. The end of the first war was negotiated in Ethiopia, and the end of the second in Kenya. As part of the latter deal, the people of South Sudan could vote to secede, which is precisely what they did in a referendum, and South Sudan became Africa's newest state in 2011. Tragically, it too then experienced its own civil war between rival factions under Riek Machar and Salva Kiir (the latter known for always wearing a cowboy hat, which was a gift from George W. Bush). Meanwhile, in Sudan itself President Omar al-Bashir, who assumed office in Khartoum in 1989, kept power for thirty years.

Sudan and South Sudan's woes seem to be the fault of Bashir, Machar and Kiir, but imperial legacies have played their own role. The British had neglected to rule large parts of the south. Just before independence in 1956, the British effectively lost control as northern Sudanese positioned themselves to monopolize power in Khartoum, while the south was left ungoverned. In the late 1970s oil was discovered in the south, which further compounded tensions between north and south, and is another reason why South Sudan erupted into war after it seceded.[50]

Contemporary Sudanese leaders in Khartoum and the south have been the agents of these crises. But it is hard to escape the conclusion that colonialism was an ill-suited precursor to the creation of modern sovereign states. Rather than the term 'failed state', which heaps the blame on the present day, it is wiser to think about the inheritance of colonialism in setting up these states to fail.

When it became independent in 2011 the omens for South Sudan's future were mixed. The rebels who had long fought for freedom from Khartoum displayed a poor aptitude to rule when given that freedom, and struggled to transition from being an armed group into a political party. Hence the mentalities of Kiir and Machar, which have been exacerbated by their respective ethnic affiliations among the Dinka and Nuer peoples. After 2011

Western specialists in development, diplomacy and security travelled to South Sudan to help make its independence work, but several of them have since written about their disillusionment concerning the severity of the problems encountered, and how South Sudan's stability somehow seemed doomed from the start.[51]

Would Sudan's various parts have fought each other anyway? Did the imperial era make a difference in terms of the combustible borders it set? Was pre-colonial Africa, with its arrangements of kingdoms and centres of powers that blurred from one to the next, more suitable to the continent than the imposition of hard borders? While these hypothetical questions cannot be answered, they highlight why the ahistorical snapshot implied by the 'state failure' jargon is misleading, is ignorant of the roots of modern problems and even insulting.

Colonial memories and African migration to Europe

Wars, such as those afflicting Sudan, make it no surprise that people might have to leave their homes. The privations of armed conflict, and instances of political repression, create refugees. Other people may leave Africa because of a poverty of opportunities, which makes them economic migrants. Some – but by no means all – of these people have left Africa for Europe. Traffickers, exploiting people's dreams and desperation to enter Europe, have then charged them extortionate fees, only to pack the hopeful into overloaded boats, some of which have capsized while crossing the Mediterranean, causing terrible loss of life.

These heart-rending stories, images and realities have become widely familiar. Both types of migrants (forced and economic) have moved at the same time, using the same routes and the same people traffickers. This is perhaps why European countries have perceived the phenomenon as a 'crisis' – confused European publics have been unsure whether they are on a mercy mission to help the persecuted or are being taken advantage of by the poor.

The migrant crisis has included people from across Africa, the Middle East and Asia trying to come and live in Europe. Focusing on Africa, there are both push and pull factors explaining why a migrant might want to set out for Europe. Pew, the polling company, conducted a survey of attitudes that offered an insight: 'The survey asked respondents whether they would go to live in another country, if they had the means and opportunity. At least four-in-ten in each sub-Saharan country surveyed answered yes, including roughly three-quarters of those surveyed in Ghana (75%) and Nigeria (74%).'[52] In a 2018 preliminary report of surveying, Afrobarometer uncovered the following: 'Initial data from nine countries – Ghana, Benin, Côte d'Ivoire, Kenya, Malawi, Uganda, Mali, Zambia, and Zimbabwe – show that on average, one-third of respondents have considered emigrating, including 16% who have given it "a lot" of thought.'[53]

Pew and Afrobarometer qualify these findings by pointing out that only a subset of those who have considered leaving Africa actually do so, and these have tended to be younger people. And it does not assume that Europe is their preferred destination. Migration can involve many directions of travel for all sorts of reasons, from family reunions, to jobs and refuge.

For those Africans migrating to Europe for economic reasons, however, it looks uncannily like an inversion of the migration patterns of colonization. An EU study on migration from Africa was historically aware enough to employ the subtitle 'From Europeans in Africa to Africans in Europe'. Previously, colonialism saw European civil servants, soldiers and settlers emigrating to Africa in large numbers. Immigration from Africa into Europe first took off when countries like France recruited labourers and soldiers from Africa in the early twentieth century. When independence came in the second half of the century, the European soldiers and officials moved back to their countries of origin, and large numbers of African-born descendants of colonial settlers came with them.

Since independence, Africans who migrate to Europe have

tended to favour their former colonizer's country. Whether as students, workers or as dependent family members, migration meant that, as of 1960, there were already an estimated 1.3 million African people living in today's EU states. The EU study also found that more than half of African migrants lived in another African country – no doubt it published this to try and calm populist nerves in Europe with statistical evidence.[54]

For some of the African migrants who try entering Europe, it is worth recalling the words of the social philosopher Frantz Fanon: 'The wealth of imperial countries is our wealth too.'[55] Given that Europe's wealth was partly dependent on its African colonies, there is more than simply a symbolic connection to modern African economic migration to Europe. Although imperial history is unlikely to be an active reference point for modern economic migrants, it may well feature somewhere in their subconscious, simply in terms of how Europe has long been associated with progress.

The academics Charles Adeyanju and Temitope Oriola decided to study the motivations around voluntary international migration by Africans. They surveyed the evidence of letters, social-media posts and suchlike to give an insight, and found that the perception of disparity between European wealth and African poverty featured, as did mentions of popular culture and media presentations of the lifestyles enjoyed by Europe's young and enterprising people. The academics point out that: 'Africans' encounter with European colonialism had a lasting effect on their lifeworld ... by associating progress with European culture and primitivism and backwardness with the African other. But colonialism was also about the material relations that existed within the larger context of global economic inequality that made the whites look superior.'[56] Colonial legacies may not be active reference points, but it is absurd to assume their impact is negligible.

The wide-ranging phenomenon of African migration to Europe has evolved between the 1960s and the 2010s, in some senses beyond all recognition. Previous generations of migrants could not view images of their potential destinations online and share them easily with their peers. One thing that has remained unchanged is the underlying imbalance between the levels of development in the two continents.

The post-colonial lens remains crucial to understanding modern migration from Africa to Europe. After all, it is not mere coincidence that a young citizen of an African country might develop a desire to travel to the place that once dominated his or her country and continent, exploiting the labour of their grandparents to enrich Europe at Africa's expense.

China's scramble and Africa's future

From the outlines of Africa's borders, to the English, French and Portuguese that is spoken, the European influence is unambiguous. Imperial legacies persist in the shape of its post-colonial states, which remain as a leitmotif to decolonization on the map, even as their origins may fade one day in the collective memories of future generations.

The demography of the continent tells its own story. Slavery and colonization negatively affected population growth for several generations, slowing it notably in the nineteenth century.[57] In 1961, as Wallerstein estimated, 'the population of Africa was very small in proportion to the rest of the world'.[58] It is now 1.2 billion (16 per cent of world population). By 2050 it will double to 2.4 billion and, according to UN estimates, Africa will account for more than half of global population growth.[59]

By then, active memories of European rule in Africa will have faded. Is this the cut-off point for Europe's sense of responsibility in having modernized and distorted Africa's development? Is this when moral responsibility for Africa's fate becomes entirely vested in the continent's inhabitants, no matter their colonial inheritances? Taking into consideration the debts and dependencies between former colonies and colonizers, managing the legacies of colonization has been a multi-generational undertaking, and one that passes now to generations that had no direct involvement in it.

China's involvement in Africa may eventually rewrite the script by ushering in a new era of foreign dependence. Transactional rather than colonial, China is hungry for resources that African countries are willing to sell. In a quid pro quo, China offers its African client states investment in roads, railways, ports and factories.

Such has been the growth of Chinese investment that it has become Africa's most important economic partner in the space of just two decades. The management consultancy firm McKinsey found that Chinese investment in Africa had grown so sharply that it was impossible to analyse this growth with statistical precision. McKinsey estimated that there were 10,000 mainly private Chinese firms operating across Africa, with a hefty emphasis on such sectors as manufacturing, trade, construction and real estate. As of 2017, Chinese firms handled an estimated 12 per cent of Africa's total industrial production and almost half Africa's internationally contracted construction market.[60]

Africa's telecoms infrastructure was built by the giant Chinese telecommunications firms Huawei and ZTE. These firms (which, in 2013, had annual turnovers of $9.2 billion and $13 billion respectively[61]) are so vital to the 'Ministry of Commerce People's Republic of China' that, despite being privately run, they are integral to the Chinese government as flagship companies. Huawei and ZTE have sold a huge number of smartphones in Africa and built a significant portion of the continent's 4G mobile-phone network.

China has not only helped enable Africans to communicate, but also to travel. One example of Chinese-built transport infrastructure is a new railway line connecting Nairobi with the coastal city of Mombasa. In 2013 the China Road and Bridge

Corporation won the project to build the railway, and claimed that the project would employ 2,000 Chinese employees and 30,000 Kenyans. The Chinese firm laid the tracks, supplied the trains and trained Kenyan drivers. As the Chinese workers arrived, they lived in self-contained compounds, eating their own cuisine, aloof from the local culture.

Given that China has expressly stated it is not interested in creating colonies, perhaps this is an obvious arrangement – except that the Europeans were at first also supposedly interested just in business opportunities. 'We're going to sell our national treasure to these people' was the premonition of a Kenyan senator in 2018; '66 per cent of our national debt and growing is to the Chinese ... History is going to judge us so harshly. When we begin selling our country to the Chinese is when we give them the port of Mombasa and Jomo Kenyatta Airport,' warned Mutala Kilonzo Junior.[62]

The dangers of dependency on China are real, based on China's debt-fuelled model of infrastructure provision. McKinsey highlighted the possibility of some African countries defaulting on Chinese debt in the future, and speculated on how this would force China into debt forgiveness.[63] This would create further dependences, and indicates that we cannot yet know how a prolonged exposure to Chinese ways of doing things will shape Africa's development.

Authoritarian China might also eventually offer political lessons to Africa, especially if Beijing is not perturbed by leaders who refuse to give up their power. Across Africa the average age of presidents is rising, and between 2010 and 2018 five were so old that they died in office. In some sense, things are more stable now than they were during the 1960s when many African republics were entering their post-colonial period, because at least the number of coups has reduced.[64] Nevertheless, it would be unwise to predict an end to disputed elections and dictatorships altogether. Future African dictators might gaze longingly at Beijing for endorsement of their one-party rule. After all, why look to the sanctimonious Euro-American world, which has the gall to stress democracy after the eras of imperialism and neo-colonialism – or so the argument could run. China's economic engagement is already generating legacies that will shape the lives of future Africans, and China's political impact on Africa is a history that is yet to be written. Democracy, after all, came to Africa in its current form through colonialism and subsequent independence, and there is no inevitability that democracy will remain Africa's fate.

The Chinese laid new tracks when they rebuilt the Nairobi–Mombasa railway, parallel to those that my grandfather's generation had helped to lay. One set of tracks heads back into the imperial past, the other into the future.

CONCLUSION

THE WORLD'S INTERSECTING IMPERIAL LEGACIES

The past is a foreign country: they do things differently there.

L. P. Hartley (1895–1972), *The Go-Between*[1]

The past is always with us, for it feeds the present.

Ruskin Bond, 'A Song for Lost Friends' (2007)[2]

All of our lives are, in certain ways, post-imperial. We currently live in a world without formal empires, and this is a historical novelty. As citizens of the world, we can look at each other and wonder about the post-imperial inheritances that others carry as part of their heritage, from the newest refugee to the richest captain of industry, from the lowest-ranked soldier to the mightiest statesman.

If the stories in the preceding chapters have seemed to be in tension, or to contradict each other outright, that is precisely the point. It illustrates why people raised on one set of stories might struggle to empathize with others, and why potentially huge misunderstandings arise between governments, when one assumes right of way on a particular issue where others deny it.

World order today comprises numerous post-imperial visions colliding with one another. These movements are akin to shifts in the tectonic plates that underlie world affairs, but on a much smaller level, every one of us carries an imperial inheritance that is personal to them. Working out the various elements that form that inheritance requires a dispassionate sense of perspective.

Much depends on the histories that we enshrine in our education systems and in popular culture, and which are handed down from one generation to the next. The selectivity of these stories helps to create a national culture. For my part, as a schoolboy in London I was fed enough German and Russian imperial history, and books by George Orwell, to leave me acutely aware of the Second World War and wary of fascist and communist totalitarian rule. Even those of us who fell asleep in class will have picked up stories from our families talking about the privations or privileges of their early lives. Hence I received another set of stories at home, this time about India and East Africa, which was handy, because my school taught me nothing at all about the impact of the British Empire around the globe. Outside school and home, all of us will have gleaned a sense of the post-imperial order of things in the nations we were raised in, which is implicit in the way our society carries itself and how our public figures operate in the modern world and on the international stage.

The preceding chapters have moved between those nations whose forebears had done the conquering and those who had been conquered. The resulting legacies can be debated (in open societies at least) and may be subject to different interpretations. Nevertheless, government-approved narratives always try to show the nation in a broadly positive historical light. In a free society this doesn't preclude some of us from forming contradictory views, but accusations of being 'unpatriotic' might be levelled at fellow citizens who do not buy into the popularly accepted post-imperial narratives.

Proximity to history matters to a great extent, and it is obvious that modern Britons are conditioned by the experiences of their empire from sixty years ago in a way that modern Italians cannot be by the western Roman Empire, which ended nearly 2,000 years ago. The passage of time untethers us from certain memories. The writer David Rieff has estimated that after roughly four generations, collective memories lose their sense of direct relevance.[3] But while this is perhaps true of remembrance of specific events, the character-forming impressions generated by centuries of imperial history can have an impact that persists for much longer.

These themes have been clear as we have considered the dominant imperial legacies around the world. The European countries once helmed their own empires, and many now belong to the EU, where they have jettisoned imperialism and some of the nationalistic impulses that led to the horrific world wars Europe suffered from in the twentieth century. Some imperial traits remain manifest in the EU, however, because it now acts as a docking station for parts of Europe – just as previous focal points like the Holy Roman crown never united the whole continent, but simply sections of it.

Britain is a country still in partial denial of the power its imperial experiences have had on its character, and how they have influenced such monumental decisions as the UK entering the Iraq War, and the UK public voting for Brexit. Conversely, Russia's elites have actively embraced its imperial legacies, partly to recover from the shattering of its empire in 1991, but also to continue holding together a vast country acquired through conquest.

The legacies of once having been imperialists can have a particular impact on the ruling elites, because of implicit pressures to live up to the past. They may still be in thrall to the former imperial governing philosophy, knowingly or unknowingly channelling it in the way a country is run and the way it orders others about, firm in the belief that it knows best.

The USA's ancestors in this regard are not the founding fathers, but the Europeans whose imperial instincts were refashioned for conquering North America. Later, the imperial instinct was rethought in order to build an informal empire that has enabled the country to remain at once globally engaged and largely self-absorbed, because it doesn't have to run other countries.

Those elites whose forebears were relatively recently conquered by other empires will have inherited very different lessons about how the world got to its present state. China has had both experiences, and can draw on its own grand imperial past to recover its confidence from a more recent century of humiliation. India, on the other hand, has had to build its self-confidence at the same time as accommodating Mughal and British legacies. It is a matter of great significance that two of the major world powers of this century, which will account for one-third of the global populace, have experienced some form of imperial subjugation during the last century.[4]

This dynamic will provide a new undercurrent to global politics, influencing Chinese or Indian mentalities in engaging with the wider post-colonial world and, at a basic level, challenging the notion that has been held for so long that describing something as 'Western' is synonymous with saying it is modern. To the extent that China and India offer regional or global leadership in the future, this will widen the main reference points in global politics.

Across the Middle East and Africa, modern nations remain constrained by borders that were influenced, or completely determined, by the European colonialism of a century ago. The Middle East is riven by the frustrations that have accrued from the extinguishing of its once-dominant imperial cultures. And while African countries cannot offset on imperial legacies all the blame for the challenges they face, it is telling that China – a country that has no cultural connections to Africa – has become Africa's chief financier of development work that supplants some of the post-colonial dependencies on the Western world.

'At least our imperialism wasn't as bad as theirs . . . '

Comparing each other's imperial experiences is not an everyday topic of conversation, but it can be the elephant in the room when people of different national backgrounds meet. Whether this manifests itself in feelings of superiority or inferiority, or in the kinds of miscomprehension that cannot be fixed by a translation app, people from different parts of the world can find themselves talking past each other on certain subjects.

This is not just true for people of different nationalities. Those within the same country can often misunderstand each other completely; and even if they have received the same post-imperial inheritances, people may come to very different conclusions as to their significance. This is one reason why modern political tribes and interest groups come to exist, and why individuals and groups band together, or think differently about where their country should be slotting into the post-imperial age.

For those who derive residual pride from their ancestral imperial triumphs, relativizing the good and bad of this historical record is important. 'Times were different back then . . . ', 'They had no choice but . . . ' or 'At least our empire wasn't as bad as *theirs* . . . ' are examples of the different responses that are often expressed in order to compensate for past misdeeds. Even if not articulated as active statements, these feelings surface when pressed to justify why a controversial period of imperial history ought still to be thought well of, for the way it helped build the modern world.

Nazi Germany's attempted 'Thousand-Year Reich' remains a benchmark of modern evil for many, and especially for Westerners. The countless horrors it unleashed through Hitler's war, and the genocide against Jews, Slavs and others, makes almost everyone else's empires look less bad in comparison. The British always know that for all their own empire's past misdeeds, it fought the Nazis. Yes, the Raj may have been bad, but it was never *that* intentionally bad – after all, didn't the British Indian Army contribute to defeating the Axis powers, including the Japanese Imperial Army? Hence my English education told me much about British heroics in the Second World War and nothing about the power and cruelty of the British Empire. For their part, the Russians always know that for all Stalin's purges and murders, at least the USSR fought the fascists in the Second World War. And so on.

Then there is the opposite, where a colonized people might find themselves thinking that their ancestral suffering was in a league of its own. The Indian author Pankaj Mishra has written that 'European subordination of Asia was not merely economic or political. It was also intellectual and moral and spiritual: a completely different kind of conquest than had been witnessed before, which left its victims resentful but also envious of their conquerors ... " Had he not recalled Ibn Khaldun, who centuries earlier observed that 'the vanquished always want to imitate the victor'?[6] This is not to pick on Mishra (his books are great), but to illustrate a wider tendency of sensationalizing one experience over others.

When discussing imperial legacies it is tempting to get carried away, and understandably so, because few themes are as consequential to our sense of identity as to whether our ancestors dictated their fates or were dictated to. It is no fault of ours that human perception tends to relativize topics of this kind in order to try and grasp their significance.

However, there can be no leader board of imperial legacies. Even if we do not actively rank and order them, the implicit sense of relativization is part and parcel of looking out at the world. Those who think all empires were equally bad all the time should think again, just as those who think some were far better than others should also think again; instead, they should judge each by its record and legacies, before considering how those legacies now intermix.

While this is good advice when settling down to read a book on the subject, or in the wonderfully cloistered world of universities, it is more difficult amidst the cut and thrust of real-world catastrophes, where raw passions, unyielding emotions and fate rule the day. History can often turn on what appears to be irrational calculations by the protagonists. This is especially noticeable in a crisis, when nations and public alike can fall back on instinctive responses, which often reflect the imperial instincts they have unwittingly inherited. When the chips really are down, a nation's traditional proclivities, points of reference and parochial attitudes often become more apparent. An obvious example would be the USA after 9/11, and how its government settled on using its globe-straddling military presence to confront 'terrorists', with many of its citizens settled on backing this strategy in the name of patriotism. Or how about after the 2008 global financial crisis, when different European nations set upon each other in trying to clear up the mess, and the EU dictated the terms of austerity to its financially weaker members. Or after Russia saw Ukraine pull closer to the EU, and responded by annexing Crimea in 2014. And so on – the role of imperial legacies in *causing* the crises is not the focus in these instances, but rather how these legacies have influenced the *response*.

Civilizations don't clash; imperial legacies collide

Such is the power of these inherited histories of empire that while we all belong to the same species, it can sometimes feel otherwise, in ways that are deeply unsettling. Our various post-imperial legacies continue to collide on all kinds of issues, leaving world order to be shaped by these interactions. Some of the biggest collisions are between countries with contending imperial legacies, and especially between aspirant or actual great powers.

As I write, there are numerous examples of great geopolitical problems that bedevil the world today and have their genesis in imperial legacies. Take, for example, the collapse in Russia–UK relations. Since the Ukraine War began in 2014, Russia's post-imperial pugnaciousness has grown. Amongst the clashes this has provoked has been one with Britain's equally stiff-backed post-imperial elite. The events this has led to seem absurd by modern standards, and probably to many citizens of both countries, but make sense if we see them as a tussle between two elites that are influenced by residual post-imperial pride. In 2018 Russian intelligence officers travelled to the UK and attempted to administer a nerve agent to kill one of their own who had defected to the UK years ago. Trying to stage a chemical attack on British soil is an extreme way to aggravate a rival; for its part, Britain has tried to sanction Russia for all its rule-breaking behaviour, from alleged online manipulation of Western public opinion to the Ukraine War. Neither London nor Moscow has readily been able to back down from this staring contest, such is the post-imperial pride at stake for both countries.

We are also witness to a simmering USA–China rivalry in the world today. How these behemoths interact will be deeply influenced by their radically different visions for the world after formal empires. The USA does not consider itself to be an empire, but believes it is historically taking a stand against various manifestations of tyranny. China, on the other hand, sees its present ascent as historically consistent with its long lineage of imperial history. There are specific debates to be had between the USA and China concerning human rights, security in the Pacific Ocean, the terms of trade, and so on. Lurking in the background for China will be a sense derived from history that it is to be respected, as a great power around which smaller countries orbit, whereas the US will expect others to agree that its global dominance is a consensual affair based on guaranteeing freedoms. Both countries have particular post-imperial mentalities that manifest in their own versions of informal empire. So long as there is space enough for both of them, these visions will not collide, but as soon as they do, we can expect intransigence on both sides.

'The clash of civilizations' has been one of the most influential one-line phrases to enter the lexicon, by purporting to explain what might be going wrong in the world. Thanks to political scientist Samuel Huntington, who coined the phrase, the clash sounds rather inevitable. The flaw in this logic is that civilizations do not animate and organize themselves to clash with each other – historically, it has been the role of empires to do so on their behalf, and today it is the after-images of empires that set the clashes in motion.

Managing great power contests in the coming decades will demand an acknowledgement of how great powers interpret the meaning of the world without empires, and how they try and build new lines of domination and control in different dimensions of the human experience.

Post-imperial visions clashing online and in AI

With the passage of time, we can see a clear example of how a once-new technology has been absorbed and appropriated in the post-imperial world.

Just before the Internet became a daily reality, a major innovation in global communication was the twenty-four-hour rolling news channel. This was considered revolutionary in the early 1990s, when pioneered by America's CNN. During the 1991 Gulf War, CNN's running commentary of US military operations, replete with airborne footage of precision aerial strikes on Iraqi forces, seemed to herald a new frontier in the propaganda potential to demonstrate national strength. Since then other nations have got in on the act, competing in the global English-language news arena, including RT, France 24, Al Jazeera, Turkey's TRT World, and so on. Surfing the news channels reveals a simultaneous stream of parallel perspectives on the breaking news items, with some stories receiving more attention than others. Some of these channels have government backing, while others might be freer to pursue their own editorial line. Regardless, this has resulted in rival contending streams of information, each with its own broad national and civilizational concerns.

Rather than technology bringing our species closer together, it risks entrenching how far apart we are. It is precisely *because* of the modernity of the information age that we will not witness a merging of identities, but a likely redoubling of allegiances based on nationally specific portrayals, each built on the foundations of a different interpretation of history. Current affairs can be reduced to soundbites and Internet memes that only have traction with audiences steeped in certain post-imperial traditions.

This is already visible in the recourse to nationalism that has swept across several parts of the world in the 2010s, and how it has been catalysed by the rapid diffusion of targeted messages to select constituencies. Post-imperial mentalities can often be detectable in nationalism, for instance in nations that suffered painfully when shedding their occupiers, such as the Philippines, where part of President Duterte's nationalistic appeal was built on critiquing the US, the former colonial power. Elsewhere, leaders like Putin in Russia and Erdogan in Turkey can whip up nationalist storms that dig deep into the well of residual pride in an old imperial identity. In the UK the political movement around Brexit built its nationalist allure by appealing to a British pride independent from continental Europe, the foundations of which lie in Britain's imperial past. For Donald Trump, his nationalism has been stoked by the desire to build a wall along the border with Mexico – a move that invokes white America's settler past along its frontier. Even Modi's stunning landslide re-election in 2019 shows in its own way how nationalism relies on offering messages that appease a post-imperial unease, which people of newer generations often don't even know they are experiencing.

The clash that erupted in 2019 over the Chinese telecoms company Huawei offers a vision of colliding post-imperial visions in a different arena. The US government's intelligence community came to an assessment that Huawei's telecoms infrastructure was vulnerable to Chinese government manipulation, citing a provision in Chinese law that obliged the company always to cooperate with its government. The fear propagated by the US government was of the Chinese government having the potential to harvest communications data, or perhaps to block communications in parts of the world where Huawei built the telecoms infrastructure. There was also a clear commercial incentive: knocking Huawei for six, by having the firm's heir arrested in Canada, and by threatening to deny Huawei access to the US-designed Android software, would remove a competitor for US companies. But at its heart, this was a tussle for global dominance in one of several technology realms, which previews how the latest empires of commerce and influence are being built.

Technology is already moving from the information age to the artificial-intelligence age, but even then humans will be involved in programming AI algorithms, and in deciding how these devices should be employed. For these reasons, the AI age will also reflect imperial legacies in the way different parts of the world control and copy these technologies, and adapt them to their national cultures. Former Google China president Kai-Fu Lee spots an imperial tradition of copying technology, found in Beijing's Forbidden City: 'The Hall of the Ancestors dates back to the Ming Dynasty, and the story of China's own copycat clockmakers played out hundreds of years in the past. But the same cultural currents continue to flow into the present day' in the way Chinese tech companies appropriate Western technologies.[7] As AI increasingly affects everything from warfare to education and workplace productivity, those countries able to enter the race as hubs of this technology – and as suppliers to others – will be able to forge new domains of influence and control. Those countries that are left out, or left behind, might find that they become subservient to the providers of the most vital advanced technologies, and in this way AI would accentuate the inequalities between nations.

The most forward-looking technologists should therefore consult the imperial past, if they wish to understand the causes to which their innovations may eventually be put.

Authoritarianism is one such cause. From China's perspective, authoritarianism is not automatically bad. Hierarchy is how order has been achieved and expanded, not through quests for equality. The origins of these attitudes are quintessentially historical and imperial – the imposition of hierarchy was crucial to China's experience of achieving its own unity and avoiding the perils of disunity. Communist rule has embedded and hardened these lessons for the modern world, and they will influence how it puts new technologies to use.

Outside its borders, the historical pattern of Chinese expansion has generated an expectation that others pledge fealty to its civilization, but don't necessarily convert to it. Contrastingly, Western expansion in the past has encouraged and expected a degree of conversion to Western ways. Whether it relates to political, economic, linguistic or other ways of operating, the West has wanted to be mimicked, which is why growing Chinese influence will generate resistance from the West. The USA and Europe want to maintain their privileged positions in global commerce and political culture, and feel that it is morally correct to do so, because China is an authoritarian country.

Such is the nature of Western pride in its own cultural and historical accomplishments that there is little prospect of it ever really accepting a Chinese post-imperial vision of world order. Instead, the USA and Europe will have to accept changes – for example, in losing their monopolization of the term 'international community'. This term has been used to convey Western leadership of the post-imperial world as it came into focus after 1945 and 1991, but it already has less traction.

Back in the 1940s, while sitting in a British jail, Nehru pondered the following: 'About 500 years ago Europe revived and slowly spread eastward and westward till, in the course of centuries, it became the dominant content of the world in power, wealth, and culture. Was there some cycle about this change and is that process now being reversed?"[8] The answer was no, since Europe's dominance was followed by America's, which has delayed the coming into focus of this broad historical cycle. Even if the era of Western global expansion may have peaked, and its norms will not be diffused as wantonly as in the past, this does not spell terminal decline for the West. Instead, it spells an era of interplay between many post-imperial visions, evident in everything from geopolitics, to commerce and inter-cultural exchanges. Rather than the future being Asia, the future will feature more two-way streets of reciprocal influence between different nationalities.

Consciousness is the first step to taming imperial legacies

Nations are certainly not the only source of a person's identity. Many of us have mixed backgrounds and live in an interconnected world in which social media and readily available travel options mean that we increasingly interact with other cultures, even if only by passively consuming stories from around the world online. But on which terms are these interactions taking place? Against which pre-existing sympathies are new stories being assimilated? And are people culturally cognisant enough to turn off their own biases during these everyday cross-border experiences?

Some people are true chameleons, either being born into multiple cultures or shedding the cultures of their birth for something constructed from an amalgam of other identities. For other people, no matter the amount of travel and foreign cultural assimilation they open themselves up to, they retain the cultural ballast from their past. Perhaps later in life, or in times of personal crisis, stories of their ancestral experiences, last heard when they were children, may resonate again in the shape of a dominant culture.

Cultures are not discrete. Ethnic mixing is one of the most enduring legacies of empire and post-imperial connections. As parts of the world move away from expressly racialist conceptions of identity, so the notion of a 'thoroughbred' member of a given community may erode in some parts of the world. That said, there are still core national and civilizational myths that even people of mixed heritage may have to buy into, not least to be accepted into the cultures in which they choose to live. The majority of the world's populace are not jet-setters anyway. And for those of you who are jet-setting cultural chameleons, never underestimate the extent to which national tradition still rules over parts of your life and your own mind.

Even if different world cultures each produce their own version of a travelling elite, it is hardly going to 'convert' their brethren en masse to see the world through someone else's eyes. The only intellectually responsible way to belong to the privileged globe-trotting elite who study in foreign universities and work between several countries is to understand how unrepresentative such a life might be. It is far wiser to hold an enlightened perspective of privilege than to think badly of your country folk for staying at home.

Governments too should certainly be aware of how homogenous they are, and the extent to which the strongest of them effectively trade off cultural overconfidence. A theme that resurfaces, wherever in the world one looks, is how past imperial successes have deposited the habit of authority within certain groups of people. Not that these people have conquered or occupied anything personally; just that they have inherited the sense of having done so, through their cultural DNA. Politicians, civil servants and militaries around the world operate on the basis of some sort of national pride, not because they naively believe their nations to be infallible, but because national stories will have been intrinsic to the formation of their systems. National government institutions remain bastions of cultural homogeneity because their core staff are nationals of their own country (as opposed to a modern global company, which might have a suitably global workforce).

Culturally homogeneous national government institutions are not going away. In some parts of the world, such as Russia or

China, there may be less impetus to fundamentally alter their essential assumptions. This means that the pride of an imperial inheritance can be preserved within the 'core' of the state. Imbued with such pride, it is unlikely that politicians or foreign-policy professionals are suddenly going to accept collective historical blame for past events, so instead it can produce a kind of self-confidence, bordering on arrogance.

Living with imperial legacies whilst they blend with forthcoming realities and transform once again: this is our fate. In a world of unpredictability and misunderstanding, it is better accepted and understood than downplayed or simply undetected. We are heading somewhere that differs from our past, but some of the coordinates may have already been set by history as we endeavour to navigate our unknown futures.

BIBLIOGRAPHY

INTRODUCTION

BBC News, 'Yanxi Palace: The most Googled show on Earth', 23 December 2018

Boot, Max, *The Savage Wars of Peace: Small War and Rise of American Power* (New York: Basic, 2014)

Burbank, Jane and Cooper, Frederick, *Empires in World History* (New Jersey: Princeton University Press, 2010)

Darwin, John, *After Tamerlane: The Global History of Empire* (London: Penguin, 2007)

Doyle, Michael, *Empires* (New York: Cornell University, 1986)

Harari, Yuval Noah, *Sapiens: A Brief History of Humankind* (London: Vintage Books, 2014)

Hobsbawm, Eric, *The Age of Empires* (London: Cardinal, 1991)

Hobson, J. A., *Imperialism: A History* (New York: James Pott & Company, 1902)

Howe, Stephen, *Empire: A Very Short Introduction* (Oxford: OUP, 2002)

Hürriyet Daily News, 'TV Series Suleiman the Magnificent reconquered Arab world and Balkans', 10 December 2013

Johnson, Samuel, *The Dictionary of the English Language* (1st edn, 1755)

Khanna, Paraag, *Connectography: Mapping the Future of Global Civilisation* (London: Random House, 2017)

Kumar, Krishin, *Visions of Empire: How Five Imperial Regimes Shaped the World* (New Jersey: Princeton University Press, 2017)

Lieven, Dominic, *Empire: The Russian Empire and its Rivals* (New Haven/London: Yale Nota Bene, 2002)

Memmi, Albert, *The Coloniser and the Colonised* (London: Earthscan Publications, 1990)

Nandy, Ashis, *Time Warps: Silent and Evasive Pasts in Indian Politics and Religion* (New Jersey: Rutgers University Press, 2002)

Nkrumah, Kwame, *Neo-Colonialism, The Last Stage of Imperialism* (London: Panaf, 1965)

Orwell, George, *All Art Is Propaganda: Critical Essays* (Wilmington, VA: Mariner Books, 2009)

Ridley, Matthew, *Genome: The Autobiography of a Species* (New York: HarperCollins, 2000)

Said, Edward, *Culture and Imperialism* (London: Vintage Books, 1993)

—— *Orientalism* (London: Penguin, 2003)

Seeley, J. R., *The Expansion of England* (1883)

Sharman, Jason and Phillips, Andrew, *International Order in Diversity: Trade and Rule in the Indian Ocean* (Cambridge: CUP, 2015)

ONE

America's Imperial Inheritance

Bicheno, Hugh, *Rebels and Redcoats: The American Revolutionary War* (London: HarperCollins, 2003)

Boot, Max, *The Savage Wars of Peace: Small War and Rise of American Power* (New York: Basic Books, 2014)

Chomsky, Noam, *Hegemony or Survival: America's Quest for Global Dominance* (London: Penguin, 2004)

Darwin, John, *After Tamerlane: The Global History of Empire* (London: Penguin, 2007)

Du Bois, William, *Of the Dawn of Freedom* (1903/London: Penguin, 2009)

Fair, Christine, Crane, Keith, Chivvis, Christopher and Puri, Samir, *Pakistan: Helping to Secure an Insecure State* (California: RAND, 2010)

Ferguson, Niall, *Colussus: The Rise and Fall of the American Empire* (London: Penguin, 2004)

Frankopan, Peter, *The New Silk Roads* (London: Bloomsbury, 2015)

Greene, Graham, *The Quiet American* (New York: Penguin, 1955)

Hahn, Steven, *A Nation Without Borders: The US and its World in an Age of Civil Wars, 1830–1910* (New York: Penguin, 2017)

Hoock, Holger, *Scars of Independence: America's Violent Birth* (New York: Broadway Books, 2017)

Hopkins, A. J., *American Empire: A Global History* (New Jersey: Princeton University Press, 2018)

Huntington, Samuel, *Who Are We? The Challenges to America's National Identity* (Simon & Schuster, 2004)

Ikenberry, John G., 'Power and Liberal Order: America's Postwar World Order in Transition', *International Relations of the Asia-Pacific*, January 2005, 5:2

Immerwahr, Daniel, *How to Hide an Empire: A Short History of the Greater United States* (London: The Bodley Head, 2019)

Johnson, Chalmers, *Blowback: The Costs and Consequences of American Empire* (New York: Henry Holt, 2000)

Kaplan, Robert, *Imperial Grunts: On the Ground with the American Military, from Mongolia to the Philippines to Iraq and Beyond* (New York: Vintage, 2006)

Karp, Matthew, *This Vast Southern Empire: Slaveholders at the Helm of American Foreign Policy* (Massachusetts: Harvard University Press, 2016)

Kinzer, Stephen, *The True Flag: Theodore Roosevelt, Mark Twain, and the Birth of American Empire* (New York: St Martin's Griffin, 2017)

Layne, Christopher and Thayler, Bradley, *American Empire: A Debate* (New York: Routledge, 2007)

Lieven, Anatol, *America Right or Wrong?* (Oxford: OUP, 2012)

Lincoln, Abraham, *The Gettysburg Address* (London: Penguin, 2009)

Mahan, Alfred T., *Lessons of the War with Spain* (Boston: Little, Brown, and Company, 1899)

Morris, Ian, *War: What is it Good For?* (London: Profile Books, 2014)

Munkler, Herfried, *Empires: the Logic of World Domination from Ancient Rome to the United States* (Cambridge: Polity Press, 2007)

Northup, Solomon, *Twelve Years a Slave* (1853/London: HarperCollins, 2014)

Obama, Barack, *The Audacity of Hope* (New York: Crown, 2006)

Pedersen, Susan, *The Guardians: The League of Nations and the Crisis of Empire* (Oxford: OUP, 2015)

Porter, Bernard, *Empire and Subempire: Britain, America and the World* (New Haven: Yale University Press, 2006)

Power, Samantha, *'A Problem from Hell': America and the Age of Genocide* (New York: Perennial, 2003)

Public Religion Research Institute, 'Partisan Polarization Dominates Trump Era: Findings from the 2018 American Values Survey', 29 October 2018

Stephanson, Anders, *Manifest Destiny: American Expansion and the Empire of the Right* (New York: Hill and Wang, 1995)

Trump, Donald, *Crippled America: How to Make America Great Again* (New York: Threshold Editions, 2015)

Turner, Frederick Jackson, *The Significance of the Frontier in American History* (London: Penguin, 2009)

US Census Bureau, 'Older People Projected to Outnumber Children for First Time in US History', Press Release, 13 March 2018

Washington, George, 'A Great Experiment', in Stedman and Hutchinson, comps., *A Library of American Literature: An Anthology in Eleven Volumes, Vol. III: Literature of the Revolutionary Period, 1765–1787* (1891).

Weinberg, Albert K., *Manifest Destiny: A Study of Nationalist Expansion in American History* (Quadrangle Books, 1935)

Zakaria, Fareed, *From Wealth to Power: The Unusual Origins of America's World Role* (New Jersey: Princeton University Press, 1999)

TWO

Britain's Grandeur and Guilt of Empire

Bell, Duncan, *The Idea of Greater Britain 1860–1900* (New Jersey: Princeton University Press, 2007)

—— 'The Anglosphere: New enthusiasm for an old dream', *Prospect*, 19 January 2017

Biggar, Neil, 'Don't feel guilty about our colonial history', *The Times*, 30 November 2017

Brandon, Piers, *The Decline and Fall of the British Empire; 1781–1997* (London: Vintage, 2008)

Callwell, Charles, *Small Wars: Their Principles and Practice* (1896)

Churchill, Winston S., *Never Give In!: Winston Churchill's Speeches* (London: Bloomsbury, 2013)

Colley, Linda, *Britons: The Forging of a Nation* (London: Pimlico, 1992)

Darwin, John, *Unfinished Empire: The Global Expansion of Britain* (London: Penguin, 2012)

Dorling, Danny and Tomlinson, Sally, *Rule Britannia: Brexit and the End of Empire* (London: Biteback Publishing Limited, 2019)

The Economist, 'A Peal for Friendship', 10 August 2018

Ferguson, Niall, *Empire: How Britain Made the Modern World* (London: Penguin, 2004)

Gilley, Bruce, 'Case for Colonialism' in *Third World Quarterly* (published 2017, later withdrawn)

Hall, Catherine, 'Culture and Identity in Imperial Britain' in Stockwell, Sarah (2008)

Howe, Stephen, 'Empire and Ideology' in Stockwell, Sarah (2008)

James, Lawrence, *Churchill and Empire: Portrait of an Imperialist* (London: Weidenfeld & Nicolson, 2013)

Johnson, Boris, 'UK and America can be better friends than ever Mr Obama . . . if we LEAVE the EU', *The Sun*, 22 April 2016

Johnston, Alastair Iain, *Cultural Realism: Strategic Culture and Grand Strategy in Chinese History* (New Jersey: Princeton University Press, 1995)

Kipling, Rudyard, *Kim* (1901/Hertfordshire: Wordsworth Editions, 2009)

Kwarteng, Kwasi, *Ghosts of Empire: Britain's Legacies in the Modern World* (London: Bloomsbury, 2012)

Ledwidge, Frank, *Losing Small Wars: British Military Failure in Iraq and Afghanistan* (New Haven/London: Yale University Press, 2011)

Marr, Andrew, *A History of Modern Britain* (London: Macmillan, 2007)

Mills, J. Saxon, *The Future of the Empire: An Account of the Growth and Extent of the British Empire* (1918)

Murphy, Philip, 'Britain as a Global Power in the Twentieth Century', in Thompson, Andrew (2012)

Orwell, George, *Burmese Days* (1934/London: Penguin, 1996)

Oswald, Michael, *The Spider's Web: An investigation into the world of Britain's secrecy jurisdictions and the City of London* (documentary, 2017)

Palan, Ronen, 'The Second British Empire' in Palan, Ronen and Halperin, Sandra (eds), *Legacies of Empire: Imperial Roots of the Contemporary Global Order* (Cambridge: CUP, 2015)

Patten, Chris, *East and West* (London: Macmillan, 1998)

Porter, Bernard, *British Imperial: What the Empire Wasn't* (London/New York: I. B. Taurus, 2016)

Reynolds, David, '1940: Fulcrum of the Twentieth Century?', *International Affairs*, 1990, 66:2

Seeley, J. R., *The Expansion of England* (1883)

Seymour, Richard, 'The Real Winston Churchill', *Jacobin*, 1 November 2018 (accessed 1 February 2019): https://www.jacobinmag.com/2018/01/winston-churchill-british-empire-colonialism

Shepherd, Robert, *Enoch Powell: A Biography* (London: Hutchinson, 1996)

Shilliam, Robbie, *Race and the Undeserving Poor* (Newcastle: Agenda Publishing, 2018)

Simms, Brendan, *Britain's Europe* (London: Allen Lane, 2016)

Stockwell, Sarah (ed.), *The British Empire: Themes and Perspectives* (Oxford: Blackwell Publishing, 2008)

Tharoor, Shashi, *Inglorious Empire: What the British did to India* (London: C. Hurst & Co., 2017)

Thompson, Andrew, 'Empire and the British State', in Stockwell, Sarah (2008)

—— (ed.), *Britain's Experience of Empire in the Twentieth Century* (Oxford: OUP, 2012)

Toye, Richard, *Churchill's Empire* (London: Pan Books, 2011)

Toynbee, Arnold, *The Conduct of British Empire Foreign Relations Since the Peace Settlement* (London: OUP, 1928)

Walton, Calder, *Empire of Secrets: British Intelligence, the Cold War and the Twilight of Empire* (London: Harper Press, 2013)

YouGov, 'The British Empire is "something to be proud of"', polling from 2014 (accessed 1 February 2019): https://yougov.co.uk/news/2014/07/26/britain-proud-its-empire/

Young, Hugo, *This Blessed Plot: Britain and Europe from Churchill to Blair* (London: Macmillan, 1998)

THREE

The European Union's Post-Imperial Project

D'Appollonia, Ariane Chebel, 'European Nationalism and European Union' in Pagden, Anthony (2002)

Asad, Talal, 'Muslims and European Identity' in Pagden, Anthony (2002)

Ascherson, Neal, *Black Sea* (New York: Hill and Wang, 1995)

Beard, Mary, *SPQR: A History of Ancient Rome* (London: Profile Books, 2016)

Bhambra, Gurminder K., 'Postcolonial Europe: Or, understanding Europe in times of the postcolonial' in Rumford, Chris (ed.), *Sage Handbook of European Studies* (London: Sage, 2009)

Blaut, James Morris, *The Colonizer's Model of the World: Geographical Diffusionism and Eurocentric History* (New York: Guilford Press, 1993)

Crowley, Roger, *Conquerors: How Portugal Seized the Indian Ocean and Forged the First Global Empire* (London, Faber: 2015)

Doyle, Michael, *Empires* (New York: Cornell University, 1986)

Du Bois, William, *Of the Dawn of Freedom* (1903/London: Penguin, 2009)

Duchêne, François, *Jean Monnet* (New York/London: W. W. Norton and Co., 1994)

European Commission, 'White Paper on the Future of Europe: Reflections and scenarios on the EU 27 by 2015' (Brussels, 1 March 2017)

Frankopan, Peter, *The New Silk Roads* (London: Bloomsbury, 2015)

Fukuyama, Francis, *Political Order and Political Decay* (London: Profile Books, 2015)

Garton Ash, Timothy, *Facts are Subversive: Political Writings from a Decade without a Name* (London: Atlantic Books, 2009)

Gravier, Magali, 'Empire vs federation: which path for Europe?', *Journal of Political Power*, 2011, 4:3, pp.413–31

—— 'Imperial Administration: Comparing the Byzantine Empire and the EU', in Parker, Noel (ed.), *Empire and the International Order* (Aldershot: Ashgate, 2013)

Gress, David, *From Plato to Nato: The Idea of the West and its Opponents* (New York: The Free Press, 1998)

Habermas, Jurgen, *Europe: The Faltering Project* (Cambridge: Polity Press, 2009)

—— trans. Ciran Cronin, *The Lure of Technocracy* (Cambridge: Polity Press, 2015)

Heer, Friedrich, trans. Janet Sondheimer, *The Holy Roman Empire* (London: Phoenix, 1968/1995)

Hochschild, Adam, *King Leopold's Ghost: A Story of Greed, Terror and Heroism in Colonial Africa* (London: Pan Macmillan, 2006)

Kumar, Krishin, *Visions of Empire: How Five Imperial Regimes Shaped the World* (New Jersey: Princeton University Press, 2017)

Middelaar, Luuk van, trans. Liz Waters, *The Passage to Europe: How a Continent Became a Union* (New Haven/London: Yale University Press, 2013)

Milward, Alan, *The European Rescue of the Nation-State* (Oxon: Routledge, 1992/2000)

Monnet, Jean, trans. Richard Mayne, *Memoirs* (London: Third Millennium Publishing, 2015)

Pagden, Anthony, *Lords of All the World: Ideologies of Empire in Spain, Britain and France c.1500–c.1800* (New Haven/London: Yale University Press, 1995)

—— (ed.), *The Idea of Europe: From Antiquity to the European Union* (Cambridge: CUP, 2002)

Parker, Noel, 'Imperialism, territory, and liberation: on the dynamics of empire stemming from Europe', *Journal of Political Power*, 2011, 4:3, pp.355–74

Passerini, Luisa, 'From the Ironies of Identity' in Pagden, Anthony (2002)

Pinder, John and Usherwood, Simon, *The European Union: A Very Short Introduction* (Oxford: OUP, 2013)

Porter, Roy, *The Enlightenment in National Context* (Cambridge: CUP, 1981)

Roper, Hugh Trevor, *The Rise of Christian Europe* (London: Thames and Hudson, 1965)

Simms, Brendan, *Britain's Europe* (London: Allen Lane, 2016)

Tharoor, Shashi, *Pax Indica: India and the World of the 21st Century* (New Delhi: Allen Lane, 2012)

Tilly, Charles, *Coercion, Capital and European States, AD 990–1990* (Oxford: Wiley-Blackwell, 1993)

Varoufakis, Yanis, *And the Weak Suffer What They Must? Europe, Austerity and the Threat to Global Stability* (London: Vintage, 2017)

Walter, Dierk, *Colonial Violence: European Empires and the Use of Force* (London: Hurst, 2017)

Zamoyski, Adam, *Poland: A History* (London: William Collins, 2015)

Zielonka, Jan, *Europe as Empire: The Nature of the Enlarged European Union* (Oxford: OUP, 2006)

—— 'Europe's new civilizing missions: The EU's normative power discourse', *Journal of Political Ideologies*, 2013, 18:1, pp.35–55

—— *Is The EU Doomed?* (Cambridge: Polity, 2014)

FOUR

Russia's Embrace of its Imperial Legacy

Berlin, Isaiah, *The Hedgehog and the Fox: An Essay on Tolstoy's View of History* (London: Phoenix, 1999)

Darwin, John, *After Tamerlane: The Global History of Empire* (London: Penguin, 2007)

d'Encausse, Hélène Carrère, *The End of the Soviet Empire: The Triumph of the Nations* (New York: HarperCollins, 1993)

Figes, Orlando, *Natasha's Dance: A Cultural History of Russia* (London: Penguin, 2002)

Gessen, Masha, *The Future is History: How Totalitarianism Reclaimed Russia* (London: Granta Books, 2017)

Goldfarb, Alex with Litvinenko, Marina, *Death of a Dissident* (London: Simon & Schuster, 2007)

Grigas, Agina, *Beyond Crimea: New Russian Empire* (New Haven/London: Yale University Press, 2016)

Hill, Fiona and Gaddy, Clifford, *Mr Putin: Operative in the Kremlin* (Washington DC: Brookings, 2013)

Howard, Michael, *The Causes of War* (Farnham: Ashgate Publishing Limited, 1983)

Kapuscinski, Ryszard, *Imperium* (New York: Vintage Books, 1994)

Klyuchevsky, Vasili, trans. Liliana Archibald, *Peter the Great* (New York: St Martin's Press, 1969)

Kumar, Krishin, *Visions of Empire: How Five Imperial Regimes Shaped the World* (New Jersey: Princeton University Press, 2017)

Laruelle, Marlene, *Russian Eurasianism: An Ideology of Empire* (Maryland: Johns Hopkins University Press, 2012)

Lavrov, Sergei, 'Russia's Foreign Policy in Historical Perspective', *Russia in Global Affairs*, March 2016

Lenin, Vladimir Ilyich, *Imperialism: The Highest Stage of Capitalism* (1917/London: Penguin, 2010)

Lieven, Dominic, *Empire: The Russian Empire and its Rivals* (New Haven/London: Yale Nota Bene, 2002)

Lo, Bobo, *Russia and the New World Disorder* (London: Chatham House, 2015)

Makarychev, Andrey, 'Imperial discourse in a post-imperial Russia' in Parker, Noel (ed.), *Empire and International Order* (Oxon: Routledge, 2016)

Motyl, Alexander, *Imperial Ends: The Decay, Collapse, and Revival of Empires* (New York: Columbia University Press, 2001)

Munkler, Herfried, *Empires: the Logic of World Domination from Ancient Rome to the United States* (Cambridge: Polity Press, 2007)

Neuman, Iver B. and Wigen, Einar, 'The legacy of Eurasian nomadic empires' in Palan, Ronen and Halperin, Sandra, *Legacies of Empire: Imperial Roots of the Contemporary Global Order* (Cambridge: CUP, 2015)

Plokhy, Serhii, *Lost Kingdom: A History of Russian Nationalism from Ivan the Great to Vladimir Putin* (London: Penguin Random House, 2018)

Putin, Vladimir, 'Annual Address to the Federal Assembly of the Russian Federation', 25 April 2005 (accessed 1 February 2018): http://en.kremlin.ru/events/president/transcripts/22931

Reynolds, Michael, *Shattering Empires: The Clash and Collapse of the Ottoman and Russian Empires 1908–1918* (Cambridge: CUP, 2011)

Stone, Oliver, 'The Putin Interviews: Part Three', Showtime, 2017

Tolstoy, Leo, *War and Peace*, trans. Louise and Aylmer Maude (1869/ Hertfordshire: Wordsworth Classics, 1993)

Tsygankov, Andrie, *Russia's Foreign Policy: Change and Continuity in National Identity* (Maryland: Rowman & Littlefield, 2nd revised edn 2010)

Watson, Hugh Seaton, *The Decline of Imperial Russia, 1855–1914* (New York: Praeger, 1952)

FIVE

China's Janus Faces of Empire

Allison, Graham, *The Thucydides Trap: Can China and America Escape War?* (New York: Houghton, 2017)

BBC News, 'Hong Kong protests: China tells UK not to interfere in "domestic affairs"', 3 July 2019 (accessed 5 August 2019): https:// www.bbc.co.uk/news/uk-politics-48855643

Benjamin, Craig, *Empires of Ancient Eurasia: The First Silk Roads Era, 100 BCE–250 CE* (Cambridge: CUP, 2018)

Chang, Jung, *Wild Swans: Three Daughters of China* (London: Harper-Collins, 1991)

—— and Halliday, Jon, *Mao: The Unknown Story* (London: Vintage, 2007)

Chih-Yu Shih, *China's Just World: The Morality of Chinese Foreign Policy* (Colorado and London: Lynne Rienner, 1993)

Darwin, John, *After Tamerlane: The Global History of Empire* (London: Penguin, 2007)

The Economist, UK print edition, 25 May 2019

Feng Zhang, *Chinese Hegemony: Grand Strategy and International Institutions in East Asian History* (California: Stanford University Press, 2015)

Ford, Matthew, *The Mind of Empire: China's History and Modern Foreign Relations* (Kentucky: University Press of Kentucky, 2010)

French, Howard, *Everything Under the Heavens: How the Past Helps China's Push for Global Power* (Victoria: Scribe, 2017)

Fukuyama, Francis, *The Origins of Political Order* (London: Profile Books, 2011)

Ge Zhaoguang, *What is China?*, trans. Michael Gibbs Hills (Cambridge: Belknap Press, 2018)

Harari, Yuval Noah, *Sapiens: A Brief History of Humankind* (London: Vintage Books, 2014)

Hinton, David (trans.), *The Four Chinese Classics: Tao Te Ching, Chuang Tzu, Analects, Mencius* (Berkeley: Counterpoint, 2013)

Jacques, Martin, *When China Rules the World* (London: Penguin, 2nd edn 2012)

Johnston, Alastair Iain, *Cultural Realism: Strategic Culture and Grand Strategy in Chinese History* (New Jersey: Princeton University Press, 1995)

—— *Social States: China in International Institutions, 1980–2000* (New Jersey and Oxford: Princeton University Press, 2008)

Kang, David, *China Rising* (New York: Colombia University Press, 2007)

—— *East Asia Before the West* (New York: Colombia University Press, 2010)

Keay, John, *China: A History* (London: HarperCollins, 2008)

Kissinger, Henry, *On China* (New York: Penguin Press, 2011)

Lovell, Julia, *The Opium War* (London: Picador, 2011)

Luo Guanzhong, *The Romance of the Three Kingdoms*, trans. Martin Palmer (London: Penguin, 2018)

Man, John, *The Mongol Empire: Genghis Khan, His Heirs and the Founding of Modern China* (London: Bantam Press, 2014)

Mearshimer, John, 'The Gathering Storm: China's Challenge to US Power in Asia', *The Chinese Journal of International Politics*, 2010, 3, pp.381–96

Miller, Tom, *China's Asian Dream* (London: Zed Books, 2017)

Mitter, Rana, *A Bitter Revolution: China's Struggle with the Modern World* (Oxford: OUP, 2004)

Morris, Ian, *Why the West Rules . . . For Now: The Patterns of History and What they Reveal About the Future* (London: Profile Books, 2011)

Parello-Plesner, Jonas and Duchatel, Mathieu, *China's Strong Arm: Protecting Citizens and Assets Abroad* (Oxon: Routledge, 2015)

Platt, Stephen, *Imperial Twilight: The Opium War and the End of China's Last Golden Age* (London: Atlantic Books, 2018)

Puri, Samir, 'The strategic hedging of Iran, Russia and China: Juxtaposing participation in the global system with regional revisionism', *Journal of Global Security Studies*, 2017

Sun Tzu, *The Art of War*, trans. John Minford (London: Penguin Classics, 2014)

Wood, Frances, *Great Books of China: From Ancient Times to the Present* (London: Head of Zeus, 2017)

Xi Jinping, *Governance of China* (Beijing: ICP Intercultural Press, 2014)

Yan Xuetong, *Ancient Chinese Thought, Modern Chinese Power* (New Jersey: Princeton University Press, 2011)

Zhao Tingyang, 'Rethinking Empire from the Chinese Concept "All Under Heaven"' in Callahan, William A. and Barabantseva, Elena (eds), *China Orders the World* (Baltimore: Johns Hopkins University Press, 2011)

—— 'Political Realism and the Western Mind' in Schuett, Robert and Hollingworth, Miles (eds), *The Edinburgh Companion to Political Realism* (Edinburgh: Edinburgh University Press, 2018)

Zheng Wang, *Never Forget National Humiliation: Historical Memory in Chinese Politics and Foreign Relations* (New York: Colombia University Press, 2012)

SIX

India's Overcoming of the 'Intimate Enemy'

Barkawi, Tarak, *Soldiers of Empire: Indian and British Armies in World War II* (Cambridge: CUP, 2017)

Bayly, C. A., *Origins of Nationality in South Asia: Patriotism and Ethical Government in the Making of Modern India* (New Delhi: OUP, 2001)

Faruqui, Munis D., *The Princes of the Mughal Empire, 1504–1719* (Cambridge: CUP, 2012)

Fukuyama, Francis, *The Origins of Political Order* (London: Profile Books, 2011)

Gandhi, Mohandas, *An Autobiography: Or the Story of My Experiments With Truth*, trans. Mahadev Desai (1927/Ahmedabad: Navajivan

Publishing House, 2008)

Guha, Ramachandra, *India After Gandhi: The History of the World's Largest Democracy* (London: Pan, 2008)

James, Lawrence, *Raj: The Making and Unmaking of British India* (Boston: Little, Brown and Company, 1998)

Keay, John, *India: A History* (London: HarperCollins, 2001)

Khilnani, Sunil, *The Idea of India* (London: Penguin, 2012)

Mohan, C. Raja, *Crossing the Rubicon: The Shaping of India's New Foreign Policy* (New York: Palgrave, 2004)

Naipaul, V. S., *An Arena of Darkness: His Discovery of India* (1964/ London: Picador, 2010)

—— *India: A Wounded Civilisation* (1977/London: Picador, 2010)

Nandy, Ashis, *The Intimate Enemy: Loss and Recovery of Self Under Colonialism* (Delhi: OUP, 1983)

—— *Time Warps: Silent and Evasive Pasts in Indian Politics and Religion* (New Jersey: Rutgers University Press, 2002)

Nehru, Jawaharlal, *The Discovery of India* (1946/New Delhi: Penguin Books India, 2004)

Price, Lance, *The Modi Effect: Inside Narendra Modi's Campaign to Transform India* (London: Hodder, 2015)

Raghavan, Srinath, *A Global History of the Creation of Bangladesh* (Massachusetts: Harvard University Press, 2013)

Richards, John, *The Mughal Empire* (Cambridge: CUP, 1995)

Savakar, V. D., *Hindutva* (1923/New Delhi: Hindi Sahita Sadan, 2009)

Sen, Amartya, *The Argumentative Indian: Writings on Indian Culture, History and Identity* (London: Penguin, 2005)

Tagore, Rabindranath, *Nationalism: All the Great Nations of Europe Have their Victims in Other Parts of the World* (1917/London: Penguin, 2010)

Tharoor, Shashi, *The Elephant, The Tiger and the Cellphone: Reflections on India the Emerging 21st-Century Power* (New York: Arcade Publishing, 2011)

—— *Pax Indica: India and the World of the 21st Century* (New Delhi: Allen Lane, 2012)

—— *Inglorious Empire: What the British did to India* (London: C. Hurst & Co., 2017)

Tunzelmann, Alex von, *Indian Summer: The Secret History of the End of the Raj* (London: Simon & Schuster, 2017)

Various authors (Rajiv Kumar, Sunil Khilnani, Pratap Bhanu Mehta, Nandan Nilekani, Shyam Saran, Siddharth Varadarajan), *Non-alignment 2.0* (Haryana: Penguin Books, 2013)

SEVEN

The Middle East's Post-Imperial Instability

Axworthy, Michael, *Iran: Empire of the Mind* (London: Penguin, 2008)

Barr, James, *A Line in the Sand: Britain, France and the Struggle that Shaped the Middle East* (London: Simon & Schuster, 2011)

bin Muhammad, Ghazi, *A Thinking Person's Guide to Islam* (London: White Thread Press, 2017)

British Museum, London, for chronologies and archaeological evidence of the ancient Middle East

Crowley, Roger, *1453: The Holy War for Constantinople and the Clash of Islam and the West* (New York: Hyperion, 2005)

Darwin, John, *After Tamerlane: The Global History of Empire* (London: Penguin, 2007)

de Bellaigue, Christopher, *The Islamic Enlightenment: The Modern Struggle Between Faith and Reason* (London: Vintage, 2018)

Fanon, Frantz, *The Wretched of the Earth* (London: Penguin, 2001)

Feldman, Noah, *The Rise and Fall of the Islamic State* (New Jersey: Princeton University Press, 2008)

Frankopan, Peter, *The New Silk Roads* (London: Bloomsbury, 2015)

Gibran, Khalil, *The Prophet* (New Delhi: Full Circle, 2011)

Glubb, John Bagot, *The Fate of Empires and Search for Survival* (Edinburgh: William Blackwood & Sons, 1977)

Goodwill, Jason, *Lords of the Horizons: A History of the Ottoman Empire* (London: Vintage, 1999)

Hokayem, Emile and Dodge, Toby (eds), *Middle Eastern Security, the US Pivot and the Rise of ISIS* (Oxon: Routledge, 2014)

Hourani, Albert, *A History of the Arab Peoples* (London: Bloomsbury, 1991)

Herzl, Theodor, *The Jewish State* (London: Penguin, 2010)

Karsh, Efraim, *Empires of the Sand: The Struggle for Mastery in the Middle East, 1789–1923* (Massachusetts: Harvard University Press, 2001)

—— *Islamic Imperialism: A History* (New Haven/London: Yale University Press, 2007)

Khaldun, Ibn, *The Muqaddimah*, trans. Frank Rosenthal (1377/Oxon: Routledge and Kegan Paul, 1958)

Khalid, Rashid, *Resurrecting Empire: Western Footprints and America's Perilous Path in the Middle East* (London/New York: I. B. Taurus, 2004)

Kumar, Krishin, *Visions of Empire: How Five Imperial Regimes Shaped the World* (New Jersey: Princeton University Press, 2017)

Lewis, Bernard, *The Middle East: 2000 Years of History from the Rise of Christianity to the Present Day* (London: Weidenfeld & Nicolson, 1995)

Lockman, Zachary, *Contending Visions of the Middle East* (Cambridge: CUP, 2009)

Mango, Andrew, *Atatürk* (London: John Murray, 1999)

Mansfield, Peter, *A History of the Middle East* (London: Penguin, 4th edn 2013)

Nasr, Vali, *The Shia Revival: How Conflicts Within Islam Will Shape the Future* (London/New York: Norton, 2006)

Oliver, Roland and Fage, J. D., *A Short History of Africa: Sixth Edition* (London: Penguin, 1990)

Pedersen, Susan, *The Guardians: The League of Nations and the Crisis of Empire* (Oxford: OUP, 2015)

Puri, Samir, *Fighting and Negotiating with Armed Groups: The Difficulty of Security Strategic Outcomes*, IISS Adelphi Series (London: Routledge, 2016)

Al-Rasheed, Madawi, *A History of Saudi Arabia* (Cambridge: CUP, 2010)

Rogan, Eugene, *The Arabs: A History* (London: Penguin, 2012)

—— *The Fall of the Ottomans: The Great War in the Middle East, 1914–1920* (London: Penguin, 2016)

Shafak, Elif, 'In Search of Untold Stories' in Lavinia Greenlaw (ed.), *1914: Goodbye to All That: Writers on the Conflict Between Life and Art* (London: Pushkin Press, 2014)

Tibi, Bassam, *Arab Nationalism: A Critical Inquiry* (Basingstoke: Macmillan, 1990)

World Bank, *Expectations and Aspirations: A New Framework for Education in the Middle East and North Africa. Overview* (Washington DC: International Bank for Reconstruction and Development/ The World Bank, 2019)

EIGHT

Africa's Scramble Beyond Colonialism

Achebe, Chinua, *Things Fall Apart* (1958/London: Penguin, 2010)

—— *An Image of Africa: Racism in Conrad's Heart of Darkness and The Trouble with Nigeria* (1977/1983/London: Penguin, 2010)

Acemoglu, Daron and Robinson, James, *Why Nations Fail* (London: Profile Books, 2013)

Adeyanju, Charles T. and Oriola, Temitope B., 'Colonialism and Contemporary African Migration: A Phenomenological Approach', *Journal of Black Studies*, 2011, 42:6

Adi, Hakim, *Pan-Africanism: A History* (London: Bloomsbury Academic, 2018)

Akyeampong, Emmanuel, Bates, Robert, Nunn, Nathan and Robinson, James, *Africa's Development in Historical Perspective* (Cambridge: CUP, 2014)

Boahen, Adu, *African Perspectives on Colonialism* (Baltimore: Johns Hopkins University Press, 1987)

Connor, Phillip, 'At Least a Million Sub-Saharan Africans Moved to Europe Since 2010', Pew Research Centre, March 2018

Conrad, Joseph, *Heart of Darkness* (1902/London: Penguin Classics, 1994)

Davidson, Basil, *The Story of Africa* (London: Mitchell Beazley, 1984)

—— *Africa, The Story of a Continent*, documentary episodes 1–8, Michael Beazley Television, Public Media Incorporated, RM Arts

Desai, Gaurav and Masquelier, Adeline, *Critical Terms for the Study of Africa* (Chicago: University of Chicago Press, 2018)

Diop, Birago, *Black Africa: The Economic and Cultural Basis for a Federated State*, trans. Harold J. Salemson (1978/Chicago: Lawrence Hill, 1987)

Dixon, Peter, *Divided by History: Roots of the Sudanese Conflict* (London: Cloudshill Press, 2019)

Ehret, Christopher, 'Africa in World History before ca. 1440' in Akyeampong, Bates, Nunn and Robinson (2014)

Fanon, Franz, *The Wretched of the Earth* (London: Penguin, 2001)

Gifford, Prosser and Louis, Roger W. M., *Decolonisation and African Independence: The Transfers of Power, 1960–1980* (New Haven/London: Yale University Press, 1988)

Hargreaves, J. D., *Decolonisation in Africa* (London/New York: Longman, 1988)

Hegel, Friedrich, *Lectures on the Philosophy of World History* (Cambridge: CUP, 1975)

Hochschild, Adam, *King Leopold's Ghost: A Story of Greed, Terror and Heroism in Colonial Africa* (London: Pan Macmillan, 2006)

Kabongo, Ilunga, 'The Catastrophe of Belgian Decolonisation' in Gifford and Louis (1988)

Kenyatta, Jomo, *Facing Mount Kenya* (1938/New York: Vintage Books, 1965)

Kwarteng, Kwasi, *Ghosts of Empire: Britain's Legacies in the Modern World* (London: Bloomsbury, 2012)

Lamphear, John and Falola, Toyin, 'Aspects of Early African History' in Martin and O'Meara (1995)

McKinsey & Company report, 'Dance of the lions and dragons: How are Africa and China engaging, and how will the partnership evolve?', June 2017

Mamdani, Mahmood, *Citizen and Subject: Contemporary Africa and the Legacy of Late Colonialism* (New Jersey: Princeton University Press, 1996)

Mandela, Nelson, *Long Walk to Freedom, Volume 1: 1918–1962* (London: Abacus, 2002)

Manning, Patrick, 'African Population, 1650–2000: Compilation and Implications of New Estimates' in Akyeampong, Bates, Nunn and Robinson (2014)

Martin, Phyllis M. and O'Meara, Patrick, *Africa: Third Edition* (Indiana: Indiana University Press, 1995)

Meredith, Martin, *The State of Africa: A History of Fifty Years of Independence* (London: Free Press, 2005)

Moyo, Dambisa, *Dead Aid* (London: Penguin, 2010)

Mwakikagile, Godfrey, *Africa and the West* (Huntington, NY: Nova Science Publishers, 2000)

Naipaul, V. S., *In a Free State* (1971/London: Picador, 2008)

——*A Bend in the River* (1979/London: Picador, 2008)

Natale, Fabrizio, Migali, Silvia and Munz, Rainer, 'Many more to come? Migration from and within Africa', European Commission (Luxembourg: Publications Office of the European Union, 2018)

Ndlovu-Gatsheni, Sabelo J. and Mhlanga, Brilliant (eds), *Bondage of Boundaries and Identity Politics in Postcolonial Africa* (Africa Institute of South Africa, 2013)

Nkrumah, Kwame, *Neo-Colonialism: The Last Stage of Imperialism* (London: Panaf, 1965)

Nyerere, Julius, *Man and Development* (Dar es Salaam: OUP, 1974)

Oliver, Roland and Fage, J. D., *A Short History of Africa: Sixth Edition* (London: Penguin, 1990)

—— *The African Experience* (London: Pimlico, 1993)

Pakenham, *The Boer War* (London: Weidenfeld & Nicolson, 1979)

Parello-Plesner, Jonas and Duchatel, Mathieu, *China's Strong Arm: Protecting Citizens and Assets Abroad* (Oxon: Routledge, 2015)

Reid, Richard J., *A Modern History of Africa: 1800 to the Present* (Chichester: Wiley-Blackwell, 2012)

Rodney, Walter, *How Europe Underdeveloped Africa* (Dar es Salaam: Tanzania Publishing House, 1972)

Schick, Kathy D., 'Prehistoric Africa' in Martin and O'Meara (1995)

Stearns, Jason, *Dancing in the Glory of Monster: The Collapse of the Congo and the Great War of Africa* (New York: Public Affairs, 2012)

United Nations, 'World Population Prospects: The 2015 Revision' (New York: UN, 2015)

Wa Thiong'o, Ngugi, *Moving the Centre: The Struggle for Cultural Freedoms* (Oxford: James Curry, 1993)

—— *Decolonising the Mind: The Politics of Language in African Literature* (1986/Oxford: James Curry, 2005)

Wallerstein, Immanuel, *Africa: The Politics of Independence and Unity* (Nebraska: Bison Books, 2005)

CONCLUSION

The World's Intersecting Imperial Legacies

Bond, *Book of Verse* (New Delhi: Penguin India, 2007)

Hartley, L. P., *The Go-Between* (Norfolk: Lowe & Brydone, 1978)

Jacques, Martin, *When China Rules the World* (London: Penguin, 2nd edn 2012)

Kai-Fu Lee, *AI Superpowers: China, Silicon Valley, and the New World Order* (New York: Houghton Mifflin Harcourt, 2018)

Khaldun, Ibn, *The Muqaddimah*, trans. Frank Rosenthal (1377/Oxon: Routledge and Kegan Paul, 1958)

Khanna, Parag, *The Future is Asian* (London: Weidenfeld & Nicolson, 2019)

Mahbubani, Kishore, *Can Asians Think?* (Singapore: Marshall Cavendish International, 2004)

Mishra, Pankaj, *From the Ruins of Empire: The Revolt Against the West and the Remaking of Asia* (London: Allen Lane, 2012)

Nehru, Jawaharlal, *The Discovery of India* (1946/New Delhi: Penguin Books India, 2004)

Rieff, David, *In Praise of Forgetting: Historical Memory and Its Ironies* (New Haven and London: Yale University Press, 2016)

NOTES

INTRODUCTION

1 Johnson (1755), *The Dictionary of the English Language*. Consulted in 'Dr Johnson's House', London.

2 Burbank and Cooper (2010), *Empires in World History*, p.61.

3 Darwin (2007), *After Tamerlane*, p.160.

4 Howe (2002), *Empire*, pp.30–1.

5 Kumar (2017), *Visions of Empire*, p.159.

6 Hobsbawm (1989), *The Age of Empire*, p.337.

7 Nkrumah (1965), *Neo-Colonialism*, p.ix.

8 193 states are listed by the UN as fully recognized by all the others, the newest being South Sudan, created in 2011. The Holy See and the Palestinian Territories hold 'UN obsesrver status'. Several others are not as widely recognized, ranging from Kosovo to Taiwan.

9 Lieven (2002), *Empire: The Russian Empire and its Rivals*, p.414.

10 Sharman and Phillips (2015), *International Order in Diversity*, p.1. 'By contrast, ours is an insistently homogenous era, the diversity of an earlier time now succeeded by a global monoculture of sovereign states.'

11 Howe (2002), *Empire*, p.82.

12 Said (2003), *Orientalism*, p.7. 'Orientalism depends for its strategy on the flexible *positional* superiority, which puts the Westerner in a whole series of possible relationships with the Orient without ever losing him the relative upper hand. And why should it have been otherwise, especially during the period of extraordinary European ascendancy from the late Renaissance to the present?'

13 Said (1993), *Culture and Imperialism*, pp.xxv, 9.
14 Darwin (2007), *After Tamerlane*, p.7.
15 Burbank and Cooper (2010), *Empires in World History*, p.9.
16 Boot (2014), *Savage Wars of Peace*, pp.99–102, on the 'Balangiga massacre'; *The Economist*, 'A peal for friendship', 18 August 2018, on the return of the bells.
17 Ridley (2000), *Genome: The Autobiography of a Species*, pp.13, 21, 220.
18 Nandy (2002), *Time Warps*, p.1.
19 Seeley (1883), *The Expansion of England*, pp.165–6.
20 Harari (2014), *Sapiens*, p.232.
21 Orwell (2009), *All Art Is Propaganda*, p.150.

ONE

America's Imperial Inheritance

1 Greene (1955), *The Quiet American*, p.60.
2 Obama (2006), *Audacity of Hope*, p.306.
3 Trump (2015), *Crippled America*, p.32.
4 Kinzer (2017), *The True Flag*, pp.1–3, offers a historical snapshot of this debate.
5 Kaplan (2005), *Imperial Grunts*.
6 Porter (2006), *Empire and Subempire*, p.125.
7 Washington, 'A Great Experiment' (1891).
8 Bicheno (2003), *Rebels and Redcoats*, p.xxxvii.
9 Hoock (2017), *Scars of Independence*, pp.12, 20: 'There are good reasons why Americans portray their revolution and war for independence as an uplifting, heroic tale, as the triumph of high-minded ideals in the face of imperial overreach.' A balanced view 'helps to untangle the inherent tensions between America's moral objectives and her violent tendencies'.
10 Frankopan (2011), *The Silk Roads*, p.436.
11 Hahn (2017), *A Nation Without Borders*, pp.22, 226: Patriots who waged the Independence War had 'rebelled against what they saw as Britain's violations rather than its essence', which was 'imperial, with a metropolitan centre loosely

coordinating the activities of far-flung and, for the most part, self-regulating outposts'.

12 Weinberg (1935), *Manifest Destiny*, pp.37, 41.

13 Stephanson (1995), *Manifest Destiny*, pp.1–6.

14 Hahn (2017), *A Nation Without Borders*, p.23.

15 Boot (2014), *Savage Wars of Peace*, p.124. Characterizes this action as a 'traditional counterinsurgency tactic'.

16 Turner (2009), *The Significance of the Frontier in American History*, pp.1, 10, 45–7.

17 Weinberg (1935), *Manifest Destiny*, p.116. 'The idea of individualism perhaps did more than anything else to cement the association between democracy and expansion. For the sturdiest element in democracy was its valuation of individualism – the thesis of the individual's right not only to exception from undue interference by government but also to the most abundant opportunity for self-development.'

18 Lieven (2012), *America Right or Wrong?*, p.129.

19 For example, New Mexico took sixty-two years between annexation and formally joining the USA. Other time-lags included: Arizona forty-nine years; Utah forty-six; Dakota twenty-eight; Idaho twenty-seven; Montana twenty-five; Wyoming twenty-two; Colorado fifteen.

20 Abraham Lincoln later wrote about this period; see Lincoln (2009), *The Gettysburg Address*, p.6.

21 Karp (2016), *This Vast Southern Empire*, p.112.

22 Northup (2014), *Twelve Years a Slave*, pp.233–4.

23 Karp (2016), *This Vast Southern Empire*, pp.125, 226.

24 Lincoln (2009), *The Gettysburg Address*, pp.5, 13–14.

25 Ibid., pp.115–16.

26 Du Bois (2009), *Of the Dawn of Freedom*, pp.37–8.

27 Zakaria (1999), *From Wealth to Power*, p.45.

28 Boot (2014), *Savage Wars of Peace*, p.129. 'American power had already filled up the chalice of North America and, overflowing its confines, naturally spilled into the adjacent region where there were no Great Powers to bar the way.'

29 Roosevelt's speech, 5 October 1898. Quoted in Kinzer (2017), *The True Flag*, p.76.

30 Mahan (1899), *Lessons of the War with Spain*, pp.26–7, 245–7, 249.

31 Hopkins (2018), *American Empire*, p.39; Immerwahr, *How to Hide an Empire* (2019), p.103.

32 Pedersen (2015), *The Guardians*, pp.19, 23.

33 Darwin (2007), *After Tamerlane*, p.470.

34 Du Bois (1903/2009), *Of the Dawn of Freedom*, p.42.

35 Kaine's speech, 'The Truman Doctrine at 70', Chatham House, London, 24 February 2017.

36 Immerwahr, *How to Hide and Empire* (2019), pp.262–77; Hopkins (2018), *American Empire*, p.40, explains that US history 'ought to be recast to give full weight to its own experience as an imperial power'. And that traditions of formal empire have evolved in the era of globalization to include domains of unseen control.

37 Munkler (2007), *Empires*, pp.83, 93, 118, comments that 'the US empire shifted from control of territory to the control of flows (capital and information, goods and services).

38 RAND was especially influential during the Cold War, with its analysts and academics influencing US nuclear-deterrence policy. During the Vietnam War, RAND got into hot water with the US government for its studies that showed North Vietnamese morale would never break under US military pressure. This contradicted official US government policy at the time, and Richard Nixon's administration was incensed. Thereafter RAND diversified away from being a defence think tank, into other areas of public policy too.

39 The report is available online at www.rand.org: Fair, Crane, Chivvis, Puri, *Pakistan: Helping to Secure an Insecure State* (2010).

40 Chomsky (2004), *Hegemony or Survival*, p.12.

41 Johnson (2000), *Blowback*, pp.8, 216.

42 Lieven (2012), *America Right or Wrong?*, p.52.

43 Obama (2006), *The Audacity of Hope*, p.280.

44 Lieven (2012), *America Right or Wrong?*, p.92.

45 US Census Bureau, 13 March 2018 (accessed 20 February 2019): https://www.census.gov/newsroom/press-releases/2018/cb18-41-population-projections.html

46 Public Religion Research Institute, 'Partisan Polarization Dominates Trump Era: Findings from the 2018 American Values Survey' (accessed 20 February 2019): https://www.prri.org/research/partisan-polarization-dominates-trump-era-findings-from-the-2018-american-values-survey/

47 Morris (2014), *War*,
p.365. This summarizes
PricewaterhouseCoopers'
projections of China's
economy overtaking the US
(in 2030 China's GDP will be
33.3 trillion US dollars, versus
US GDP at 21.2 trillion).
By 2060 the gap will be far
bigger (China's GDP 66.2
trillion, versus 38.8 trillion
for the US). These projections
roughly tally with the OECD
(in 2030 China's GDP will
be 30.6 trillion, versus 23.4
trillion for the US; and in
2060 China's will be 53.9
trillion, versus 38 trillion for
the US).

TWO

Britain's Grandeur and Guilt of Empire

1 Kipling (1901), *Kim*, p.134.
2 Orwell (1934), *Burmese Days*,
p.68.
3 Johnson, *The Sun*, 22 April
2016.
4 Some academics call the
manifesto of past experiences
in present political behaviour
'strategic culture'. Johnston
(1995), *Cultural Realism*,
pp.1–2, explains this as
'historically imposed inertia
on choice that makes
strategy less responsive
to specific contingencies'.
When deciding what to do
in the world, countries do
not rely on a purely rational
cost–benefit calculus. Instead,
'historical choices, analogies,
metaphors, and precedents
are invoked to guide
choice'.
5 Mills (1918), *The Future of the
Empire*, p.15.
6 Simms (2017), *Britain's
Europe*, pp.1–18.
7 Colley (1992), *Britons*, p.17.
8 Bell (2007), *The Idea of Greater
Britain*, pp.64–8, 77.
9 Ibid., pp.243, 254.
10 Callwell (1896), *Small Wars*,
p.1.
11 Napier, quoted in Kwarteng
(2012), *Ghosts of Empire*, p.91.
12 Stockwell (2008), *The British
Empire*, p.1.
13 Brandon (2008), *The Rise
and Fall of the British Empire*,
p.328.
14 Marr (2007), *A History of
Modern Britain*, p.117.
15 Howe (2008), 'Empire and
Ideology', p.166.
16 *The Economist*, 'The
Economist at 175:

Reinventing liberalism for the 21st century', 15 September 2018, p.46.

17 Brandon (2008), *The Rise and Fall of the British Empire*, p.626. See also Walton (2013), *Empire of Secrets*, p.237. Walton, who also researched MI5's official history, has documented how 'Britain fought an extremely dirty and violent war in Kenya' against the Mau Mau uprising.

18 Patten (1998), *East and West*, p.6.

19 Ferguson (2004), *Empire*, p.xxvii.

20 Tharoor (2017), *Inglorious Empire*, p.xxv.

21 Biggar, *The Times*, 30 November 2017.

22 Thompson (2012), *Britain's Experience of Empire*, pp.20–1. See also: Darwin (2012), *Unfinished Empire*, pp.293, 302; Hall (2008), 'Culture and Identity in Imperial Britain', p.205; Stockwell (2008), *The British Empire*, p.288; Porter (2016), *British Imperial*, p.71.

23 Dorling and Tomlinson (2019), *Rule Britannia*, p.10.

24 YouGov, 'The British Empire is "something to proud of"' (accessed 9 February 2019): https://yougov.co.uk/topics/politics/articles-reports/2014/07/26/britain-proud-its-empire

25 Seymour, *Jacobin*, 1 November 2018.

26 James (2013), *Churchill and Empire*, p.1.

27 Toye (2011), *Churchill's Empire*, pp.59, 112.

28 Interventions in the former Yugoslavia had helped bring its violent fragmentation to a halt in 1995. NATO's air war in 1999 had helped to stop Serbian ethnic cleansing in Kosovo. Blair had also ordered British soldiers in Sierra Leone to help UN peacekeepers out of a sticky situation in 2000.

29 'Chilcot report: Read Tony Blair's full statement in response to the Iraq war inquiry', *The Independent*, 6 July 2016 (accessed 1 February 2019): https://www.independent.co.uk/news/uk/politics/chilcot-report-tony-blair-read-response-statement-in-full-iraq-war-inquiry-a7123251.html

30 Kwarteng (2012), *Ghosts of Empire*, pp.29–66.

31 Ledwidge (2011), *Losing Small Wars*, pp.1–62.

32 Colley (1992), *Britons*, p.375.

33 Young (1998), *This Blessed Plot*, p.119.

34 Thompson (2012), *Britain's Experience of Empire*, pp.62–4; Marr (2007), *A History of Modern Britain*.

35 Bell, *Prospect*, 19 January 2017.

36 Ibid.
37 Marr (2007), *A History of Modern Britain*, p.478.
38 Office for National Statistics, 'Ethnicity and National Identity in England and Wales: 2011'.
39 Thompson (2008), 'Empire and the British State', pp.56–7.
40 Shepherd (1996), *Enoch Powell*, pp.72, 277.
41 Ibid., p.504.
42 Churchill (2013), *Never Give In!*, p.374.
43 Oswald (2017), *The Spider's Web* documentary.
44 Darwin (2012), *Unfinished Empire*, p.180: 'The City's two poles were the Bank of England and the Stock Exchange ... This was the setting in which London exerted its global supremacy ... many commercial transactions in London concerned goods that never reached it or a British port.' See also Palan (2015), 'The Second British Empire', p.54: 'The City of London could become, through the British colonial outposts, a 24-hour integrated financial centre.'
45 Porter (2016), *British Imperial*, p.182.

THREE

The European Union's Post-Imperial Project

1 Monnet (2015), *Memoirs*, Chapter 13: 'The Schuman Plan Conference'.
2 Orbán's speech, Budapest, 23 October 2018 (accessed 10 December 2018): http://www.miniszterelnok.hu/prime-minister-viktor-orbans-speech-on-the-62nd-anniversary-of-the-1956-revolution-and-freedom-fight/
3 Tusk's speech, Brussels, 6 February 2019 (accessed 7 February 2019): https://www.consilium.europa.eu/en/press/press-releases/2019/02/06/remarks-by-president-donald-tusk-after-his-meeting-with-taoiseach-leo-varadkar/
4 'The EU: Nobel Peace Prize 2012' (accessed 7 February 2019): https://www.nobelpeaceprize.org/Prize-winners/Prizewinner-documentation/The-European-Union-EU
5 Rompuy's speech, Oslo,

10 December 2012 (accessed 8 February 2019): https://www.nobelprize. org/prizes/peace/2012/ eu/26124-european-union- eu-nobel-lecture-2012/

6 Varoufakis (2017), *And the Weak Suffer What They Must?*, p.158.

7 Barroso's speech, Strasbourg, 10 July 2007 (accessed 8 February 2019): https:// www.youtube.com/ watch?v=c2Ralocq9uE; archived version of original broadcast from EUX.TV.

8 Gress (1998), *From Plato to Nato*, p.57.

9 Beard (2015), *SPQR*, p.196. See also Kumar (2017), *Visions of Empire*, pp.8–11.

10 Beard (2016), *SPQR*, pp.67, 489, 497.

11 Frankopan (2015), *New Silk Roads*, pp.42–4.

12 In the 2011 UK Census (accessed 10 February 2019) 59.3 per cent of people registered as Christian: https://www.ons.gov.uk/ peoplepopulationand community/culturalidentity/ religion/articles/ religioninenglandand wales2011/2012-12-11

13 Gress (1998), *From Plato to Nato*, pp.193–5. 'The year zero of the West, if one were to fix such a date, was 800, when the pope created a new western empire by crowning Charlemagne emperor in St Peter's basilica in Rome.'

14 Heer (1968), *The Holy Empire*, pp.48, 94.

15 Ibid., pp.95–6.

16 Gress (1998), *From Plato to Nato*, p.3.

17 Roper (1965), *The Rise of Christian Europe*, pp.21–5.

18 Frankopan (2015), *New Silk Roads*, pp.218–19.

19 Kumar (2017), *Visions of Empire*, p.72.

20 Pagden (2002), *The Idea of Europe*, p.10; Pagden (1995), *Lords of All the World*, p.13; Asad (2002), 'Muslims and European Identity', p.220.

21 Walter (2017), *Colonial Violence*, p.104: 'Active collaboration ensued between Western empires to the detriment of non-European societies, and not just with regard to China, which in practical terms could never be conquered by any single nation.'

22 Simms (2016), *Britain's Europe*, argues that Britain acquired colonies mainly to influence European balances of power, which was certainly one motivation, but is ultimately too narrow a view.

23 Darwin (2007), *After Tamerlane*, pp.51–2.

24 Pagden (1995), *Lords of All the World*, p.11; Doyle (1986), *Empire*, p.110, is even more

direct: 'Colonisation, in effect, was an entrepreneurial venture of Christendom.'

25 Kumar (2017), *Visions of Empire*, p.161.

26 Ibid., pp.167–8.

27 Darwin (2007), *After Tamerlane*, p.180; Kumar (2017), *Visions of Empire*, p.392.

28 Kumar (2017), *Visions of Empire*, pp.390, 398.

29 Hochschild (1999), *King Leopold's Ghosts*, p.296. Also: *The Economist*, 'Belgium's Africa Museum', 8 December 2018. When Belgium revamped its old 'Africa Museum', military veteran groups contested what they interpreted as a bastardization of its portrayal of Leopold II's reign.

30 Heer (1968), *The Holy Empire*, p.22: 'Although the Empire was at no time a German national state, Germany was to be its chief prop.'

31 Fukuyama (2015), *Political Order and Political Decay*, pp.94–125, explains the prevalence of Greek and Italian patronage.

32 Middelaar (2013), *The Passage to Europe*, pp.3–4.

33 Ibid., p.42.

34 Ibid., pp.45, 157.

35 Ibid., p.256.

36 Milward (1992), *The European Rescue of the Nation State*, pp.1–20.

37 Monnet speech, 9 November 1954, quoted in Duchêne (1994), *Jean Monnet*, p.398.

38 Barroso's speech, Strasbourg, 10 July 2007: https://www.youtube.com/watch?v=c2Ralocq9uE

39 Middelaar (2013), *The Passage to Europe*, p.192.

40 Zielonka (2014), *Is The EU Doomed?*, p.40.

41 Monnet (2015), *Memoirs*, p.435.

42 Duchêne (1994), *Jean Monnet*, pp.238, 363, 383.

43 D'Appollonia (2002), 'European Nationalism and European Union', pp.171–88; Zielonka (2014), *Is The EU Doomed?*, p.10.

44 Gravier (2013), 'Imperial Administration', pp.61–2; Middelaar (2013), *The Passage to Europe*, pp.26–7, 256.

45 Middelaar (2013), *The Passage to Europe*, p.276.

46 Zielonka (2006), *Europe as Empire*, p.1.

47 Varoufakis (2017), *And the Weak Suffer What They Must?*, p.10.

48 Ibid., p.194.

49 Habermas (2015), *The Lure of Technocracy*, p.11, warns against 'a technocracy without democratic roots'.

50 Ashton's speech before the Human Rights Council, SPEECH/11/127, Geneva, 28 February 2011.

51 Zielonka (2006), *Europe as Empire*, pp.2, 13.

52 Middelaar (2013), *The Passage to Europe*, pp.245, 249.

53 "United we stand, divided we fall": letter by President Donald Tusk to the 27 EU heads of state or government on the future of the EU before the Malta summit', 31 January 2017.

54 European Commission, 'White Paper on the Future of Europe', 1 March 2017.

55 Middelaar (2013), *The Passage to Europe*, p.246.

56 Gravier (2013), 'Imperial Administration', pp.48–50, points to Byzantium's bureaucracy and legal practices as being far more developed than its contemporary challenger, the Holy Roman Empire.

57 Gravier (2011), 'Empire vs federation', pp.415, 426. History shows that federations can coexist with empires; some empires used to devolve power consensually in order to keep their constituent national communities happy.

58 Blaut (1993), *The Colonizer's Model of the World*, p.9. This trait is not Europe's alone. 'Sino-centrism' and the 'Ulema' were also inward-looking in their day, as the ancient Chinese and the old Muslim empires interpreted their trading and military encounters with other civilizations through self-referential lenses.

59 Zielonka (2013), 'Europe's new civilizing mission', explains that 'Post-communist countries were seen as norm takers, not givers'.

60 Tharoor (2012), *Pax Indica*, p.242.

61 Garton Ash (2009), *Facts are Subversive*, pp.126–32. 'Europe's history over the last 65 years is a story of the spread of freedom. In 1942 there were only four perilously free countries in Europe ... Most Europeans now live in liberal democracies. That has never before been the case; not in 2,500 years.'

62 RAND Europe, cited in European Commission, 'White Paper on the Future of Europe', 1 March 2017, p.10.

63 Ascherson (1995), *Black Sea*, p.49. '"Civilisation and barbarism" were twins born in the Greek and above all Athenian imagination. They in turn gave birth to a ruthless mental dynasty that still holds power over the western mind. The Roman and Byzantine Empires sanctified their own struggles as the defence of "civilized" order against

"barbaric" primitivism. So
did the Holy Roman Empire
and the colonial expansions

of Spain, Portugal, Holland,
France, Italy, Germany and
Britain.'

FOUR

Russia's Embrace of its Imperial Legacy

1 Tolstoy (1993), *War and Peace*, Book IX, Chapter 10.
2 Putin (2005), 'Annual Address'.
3 Motyl (2001), *Imperial Ends*, p.1.
4 Plokhy (2018), *Lost Kingdom*, pp.vii, 37, 110. It is one reason why Russians later looked upon the Ukrainians as 'little Russians'.
5 Figes (2002), *Natasha's Dance*, p.367.
6 Munkler (2003), *Empires*, pp.56–7: 'Steppe empires had a fundamentally parasitic character.'
7 Lieven (2002), *Empire*, p.231. Also Darwin (2007), *After Tamerlane*, pp.66–73.
8 Laruelle (2012), *Russian Eurasianism*, p.3.
9 Figes (2002), *Natasha's Dance*, p.377.
10 Klyuchevsky (1965), *Peter the Great*, p.58.
11 Reynolds (2011), *Shattering Empires*, p.14.
12 Lenin (1917), *Imperialism: The Highest Stage of Capitalism*, pp.101, 104.
13 Makarychev (2013), 'Imperial discourse in a post-imperial Russia', p.113: 'Only a small minority in Russian academia would disagree that the Soviet Union was the inheritor of Russia's centuries-long imperial traditions.' See also Kumar (2017), *Visions of Empire*, pp.214, 288.
14 d'Encausse (1993), *The End of the Soviet Empire*, pp.4–6.
15 Ibid., p.102.
16 Laruelle (2012), *Russian Eurasianism*, pp.33, 41.
17 Neuman and Wigen (2015), 'The legacy of Eurasian nomadic empires', pp.103–23.
18 Kapuscinski (1994), *Imperium*, p.87.
19 Tsygankov (2010), *Russia's Foreign Policy*, pp.93–9.
20 d'Encausse (1993), *The End of the Soviet Empire*, pp.171–95; Kumar (2017), *Visions of Empire*, pp.286, 300.
21 Lo (2015), *Russia and the New World Disorder*, pp.47, 63: 'when one looks back at the sweep of Russian

history, there have been very few periods since Peter the Great when it has not been a major power'. Lo goes on to point to Russia's 'historical habits of entitlement and notions about the natural order of things'. Kapuscinski (1994), *Imperium*, pp.162–3: 'In the Imperium, the ruling elite (and often the common people as well) are preoccupied with the imperial scale of thinking and, even more, the global scale, the scale of large numbers, large spaces, of continents and oceans, of geographic meridians and parallels, of the atmosphere and the stratosphere, why, of the cosmos.'

22 Kumar (2017), *Visions of Empire*, p.231.

23 Goldfarb and Litvinenko (2007), *Death of a Dissident*, p.141.

24 Hill and Gaddy (2013), *Mr Putin: Operative in the Kremlin.*

25 Lavrov (2016), 'Russia's Foreign Policy'.

26 Laruelle (2012), *Russian Eurasianism*, p.138.

27 Lavrov (2016), 'Russia's Foreign Policy'.

28 Tolstoy (1993), *War and Peace*, Book IX, Chapter 1.

29 Berlin (1999), *The Hedgehog and the Fox*, pp.28–9.

FIVE

China's Janus Faces of Empire

1 Originally Mengzi. Translated by Hinton (2013), *The Four Chinese Classics*, p.472.

2 Luo Guanzhong (2018), *The Romance of the Three Kingdoms*, p.1.

3 Xi Jinping, 'Full text of President Xi's speech at opening of Belt and Road forum' (accessed 5 January 2019): http://www.chinese-embassy.org.uk/eng/zgyw/t1465819.htm

4 World Bank, 'China Overview' (accessed 3 January 2019): https://www.worldbank.org/en/country/china/overview

5 IMF, 'World Economic Outlook Database, October 2018' (accessed 3 January 2019): https://www.imf.org/external/pubs/ft/weo/2018/02/weodata/index.aspx

6 For example, US academics

Allison (2017), *The Thucydides Trap*; Mearshimer (2010), 'The Gathering Storm'.

7 Ge Zhaoguang (2018), *What Is China?*, p.110.

8 Jacques (2012), *When China Rules the World*, p.246, notes China's keen sense of its own history.

9 Keay (2009), *A History of China*, pp.138–9.

10 Captions correct as of a visit to the Chinese National Museum, Beijing, December 2017.

11 Jacques (2012), *When China Rules the World*, p.299.

12 Keay (2008), *China: A History*, pp.28–50.

13 According to Frances Wood, a former curator of the British Library's Chinese collection: 'the earliest significant body of Chinese writing is to be found on the "oracle bones" of the Shang dynasty . . . It is from the Zhou that the first body of literature emerges (including the Confucius and the Daoist classics), although the passage of millennia means that surviving texts may have considerably changed from their original state.' Wood (2017), *Great Books of China*, p.1.

14 Sun Tzu (2014), introduction to *The Art of War*, p.xxix.

15 Chih-Yu Shih (1993), *China's Just World*, p.30.

16 Hinton (2013), *The Four Chinese Classics*, p.472; Keay (2008), *China: A History*, p.75.

17 Keay (2008), *China: A History*, pp.52, 79, 97–8.

18 Wood (2017), *Great Books of China*, introduction; Keay (2008), *China: A History*, p.16.

19 Translated in Wood (2017), *Great Books of China*, p.97.

20 Chih-Yu Shih (1993), *China's Just World*, pp.30–1. 'According to Confucianism, the emperor is the supreme moral symbol of all under heaven . . . The emperor is the gentleman (*junzi*) and his citizens, little men (*xiaoren*). Confucius said, "The gentleman's virtue is like wind and the little men's weeds. The wind blows over the weeds, the weeds bow."'

21 Morris (2011), *Why the West Rules . . . For Now*, pp.302–4.

22 Luo Guanzhong (2018), *The Romance of the Three Kingdoms*, introduction, pp.xxi–xxxvii.

23 Wood (2017), *Great Books of China*, pp.111, 114.

24 Lou Guanzhong (2018), *The Romance of the Three Kingdoms*, pp.1, 611.

25 Visit to the Chinese National Museum, Beijing, December 2017.

26 Man (2014), *The Mongol Empire*, pp.243, 357.

27 Morris (2011), *Why the West*

Rules . . . For Now, p.408; Harari (2014), *Sapiens*, p.324.

28 Johnston (1995), *Cultural Realism*, pp.212–28.

29 Wood (2017), *Great Books of China*, pp.8–9; Keay (2008), *China: A History*, pp.409–10.

30 Scholars, both Western and Chinese, continue to puzzle over precisely why China fell behind. For example: Darwin (2007), *After Tamerlane*, pp.40–5; Morris (2011), *Why the West Rules . . . For Now*; Jacques (2012), *When China Rules the World*, p.31; Ge Zhaoguang (2018), *What Is China?*, p.116; Kang (2007), *China Rising*, p.49.

31 Wood (2017), *Great Books of China*, p.8.

32 Platt (2018), *Imperial Twilight*, pp.8–10.

33 Ford (2010), *The Mind of Empire*, pp.128–9, 134.

34 Platt (2018), *Imperial Twilight*, pp.193, 211.

35 Lovell (2011), *The Opium War*, pp.23, 80, 119.

36 Ford (2010), *The Mind of Empire*, p.157.

37 Jacques (2012), *When China Rules the World*, p.345.

38 Wording of plaque at Jifang Pavilion, Beijing, as of summer 2014.

39 Mitter (2004), *A Bitter Revolution*, pp.3–11, 133–4.

40 Zheng (2012), *Never Forget National Humiliation*, p.54.

41 Chang and Halliday (2007), *Mao*, pp.248, 380; Zheng (2012), *Never Forget National Humiliation*, p.88.

42 Chang (1991), *Wild Swans*, p.xxi.

43 Johnston (2000), *Social States*, argues that China has been socialized into some international norms through this process.

44 Hong Kong SAR minister, address to the International Studies Association Asia Conference, June 2017.

45 *BBC News*, 'Hong Kong protests', 3 July 2019.

46 'In March 2015, two Chinese frigates, the *Linyu* and *Weifang*, evacuated 629 Chinese citizens and 279 other foreign nationals from war-torn Yemen . . . it was the first time that the PLA Navy had conducted such a non-combatant evacuation operation alone.' Parello-Plesner and Duchatel (2015), *China's Strong Arm*, p.1.

47 Zhao Tingyang's views appeared in 'The Tianxia System: A Philosophy for the World Institution', translated by Callahan and Barbantseva (2011), *China Orders the World*, p.96.

48 Yan Xuetong (2011), *Ancient Chinese Thought*, p.95.

49 Ge Zhaoguang (2018), *What Is China?*, pp.53, 139, 165.

'China as a modern nation-state is precisely that which evolved out of the traditional centralised empire.' So 'the two [state and empire] are entangled throughout history'. Ge calls present-day China a 'unified, multinational state' and thinks it is perfectly suited to being ruled by a strong central authority. The fad for federal rule is not essential for China to adopt, Ge reasons.

50 Xi Jinping (2014), *Governance of China*, p.33.

51 Xi Jinping, 'Full text of President Xi's speech at opening of Belt and Road forum' (accessed 5 January 2019): http://www.chinese-embassy.org.uk/eng/zgyw/t1465819.htm

52 Author visit to Malacca, June 2019.

53 *The Economist*, UK print edition, 25 May 2019. Advert placed by *Beijing Review*.

54 Miller (2017), *China's Asia Dream*, pp.12, 17, 240; Jacques (2012), *When China Rules the World*, p.206.

55 Miller (2017), *China's Asia Dream*, pp.75–89.

56 Kissinger (2011), *On China*, pp.23, 25, 29.

57 Johnston (1995), *Cultural Realism*, p.101.

58 Ibid., p.1.

59 Feng Zhang (2015), *Chinese Hegemony*, pp.25–8. 'According to Confucian ethics, all relationships should be conducted by following the principle of respecting the superior, which will lead to hierarchical role relationships between actors.'

60 Yan Xuetong (2011), *Ancient Chinese Thought*, p.219. 'China should not adopt the US' current way of acting, saying that all states are equal while in practise always seeking to have a dominant international status ... There are more than 200 political entities in the world. The differences between them are too great.'

61 Ibid., p.108.

62 Zhao Tingyang (2011), 'Rethinking Empire ...', p.32.

63 Zhao Tingyang (2018), 'Political Realism and the Western Mind', in Schuett and Hollingworth (eds), *The Edinburgh Companion to Political Realism*, p.33.

64 Derek Watkins, 'What China has been building in the South China Sea', *New York Times*, 27 October 2015 (accessed 1 January 2018): www.nytimes.com/interactive/2015/07/30/world/asia/what-china-has-been-building-in-the-south-china-sea.html?_r=0

65 *The Economist*, 'Special report: The Pacific', 15–21 November 2014; Sarah Raine and Christiane Le Miere, *Regional Disorder: The South China Sea Disputes* (IISS Adelphi Book, 2013).

66 Luo Guanzhong (2018), *The Romance of the Three Kingdoms*, p.104.

SIX

India's Overcoming of the 'Intimate Enemy'

1 Gandhi (1927), *An Autobiography*, p.27.

2 Nehru (1946), *The Discovery of India*, p.47.

3 Modi (2015), 'PM Modi addresses British-Indian Community at Wembley Stadium' (accessed 7 January 2019): https://www.narendramodi.in/india-doesn-t-want-favours-from-the-world-india-wants-equality-pm-modi-at-wembley-375884

4 Guha (2008), *India After Gandhi*, p.515.

5 Keay (2001), *India: A History*, pp.1–36.

6 Nehru (1946), *The Discovery of India*, p.98.

7 Sen (2005), *The Argumentative Indian*, pp.3–4.

8 Nehru (1946), *The Discovery of India*, p.69.

9 Fukuyama (2011), *The Origins of Political Order*, pp.98–188, explains that whereas the Chinese state could impose itself over society in order to overcome the tyranny of war, the Indian state was always limited by the tyranny of a society that was atomized between various local religious and caste identities.

10 Keay (2001), *India: A History*, pp.237, 261, 281.

11 Faruqui (2012), *The Princes of the Mughal Empire*, p.46.

12 Richards (1995), *The Mughal Empire*, p.12.

13 Ibid., pp.151, 164, 171.

14 Ibid., pp.208–23.

15 Faruqui (2012), *The Princes of the Mughal Empire*, p.317.

16 Ibid., p.325.

17 James (1998), *Raj*, pp.118–20.

18 Tharoor (2011), *The Elephant, The Tiger and the Cellphone*, p.167.

19 Nehru (1946), *The Discovery of India*, p.312.

20 Barkawi (2017), *Soldiers of Empire*, pp.18–19, 24–5.

21 Ibid., pp.75, 114.

22 Brandon (2008), *The Decline*

and Fall of the British Empire, p.387.

23 Khilnani (2012), *The Idea of India*, p.163.

24 James (1998), *Raj*, pp.629–30.

25 Guha (2008), *India After Gandhi*, p.12.

26 Ibid., p.94.

27 Ibid., pp.5, 31.

28 Brandon (2008), *The Decline and Fall of the British Empire*, pp.413–14; Tunzelmann (2017), *Indian Summer*, pp.256–7: 'The best interests of Britain had been served by a swift exit, a slapdash partition, the creation of Pakistan, and the repatriation of British armed forces. The best interests of India might well have been served by exactly the opposite.'

29 Guha (2008), *India After Gandhi*, p.34.

30 Sen (2005), *The Argumentative Indian*, p.39. Sen, a Nobel Prize-winning scholar, was enamoured by 'Akbar's vision' in hosting inter-community discussions in Agra, and by 'the acknowledgement and recognition of the internal diversity of India' this conveyed. See also Richards (1995), *The Mughal Empire*, pp.31–6.

31 Tharoor (2011), *The Elephant, The Tiger and the Cellphone*, p.14: 'If America is a melting pot, then to me India is a *thali*, a selection of sumptuous dishes in different bowls. Each tastes different, and does not necessarily mix with the next, but they belong together on the same plate.'

32 Tagore (1917), *Nationalism*, p.73.

33 Ibid.

34 Nehru (1946), *The Discovery of India*, p.255.

35 Naipaul (1964), *An Arena of Darkness*, p.215.

36 Seeley (1888), *The Expansion of England*, p.234.

37 Nehru (1946), *The Discovery of India*, p.254.

38 Sen (2005), *The Argumentative Indian*, p.39.

39 Tharoor (2017), *Inglorious Empire*, p.37.

40 Nandy (1983), *The Intimate Enemy*, pp.1–3.

41 Gandhi (1927), *An Autobiography*, pp.158, 198.

42 Naipaul (1964), *An Arena of Darkness*, p.74.

43 Khilnani (2012), *The Idea of India*, p.3.

44 Guha (2008), *India After Gandhi*, pp.313, 338.

45 Price (2015), *The Modi Effect*, pp.39–46.

46 rss.org

47 Savarkar (1923), *Hindutva*, pp.4–5.

48 Ibid., pp.56, 58.

49 Ibid., p.63.

50 Ibid., p.90.

51 Golwalkar (1952), 'Total

Prohibition of Cow Slaughter', *Hitavada*, 26 October 1952.

52 Pankaj Mishra (2014), 'Narendra Modi and the new face of India', *The Guardian* (accessed 10 January 2019): https://www.theguardian.com/books/2014/may/16/what-next-india-pankaj-mishra. See also Sen (2005), *The Argumentative Indian*, pp.x, 49–51.

53 Naipaul (1977), *India: A Wounded Civilisation*, p.51.

54 Modi speech in Port Blair, Andaman and Nicobar Islands, on the seventy-fifth anniversary of hoisting the tricolour on Indian soil. Streamed live, 30 December 2018 (accessed 14 January 2019): https://www.youtube.com/watch?v=GcScEUIVusM

55 Khilnani (2012), *The Idea of India*, p.114.

56 K. Subrahmanyam, quoted in Tharoor (2012), *Pax Indica*, p.416.

SEVEN

The Middle East's Post-Imperial Instability

1 Khaldun (1958), *Al Muqaddimah*, Chapter 2, Section 22.

2 Gibran (2011), 'On Freedom', *The Prophet*.

3 World Bank (2019), *Expectations and Aspirations*, p.2.

4 Oliver and Fage (1990), *A Short History of Africa*, p.56.

5 bin Muhammad (2017), *A Thinking Person's Guide to Islam*, p.80; Khaldun (1958), Introduction, *The Muqaddimah*, pp.825–40.

6 British Museum, London, for chronologies and archaeological evidence of the ancient Middle East.

7 Frankopan (2015), *The New Silk Roads*, pp.4, 22. 'Not for a moment did he look to Europe, which offered nothing at all: no cities, no culture, no prestige, no reward. For Alexander, as for all ancient Greeks ... It was no surprise that his gaze fell on the greatest power of antiquity: Persia.'

8 Hourani (1991), *A History of the Arab Peoples*, p.5.

9 Lewis (1995), *The Middle East: 2000 Years of History*, p.35.

10 Nasr (2006), *The Shia Revival*, pp.32–40.

11 Lockman (2009), *Contending Visions of the Middle East*, pp.36–7. One example of scientific accomplishment in this period was Ibn Sina, or Avicenna (980–1037), a Persian physician, astronomer and writer who is considered to be founding father in the practice of modern medicine.

12 Crowley (2005), *1453*, pp.6, 234.

13 Rogan (2012), *The Arabs*, pp.8, 33.

14 Darwin (2007), *After Tamerlane*, pp.78–82.

15 Axworthy (2008), *Iran: Empire of the Mind*, p.141.

16 Lockman (2009), *Contending Visions of the Middle East*, pp.42, 55.

17 Hourani (1991), *A History of the Arab Peoples*, p.259; Kumar (2017), *Visions of Empire*, p.122.

18 Lewis (1995), *The Middle East: 2000 Years of History*, p.57.

19 De Bellaigue (2018), *The Islamic Enlightenment*, p.268.

20 Kumar (2017), *Visions of Empire*, p.95.

21 Mango (1999), *Atatürk*, p.7.

22 Barr (2011), *A Line in the Sand*, p.375.

23 Darwin (2007), *After Tamerlane*, p.389.

24 Pedersen (2015), *The Guardians*, pp.24–5, 61.

25 Rogan (2012), *The Arabs*, p.348.

26 Ibid., p.446–54.

27 Herzl (2010), *The Jewish State*, p.18.

28 Shafak (2014), 'In Search of Untold Stories', p.78.

29 I have written on this war in *Fighting and Negotiating with Armed Groups* (2016).

30 Al-Rasheed (2010), *A History of Saudi Arabia*, pp.1–2.

31 Khalid (2004), *Resurrecting Empire*, p.102.

32 Axworthy, *Iran: Empire of the Mind*, p.298.

33 Khamaeni's words from 2007, cited in Axworthy, p.289.

34 Khamaeni, 'Open Letter . . .', 21 January 2015 (accessed 9 December 2018): https://www.leader. ir/en/content/12798/ To-the-Youth-in-Europe- and-North-America

35 Mohammad Javad Zarif, Twitter post 3.27 a.m.. 20 May 2019 (accessed 8 August 2019): https://twitter.com/ jzarif/status/113041967375 6049410? lang=en

36 Feldman (2008), *Rise and Fall of the Islamic State*, pp.1–12.

37 Qutb, quoted in Karsh (2007), *Islamic Imperialism*, p.217.

38 De Bellaigue (2018), *The*

Islamic Enlightenment,
pp.316–29.

39 Al-Zawahiri, quoted in Karsh
(2007), *Islamic Imperialism,*
p.225.

40 bin Muhammad (2017), *A
Thinking Person's Guide to
Islam,* p.264.

41 Karsh (2007), *Islamic
Imperialism,* pp.2, 9.

EIGHT

Africa's Scramble Beyond Colonialism

1 Achebe (1958), *Things Fall
Apart,* p.166.

2 Mandela, 'Africa and Its
Position in the World
Today', London School of
Economics, 6 April 2000
(accessed 9 January 2019):
http://blogs.lse.ac.uk/
africaatlse/2013/12/06/
full-text-of-nelson-mandela-
speech-at-lse-on-6-
april-2000/

3 Wallerstein (2005), *Africa,*
p.12.

4 The professor's words were
translated from French and
are unattributable, due to the
conference's strictures.

5 Davidson (1984), *Africa* TV
documentary.

6 Naipaul (1971), *In A Free
State,* pp.115–16.

7 V. S. Naipaul encapsulates
this pithily, when his Indian-
African protagonist reflects
on his knowledge of his
origins: 'If I say these things
it is because I have got them

from European books.
They formed no part of our
knowledge or pride. Without
Europeans, I feel, all our past
would have been washed
away, like the scuff-marks
of fisherman on the beach.'
Naipaul (1979), *A Bend In the
River,* p.13.

8 Schtick (1995), 'Prehistoric
Africa', pp.49–50, 63–4.

9 Hegel (1975), *Lectures on the
Philosophy of World History,*
pp.216–17.

10 Diop (1978), *Black Africa,*
pp.1–8.

11 Ibid., p.4; Lamphear and
Falola (1995), 'Aspects of
Early African History',
pp.82–3.

12 Lamphear and Falola (1995),
'Aspects of Early African
History', p.95.

13 Davidson (1984), *The Story of
Africa,* pp.79–82.

14 Lamphear and Falola (1995),
'Aspects of Early African
History', pp.74–6; Hochschild

(2006), *King Leopold's Ghost*, p.5.

15 Ibid.

16 Mwakikagile (2000), *Africa and the West*, p.63.

17 Oliver and Fage (1990), *A Short History of Africa*, p.84.

18 Davidson (1984), *The Story of Africa*, pp.127–36.

19 Manning (2014), 'African Population, 1650–2000', pp.132–3.

20 Reid (2012), *A Modern History of Africa*, pp.139, 150; Oliver and Fage (1990), *A Short History of Africa*, pp.106, 156–7.

21 Mamdani (1996), *Citizen and Subject*, p.37.

22 Oliver and Fage (1990), *A Short History of Africa*, p.161.

23 Ndlovu-Gatsheni and Mhlanga (2013), *Bondage of Boundaries*, p.1.

24 Hochschild (1999), *King Leopold's Ghost*, pp.115, 136, 233, 283.

25 Achebe (1911), *An Image of Africa*, pp.3, 12.

26 Reid (2012), *A Modern History of Africa*, p.210.

27 Ibid., p.134.

28 Rodney (1972), *How Europe Underdeveloped Africa*, p.278.

29 Mamdani (1996), *Citizen and Subject*, pp.41, 51, 59, 183.

30 Kenyatta (1938), *Facing Mount Kenya*, pp.44–5.

31 Ibid., pp.203–4.

32 Kabongo (1988), 'The Catastrophe of Belgian Decolonisation', p.381.

33 Akayeampong et al. (2014), *Africa's Development in Historical Perspective*, pp.19–20: 'Colonialism did not just impede development, it also distorted it . . . An ahistorical understanding of Africa's current developmental problems is of little value.'

34 Pakenham (1979), *The Boer War*, pp.xxi–xxii, 1–5.

35 Mandela (2002), *Long Walk to Freedom*, p.16.

36 Wallerstein (1961), *Africa*; Reid (2012), *A Modern History of Africa*, pp.259, 310.

37 Ndlovu-Gatsheni and Mhlanga (2013), *Bondage of Boundaries*, p.2.

38 Boahen (1987), *African Perspectives on Colonialism*, p.41.

39 Oliver and Fage (1990), *A Short History of Africa*, p.246.

40 Nyerere (1974), *Man and Development*, pp.43–4.

41 Hochschild (1999), *King Leopold's Ghost*, p.304.

42 Meredith (2005), *The State of Africa*, pp.386, 405, 410, 588.

43 Achebe (1983), *An Image of Africa*, pp.42, 75–6.

44 Transparency International, 'How corruption weakens democracy', 29 January 2019. 'The index, which ranks 180 countries and territories by their perceived

levels of public-sector corruption according to experts and businesspeople, uses a scale of zero to 100, where zero is highly corrupt and 100 is very clean' (accessed 1 March 2019): https://www.transparency. org/news/feature/ cpi_2018_global_analysis

45 Nkrumah (1965), *Neo-Colonialism*.

46 Acemoglu and Robinson (2013), *Why Nations Fail*, p.343.

47 Boahen (1987), *African Perspectives on Colonialism*, p.108.

48 Mandela's speech, Cambridge, UK, 2 May 2001.

49 Desai and Masquelier (2018), *Critical Terms for the Study of Africa*, p.5.

50 Kwarteng (2011), *Ghosts of Empire*, pp.253–70.

51 Three such books are reviewed here: 'Jaw-jaw, war-war', *The Economist*, 12 December 2018. See also Dixon (2019), *Divided by History*.

52 Connor (2018), 'At Least a Million Sub-Saharan Africans Moved to Europe Since 2010', p.8.

53 Afrobarometer, 'African migration: Who's thinking of going where?', 27 June 2018 (accessed 19 February 2019): http://afrobarometer. org/blogs/african-migration-whos-thinking-going-where

54 Natale et al. (2018), 'Many more to come?', pp.7–12.

55 Fanon (2001), *The Wretched of the Earth*, p.81.

56 Adeyanju and Oriola (2011), 'Colonialism and Contemporary African Migration', pp.945–962.

57 Manning (2014), 'African Population, 1650–2000', pp.131–48. 'Two hypotheses – a dense early African population and a decline in African population because of the slave trade – are linked together.' Manning finds that the transatlantic slave trade grew irregularly from 1450 and peaked in the 1790s, with the trans-Saharan and Indian Ocean slave trades peaking in the 1870s. 'Population growth was held down by the violence from 1890 to 1920 . . . Populations rose at very modest rate from 1890, then accelerated from 1920 to 1950.'

58 Wallerstein (2005), *Africa*, p.151.

59 UN Population Division (2015), p.1.

60 McKinsey report, 'Dance of the lions and dragons', June 2017, pp.16–49.

61 Parello-Plesner and Duchatel, *China's Strong Arm*, p.24.

62 Senator Mutala Kilonzo Junior, Address to the Kenyan Senate, 11 July 2018.

63 McKinsey report, 'Dance of
     the lions and dragons', June
     2017, p.74.
64 *The Economist*, 'African

Presidents: Till death do
us part', 12 January 2019,
pp.44–5.

CONCLUSION

The World's Intersecting Imperial Legacies

1 Hartley (1997), *The
    Go-Between*, p.5.
2 Bond (2007), *Book of Verse*,
    p.94.
3 Rieff (2016), *In Praise of
    Forgetting*, pp.79, 106:
    '. . . once the transmission of
    collective memories continues
    for more than three or four
    generations, it can no longer
    be called memory *other than*
    metaphorically.'
4 Jacques (2012), *When China
    Rules the World*, pp.168, 293:
    'The emergence of Chinese
    modernity will de-centre and
    relativise the position of the

West.' This is because 'For
the first time in the modern
era, the world's increasingly
dominant player will be a
civilisation state.' Moreover, it
will be 'a developing country
and a former colony of
Western powers and Japan'.
5 Mishra (2012), *From the
    Ruins of Empire*, p.45.
6 Khaldun (1958), *Al
    Muqaddimah*, Chapter 2,
    Section 22.
7 Lee (2018), *AI Super-Powers*,
    p.30.
8 Nehru (1946), *The Discovery of
    India*, p.610.

ACKNOWLEDGEMENTS

Bestowing gratitude upon those who have assisted me is no easy matter. This book channels so many accumulated experiences from years of researching and working in various parts of the world. Those who shared in these experiences and helped make them happen are too numerous to list, and I look forward to recalling their roles the next time our paths shall cross.

More pertinently, ever since I had the idea for this book in 2017 several people have helped me to navigate the extant scholarship and to refine my arguments. I had useful conversations with Banu Turnaoğlu and Tasneem Bint Ghazi about the Middle East. Natasha Kuhrt offered pointers on Russia, as did Nella Beevor on Africa. Colleagues past and present at RAND and Johns Hopkins were especially helpful regarding Europe and the USA. My time at the Commonwealth Secretariat helped me to better understand the post-independence trajectories of several African, Asian and Pacific countries. My earlier work for the OSCE was similarly beneficial to my grasp of East Europe after the USSR. Needless to say, the views and interpretations contained within this book are mine alone.

Closer to home I owe a debt of thanks to Joe Maiolo and Mike Rainsborough for marking my student work back in the day and, years later, making my time as a War Studies Lecturer a wonderful closing of this circle. Mitch Mitchell and the DCDC crew for the opportunity to contribute to their work. Jeff Michaels for years of discussions over matters of academia and policy. And Jonathan

Brown for a friendship that has continued to serve as a source of inspiration and guidance.

Darryl Samaraweera believed in this book right from the start and went above and beyond to make it happen; I hope that he and Artellus are pleased with the outcome. Mike Harpley placed his faith in this project and I cannot speak more highly of working with the team at Atlantic. I asked Mike Jones not to hold back in his edit and he certainly didn't – this is a better book for his suggestions, as it is for Mandy Greenfield's sterling work in further refining the text.

And last but most of all. My love and enduring respect to my mother for providing me with a solid foundation and a stable base in life, without which none of this would have been possible. And my love and gratitude to Anna Moore for all of our shared adventures, and for those still to come.

INDEX

About the Author

SAMIR PURI is is Senior Fellow at the International Institute for Strategic Studies, based in Singapore. Prior to this he was an academic, teaching War Studies at King's College London and later in the Johns Hopkins School of Advanced International Studies. Earlier in his career he served in the Foreign Office (2009–15) and worked at RAND (2006–09). He appears on news programmes for Al Jazeera, the BBC, CNBC, Sky and TRT World, and has written for publications including the *Guardian*.